Quantifying Quality
in
Policing

Edited by
Larry T. Hoover
Sam Houston State University

Gerald L. Williams, Executive Director
Bill Blackwood Law Enforcement Management Institute of Texas
Sam Houston State University
Huntsville, TX

Larry T. Hoover, Director
Police Research Center
Sam Houston State University
Huntsville, TX

Chuck Wexler, Executive Director
Police Executive Research Forum (PERF)
Washington, DC

This anthology was produced by the Bill Blackwood Law Enforcement Management Institute of Texas and the Police Research Center at Sam Houston State University, Huntsville, Texas. Publication is by a cooperative agreement with the Police Executive Research Forum. The views expressed in this publication are those of the authors and do not necessarily represent those of PERF's members.

ISBN 1-878734-40-7

Police Executive Research Forum
1120 Connecticut Ave. NW, Suite 930
Washington, DC 20036

Contents

Preface

One is sometimes tempted to dismiss all organizational development effort as "another passing fad." Occasionally, the feeling is justified. Too many academics and consultants involved in management development feel compelled to invent new terminology, to characterize every initiative as fresh and innovative, to overpromise and then overdiagram, and, in general, to characterize relatively straightforward approaches to improving the way organizations function with systems "techno-eze." But despite abuse in the form of pseudosophistication, organizational development does work. Organizations do genuinely renew themselves. Some approaches engender pride and motivation in employees, while others alienate. One must be very careful not to commit the proverbial sin of tossing the baby out with the bathwater.

No organizational development effort better illustrates the contrast between substance and jargon than total quality management (TQM). On the one hand, TQM is anything but a fad. It has evolved from 90 years of cumulative wisdom based on both formal and informal assessment of what works in management. At the same time, one is hard-pressed to think of any other approach to organizational development more laced with techno-eze jargon than TQM. Proactivity, empowerment, reinvention, flow-charting, feedback loops—TQM has it all. Beyond sounding "with it" in conversations with city council members, is there anything here that a police manager might practically employ?

We think there is. Not all elements of TQM can be transposed from the private sector to policing. Indeed, not all elements of TQM as originally developed in the manufacturing sector can be transposed to the private-sector service industry. But elements of TQM can be applied in any service endeavor, whether in the government or in the private sector. This book is intended to provide a comprehensive review of the potential application of total quality management to police administration.

The book was compiled under the auspices of the Bill Blackwood Law Enforcement Management Institute of Texas at Sam Houston State University. Each chapter was individually commissioned and written for this book. Each of the chapter authors served as a facilitator for one of the Executive Issues Seminar Series workshops the Law Enforcement Management Institute conducted for Texas police managers. Thus, the ideas presented have been "pretested" in the crucible of a three-day seminar involving discussion, critique and analysis by practitioners.

Publications produced by the Law Enforcement Management Institute at Sam Houston State University are designed to fill significant gaps in the literature that law enforcement administrators need. The first anthology the Law Enforcement Management Institute produced, *Police Management: Issues & Perspectives*, also published by the Police Executive Research Forum, was designed to provide a comprehensive review of endemic issues in police management. This work is designed to provide a comprehensive review of organizational development approaches across a range of police programs.

As editor, I took some risk in employing what some might regard as a buzz term, *Quantifying Quality*, as the title for the book. I could have been much more conservative and simply used the term *measuring police effectiveness*. But something really is lost in using the older terminology. We truly wanted to produce a work that examined the issues of *quality* in police programming. The simple terminology *measurement of effectiveness* is too easily interpreted as *how to count things*. As several of the chapter authors note, not all elements of quality in policing can be quantified. There are some nonmeasurable qualitative attributes of police services. About the quality of these attributes, one may say, "I know it when I see it," but beyond that be unable to offer anything in the way of measurable definition. However, this book was never intended to offer a prescription for quantifying all quality in policing. Indeed, one of our objectives is to simply make explicit what can reasonably be quantified and what cannot.

Acknowledgments

First and foremost, I want to acknowledge the irreplaceable assistance of Ms. Jamie Tillerson, program manager for the Executive Issues Seminar Series sponsored by the Bill Blackwood Law Enforcement Management Institute of Texas at Sam Houston State University. The Executive Issues Seminar Series is the foundation for this work. Second, I wish to thank Ms. Kay Billingsley, who did copy layout. A special thanks as well to Bill Streidl, retired from Tenneco, for his contributions. Mr. Streidl has donated his time selflessly to law enforcement for a number of years, and he was an integral part of the Seminar Series.

As director of the Bill Blackwood Law Enforcement Management Institute of Texas, Dr. Gerald Williams contributed to this book not only as a chapter author but also in terms of administrative support. Likewise, Dr. Timothy J. Flanagan, dean and director of the Criminal Justice Center at Sam Houston State University, provided the largely invisible administrative support that makes the production of publications such as this possible.

During the Executive Issues Seminar Series, which provided the foundation for this book, executives from several corporations participated pro bono in seminars, providing law enforcement managers with insight regarding the application of total quality management to their organizations. The executives included

William Bradford, Dresser Industries;
William J. Dickeson, Texas Governor's Center for Management
    Development;
Martin Hathaway, American Airlines;
Donald Hawk, Texas Commerce Bancshares Inc.;
Art Lacy, Texas Instruments; and
Robert Tuley, Southwestern Bell.

Our heartfelt thanks to these corporate executives for their contributions. Finally, I want to acknowledge the assistance of PERF staff, particularly Ms. Martha Plotkin, PERF's communications director, for her management of the endeavor; and Ms. Suzanne Fregly, PERF's senior editor, for a thorough and superb copy revision.

Chapter 1

Translating Total Quality Management From the Private Sector to Policing

Larry T. Hoover

The Context of Total Quality Management

Total quality management (TQM) is the first global organizational development movement. Previous organizational development approaches have had a specific national genesis. American universities were the first to develop business colleges as a standard part of their degree programming, and, consequently, the preponderance of literature on organizational development has come from the United States. The true founder of organizational analysis was, of course, a German, Max Weber. Other significant contributions have come from elsewhere in the world, but structured approaches to improving organizational effectiveness have evolved largely in the United States. If one reviews the names of theorists associated with management theory before the 20th century, one will find they are predominantly American: Taylor, Follet, Barnard, Merton, Mayo, McGreger, Argyris, Herzberg, McClelland, Simon, Likert, Fiedler, Kahn, Katz, Hersey, Blanchard, Mintzberg, Bennis. With the advent of TQM, however, we find names of a different national origin—Shingo, Ishikawa and Taguchi.

Although the *Quality Control Handbook* has been published continually since the turn of the century, almost all theorists characterize

TQM as a post-World War II phenomenon, placing its origins in Japan. As part of the post-war aid the United States provided to Japan, the U.S. government sent American management consultants there. Among those journeying to Japan during that era were Joseph M. Juran and W. Edwards Deming. Deming was to leave an indelible mark on both Japanese industry and the worldwide quality movement. Drawing on his background in mathematics, he introduced the concept of statistical process controls to Japanese manufacturing. Like $E = mc^2$, the concept is simple in expression but complex in its application. Deming believed that defects in manufactured goods were not due to poorly motivated employees or shoddy workmanship, but rather, to identifiable shortcomings in the production process itself. Using statistical process controls, one could trace production defects to their sources, and subsequently correct them. Drawing on research from the motivational school of management, Deming suggested that workers naturally wanted to produce quality products, and that management was responsible for organizing work so they could do so. His 14 principles have become tantamount to gospel for many organizations. See table 1.

While we must be careful not to exaggerate Americans' contribution to the Japanese quality revolution, some have found it ironic that Americans played a significant role. Why? Because the Japanese quality revolution sparked the same revolution in this country 20 years later. From 1945 to 1970, the bad connotation associated with Japanese brand names literally reversed. Immediately following World War II, "Made in Japan" was synonymous with "junk." However, by 1970, names like Honda, Toyota, Sony, and Hitachi implied precisely the opposite. "Made in Japan" guaranteed far more reliability than "Made in the USA." Japanese products began to command a significant portion of the American marketplace, most visibly in the automobile industry. By the late 1980s, Japanese imports constituted over 30 percent of the automobiles sold in the United States. Further, the Japanese overwhelmingly dominated the consumer electronics industry. With turnabout as fair play, American manufacturers made pilgrimages to Japan to see what the Japanese were doing. A revolution in American manufacturing resulted (Rice 1993). For example, during the 1980s, the number of consumer-reported defects in American automobiles dropped precipitously. Instead of waving good-bye at the car dealership and hoping they would never see consumers again, American manufacturers and automobile dealers contacted buyers several times to make sure they were happy with their automobiles. Lee Iacocoa went on a television advertising blitz to save Chrysler, noting its commitment to quality. At Ford, quality became "Job 1." And Buick is now the new name for quality on American highways. By 1990, the number of import automobiles sold in the United States leveled off, and it has actually declined even more since then.

The creation of the Malcolm Baldrige National Quality Award in 1987 symbolized the new American commitment to quality. Businesses compete for

Table 1

Deming's 14 Principles

1. Create constancy of purpose toward improvement of product and service, with the aim to become competitive and to stay in business, and to provide jobs.
2. Adopt the new philosophy. We are in a new economic age. Western management must awaken to the challenge, must learn their responsibilities, and take on leadership for a change.
3. Cease dependence on inspection to achieve quality. Eliminate the need for inspection on a mass basis by building quality into the product in the first place.
4. End the practice of awarding business on the basis of price tag. Instead, minimize total cost. Move toward a single supplier for any one item, on a long-term relationship of loyalty and trust.
5. Improve constantly and forever the system of production and service, to improve quality and productivity, and thus constantly decrease costs.
6. Institute training on the job.
7. Institute leadership. The aim of supervision should be to help people and machines and gadgets to do a better job. Supervision of management is in need of overhaul, as well as supervision of production workers.
8. Drive out fear, so that everyone may work effectively for the company.
9. Break down barriers between departments. People in research, design, sales, and production must (work as a team), to foresee problems of production and in use that may be encountered with the product or service.
10. Eliminate slogans, exhortations, and targets for the work force asking for zero defects and new levels of productivity. Such exhortations only create adversarial relationships, as the bulk of the causes of low quality and low productivity belong to the system and thus lie beyond the power of the work force.
11a. Eliminate work standards (quotas) on the factory floor. Substitute leadership.
b. Eliminate management by objective. Eliminate management by numbers, numerical goals. Substitute leadership.
12a. Remove barriers that rob the hourly worker of his right to pride of workmanship. The responsibility of supervisors must be changed from sheer numbers to quality.
b. Remove barriers that rob people in management and in engineering of their right to pride of workmanship. This means *inter alia*, abolishment of the annual or merit rating and of management by objective.
13. Institute a vigorous program of education and self-improvement.
14. Put everybody in the company to work to accomplish the transformation. The transformation is everybody's job.

Source: W.E. Deming, *Out of the Crisis*

the award, administered by the U.S. Department of Commerce, in terms of a complex set of criteria (Department of Commerce 1995). Winners integrate their achievement into advertising. "Defect-free" is no longer a joke in American manufacturing, but rather, is a real goal. The defense sector of Texas Instruments, one of the winners of the Baldrige Award, is trying to move from a defect ratio expressed in parts per million to one expressed in parts per billion (Lacy 1993). "Zero defect" is for real. For a synopsis of the development of the quality movement, see figure 1.

With the success of TQM in the American manufacturing sector, one would inevitably expect a migration to service industries. And, indeed, by the early 1990s, innumerable service-sector companies were implementing formal quality management programming. Federal Express, for example, has won the Baldrige Award. Transposition to government enterprise was inevitable.

Quality's Family Tree

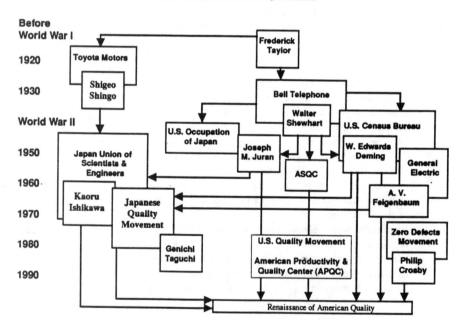

Source: Texas Department of Commerce, *Quality Texas: Investment for Survival*

Fig. 1. Development of the quality movement

TQM efforts were initiated in innumerable units of the federal bureaucracy during the Bush administration.   With the Clinton administration came the "reinventing government" nomenclature, and a continuing commitment to implementing TQM principles in the federal government (Gore 1993).   Concurrently, state and local units of government joined the quality management movement. Demands that police agencies do so are inevitable.

But police managers should be very cautious about joining any organizational development movement without carefully examining the applicability of its tenets. In the early 1980s, many units of government tried to implement management by objectives. With few exceptions, the effort failed outright, had nominal impact or fizzled out once the rhetoric wore off. Much of what works well in the manufacturing sector does not translate well to the service sector, either public or private. And what may work in the private service sector may not translate well to government. Caution should be taken regarding the application of TQM to policing. It is intrinsically difficult to quantify quality with regard to the enterprises we relegate to government.

In the private sector, inefficient pension plans are winnowed out. Try proposing elimination of Social Security. One might immediately respond, "That is an unfair comparison." But that is exactly the point. To the extent that government has different objectives, different process rules may also apply. As another example, it makes eminent economic sense for the U.S. Postal Service to eliminate Saturday delivery. But the body politic will not let that happen.   Diversity of goals begets inevitable inefficiencies in process.   One must be very careful about advocating the American government's wholesale adoption of an organizational development process originally designed to bring Japanese manufacturing to world-class status.

TQM's Basic Elements

With that cautionary note, we can proceed to a discussion of the tenets of total quality management, and the subsequent examination of their application to American police departments. There are as many lists of TQM principles as there are noteworthy authors on the topic. Sashkin and Kiser (1992) suggest that the principles various TQM consultants and theorists expound can be categorized into three broad premises: culture, customers and counting. Remembered easily as the three "C's" of TQM, this typology appears to be a useful way to capture the essence of total quality management.

TQM Culture — The First of the Three C's

Eight phrases describe the elements of TQM culture: measurement for improvement, delegation of decision authority to lowest possible organizational level, rewards for results, teamwork and cooperation, job security, perceived fairness is reality, equitable rewards, and ownership. The core of TQM is TQM culture. Each element merits definition:

Measurement for improvement. The phrase *measurement for improvement* captures two essential elements of TQM. First, there should be measurement, and measurement should be constant and routine. "How are we doing?" isn't asked sporadically or only when a particular problem arises. Second, measurement is made to improve processes, not to judge people. No one suggests that we not assess the quality of people's performance. However, mixing measurement to improve processes with measurement to judge people defeats both purposes.

Delegation of decision authority to lowest possible organizational level. A roughly synonymous term for *delegation of decision authority to lowest possible organizational level* is *organization empowerment*. However, for police managers who have been around since the 1960s, "empowerment" sounds a little too much like "power to the people." Hence, we'll stay with the phrase *delegation of decision authority*. This TQM tenet is traceable all the way back to the principles approach to management, one of the cornerstones of which was "authority should equal responsibility." Add to this Douglas McGregor's *Theory Y* and Frederick Herzberg's *Principles of Job Enrichment*, and one has in effect only the latest manifestation of a long-standing productivity principle.

Rewards for results. Employees should be rewarded for demonstrated productivity, not management judgment of potential. Obviously, it is assumed here that a reward structure exists in the first place. (*A policing application note: In policing, we reward exclusively for potential, and never for results. That is, promotions are based on written exams and/or assessment centers, which are designed to identify supervisory or management potential. Productivity in previous roles is almost never considered. When it is, the productivity rating generally accounts for less than 10 percent of the promotion rating score. It is almost impossible to change police promotion systems, since they are designed to insulate an agency's internal administration from political influence. Hence, this important element of TQM must be, for all intents and purposes, written off.*)

Teamwork and cooperation. Both the organizational structure and the reward system should be built around teamwork and cooperation. However, TQM advocates acknowledge that we cannot overcome the American cultural bias toward individualism. Indeed, we even have a bias toward *rugged* individualism (note the settings and characters employed in television advertising). But success in the modern workplace requires teamwork, not rugged individualists marching to the beats of their own drummers. Hence, compromise arrangements are suggested, blending teamwork organization and rewards with recognition of individual achievement.

Job security. One of Deming's 14 points was to "drive out fear." Operating in a TQM environment, American enterprises are advised to offer as much job security as is economically possible, and to avoid layoffs unless there are absolutely no alternatives.

Perceived fairness is reality. Perception is paramount with regard to fairness in the workplace. It matters little that management has in place bureaucratic procedures, explicated policy and the like, which hypothetically promote fairness. This is one of those phenomena where the *perception* of reality *is* the reality. Managers must respond to employee concerns in this respect if they are to foster a TQM environment.

Equitable rewards. In this context, equitable rewards are related to gross disparity. American enterprises wishing to foster a TQM environment are encouraged to flatten the salary scale. Particularly targeted should be top executives whose salaries are considered exorbitant. Although a corporate board may think that a particular executive is "worth it," employees at lower levels who earn a fraction of the executive's salary will certainly not. Additionally, corporations are urged to eliminate unnecessary but potentially controversial management perks, such as reserved parking spaces and separate cafeterias. (*A policing application note: Interestingly, this isn't even an issue in policing. The typical police chief earns only two to three times as much as a starting rookie patrol officer. Cafeterias reserved for top management use are certainly few and far between in American police departments. About the only perk that exists in most police departments is the reserved parking space, and that is hardly worth getting excited about.*)

Ownership. Work should be designed so that employees feel a personal sense of investment and ownership. In this respect, work processes should be designed to give employees responsibility for a complete "unit of work." Interestingly, this principle is probably easier to apply in the service sector than in the manufacturing. Manufacturers have struggled to implement the principle by creating work teams who assemble larger units of a manufactured product, but they have had limited success. Nevertheless, the principle still stands. To the extent that employees feel a sense of ownership, they will build or provide better products or services. (*A policing application note: Our response in policing has been to try to give patrol officers greater responsibility for case follow-up and closure, as well as to stabilize beat assignments so that patrol officers feel a sense of geographic "ownership," at least. Almost all our efforts have been directed at patrol officers. Detectives and auxiliary service staff have received almost no attention in this respect.*)

Customer Focus — The Second of the Three C's

There are three primary elements of customer focus:

Structured programs to ascertain customer perspective. With structured programs to ascertain customer perspective, the key term is *structured*. No business stays in business very long unless it is reasonably responsive to customer perspective. Further, most businesses have a great deal of insight about what customers want via informal feedback from routine contacts, as well as registered complaints. However, TQM advocates suggest that such information is usually incomplete and often static. Ongoing structured customer surveys offer more systematic and dynamic information. It should be noted, moreover, that structured programs to ascertain customer perspective do not have to be in the form of questionnaires. Texas Commerce Bank requires top executives to do their banking just as average customers do. Further, they must conduct their transactions at various branch banks. Hence, they have to stand in line at the teller counter, pull up to the drive-in window, etc., just as average customers do (Hawk 1994).

The internal customer concept. A high proportion of employees in any organization provides services exclusively to other organization employees. In a TQM environment, these members of "auxiliary services" must treat other employees as if they were external customers. In that sense, they must conduct customer satisfaction surveys, try to reduce cycle time, and the like.

Supplier/provider communication by level of operation personnel. Suppliers and providers for organizations typically work through intermediate personnel, not end users. In a TQM environment, mechanisms are put in place to provide direct communication between end-user employees and suppliers/providers. Thus, if the binder rings won't close properly on notebooks ordered for a training program, the trainer complains to the supplier, not someone from purchasing.

Counting — The Third of the Three C's

The most complex of the three C's is counting. It consists of more than simply tabulating. There are four elements:

Specify customers. The first step in measuring the quality of a manufactured product or service is carefully specifying the customer. For example, when a bank provides services to a physician's office, the physician is a customer at only a macro level. The real user of the services, the real customer, is the physician's office manager. Thus, routine measurement of quality service should be ascertained through him or her, not the physician. Further, few products or services are aimed at literally everyone in the general public. Market specialization is everywhere. Enterprises operating in a TQM environment take time to carefully identify and characterize their customer base.

Define supplier specifications. No enterprise is totally self-sufficient. Virtually all organizations, both private and public, need materials and services. Thus, every enterprise is concurrently a provider/supplier and a customer. TQM approaches suggest that most enterprises can profit by more carefully specifying supplier requirements. Defects in products or service delivery can often be traced to correctable problems with component suppliers. This is easy to visualize in the manufacturing process, where problems in the production of any of 3,000 component parts of an automobile will cause considerable customer unhappiness. The customer does not blame the supplier; instead, General Motors, Ford or Chrysler is blamed. Supplier problems in the service sector are not as tangible, but they are often as problematic. (*A policing application note: When patrol cars sit in a city garage for weeks before someone is available to perform routine maintenance, police service is likely to deteriorate. And as is the case with the automobile example, citizens won't blame city vehicle maintenance; they'll blame the police department.*)

Identify steps in work process. One of the best ways corporations have found to reduce cycle times in paperwork processing is to carefully specify each step and its value-added contribution. It is unusual for a corporation not to find that it can eliminate several steps in typical paperwork processing. Careful specification of steps in the work process also suggests points of quality measurement.

Select measurements. No organization makes all possible quality measurements. Organizations must assess the cost-effectiveness of making a measurement. Clearly, this is not always a simple process. Some measurements may cost more but provide better information. Certain quality measures may be critical under one set of circumstances but not under another. In general, however, it is important to identify a full range of potential quality measures and systematically discuss the cost-benefit of implementing each. It is an axiom of TQM that employees at the level of operation participate fully in this process.

Application of TQM Principles in Policing

During the course of the Executive Issues Seminars Series referenced in the preface to this book, Texas police managers were administered an inventory Marshall Sashkin developed to measure the extent to which an organization applies TQM principles. The inventory's design is generic, i.e., it is configured to be used in both the manufacturing and the service industries, the public and the private sector. The inventory measures the extent of the application of principles related to the three primary TQM components discussed above: culture, customers, and counting. Figure 2 shows

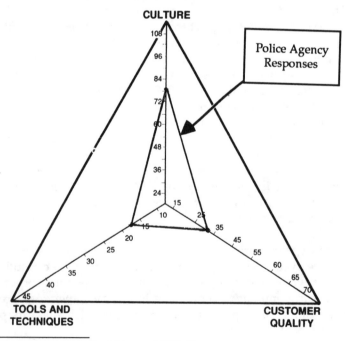

Source of Inventory: M. Sashkin and K.J. Kiser

Fig. 2. TQM assessment inventory: scale for general application of
TQM principles

the results of the questionnaire administered to a sample of 200 Texas police managers. Organizations that fully applied all the TQM principles would receive scores at the outer edge of the triangle, i.e., a score of 110 in culture, 75 in customer quality and 50 in counting (tools and techniques). The smaller the inside triangle compared with the outside, the less application of TQM principles. The purpose of diagramming responses in the triangular format is to illustrate various organizations' strengths and weaknesses with regard to the three primary TQM components. Examination of figure 2 reveals that police agencies score highest on the culture component (76), and lowest on the counting component (18), labeled "Tools and Techniques" on the graph, with customer orientation obviously in between (36). There is no reason to believe that Texas police agencies would score particularly higher or lower than those in other states on these scales.

Few organizations would score near the outside of the triangle on all three dimensions. The scores among police agencies can be interpreted as indicating reasonable application of TQM culture principles, moderate application of customer orientation techniques, and sparse application of measurement efforts.

A secondary scale in the Sashkin inventory measures the extent of application of the primary components of TQM culture. Figure 3 shows the results. Note that "job security" and "fairness" rate highest. The lowest culture element score is for "measurement for improvement." Low scores are provided for "rewards for results" and "ownership," as well. High ratings for job security and fairness are consistent with civil service personnel systems. However, since such systems literally forbid direct rewards for results, it is not surprising that this element was rated low. Police agencies could make changes that would improve ratings for measurement for improvement and ownership. For example, problem-oriented policing entails both enhanced measurement and greater ownership of work products by patrol officers.

Limitations on Applying The First C: Culture

As noted previously, it is important to carefully consider which TQM elements will translate to a police environment and which will not. Albrecht and Zemke (1985) identified 10 characteristics of service-sector enterprises that distinguish them from manufacturing organizations in terms of TQM application. See table 2. Clearly, all of these apply to policing. For example, Albrecht and Zemke note that service cannot be created in advance and stored in inventory. In law enforcement, we expend a great deal of effort to deploy resources so that they are reasonably available to citizens upon demand. The Kansas City Response Time Study notwithstanding, citizens in urgent situations expect to see an officer promptly, and in at least a limited

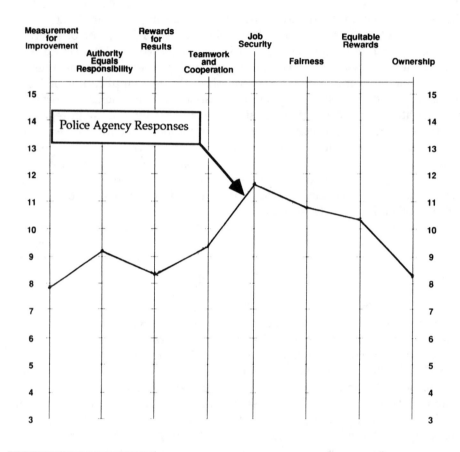

Source of Inventory: M. Sashkin and K.J. Kiser

Fig. 3. TQM assessment inventory: scale for TQM culture elements

number of instances, rapid response will make a difference in apprehension probability.   But we experience serious limitations on our ability to "stockpile" the availability of police response.

Albrecht and Zemke note that customer assessments of service quality tend to decrease in proportion to the number of employees they encounter during the delivery of services. In a TQM culture, close one-on-one customer/ employee relationships are nurtured. Again, developing organizational configurations that allow such relationships is problematic for police agencies. Policing is a 24-hour-a-day operation, and thus different people staff the given positions. Efforts at creating so-called permanent beat assignments are at least partially designed to ameliorate the problem, but

Table 2

The 10 Characteristics of Service

1. Service is produced at the instant of delivery and cannot be created in advance and stored in inventory.

2. Service cannot be centrally produced, inspected, or stockpiled.

3. Service cannot be demonstrated, nor can a sample be sent in advance for approval.

4. In the absence of tangible product, customers value service on the basis of their own personal experience.

5. The service experience cannot be resold or passed on to a third party.

6. Faulty service cannot be recalled.

7. Quality assurance is required before production.

8. Delivery of service usually requires human interactions.

9. Customers' assessments of service quality are subjective and strongly influenced by expectations.

10. Customers' assessments of service quality tend to decrease in proportion to the number of employees they encounter during the delivery of services.

Source: K. Albrecht and R. Zemke, *Service America*

they are far from a perfect solution. A customer who calls at 10 a.m. one day and 10 p.m. the next is likely to see a different police officer. Further, the process by which we handle innumerable complaints results in multiple employee contacts with police customers, e.g., referral of long-term investigations from patrol to a detective bureau. Even the manufacturing sector has difficulty in maintaining a single point of contact for customers. But in the service sector and, in particular, in a 24-hour-a-day service endeavor, it is almost impossible. This clearly limits police agencies' ability to apply the "single point of contact" methods TQM consultants suggest.

Interestingly, there are some TQM culture principles that are arguably "overapplied" in policing. One of Deming's 14 points is to "drive out fear." He is referring to fear of eminent job loss. TQM works best when employees have a reasonable sense of job security. The Japanese, of course, have taken this to the extreme of lifetime employment. As Ouchi (1981) noted in *Theory Z*, lifetime employment would never work in the United States. It is possible in Japan only through a compensation system that cuts wages dramatically during corporate difficult times. It also depends on treating large numbers of women as "permanent temporary" workers. In reality, at least until very recently, lifetime employment only applied to males.

So in any case, we have a situation where the American corporate manufacturing sector was urged to provide greater job security to its employees. In particular, corporations were cautioned to "never ever" lay off employees because other employees found more efficient ways to do the job, because suggestions for greater efficiency would stop immediately. When corporate executives visit with groups of police managers, they inevitably note how fortunate police managers are to work in an environment where employees are assured of job security. The reaction among police managers is "you've got to be kidding."

The civil service systems in place in U.S. public safety agencies come as close as any arrangement we have to guarantee lifetime employment. Motivated by the desire to protect police and fire agencies from partisan political influence, and to prevent police and fire positions from being distributed as political spoils, we have developed one of the most formalized, bureaucratized, rigid, and defined personnel administrative systems in the world. Unless there is gross malfeasance, a police officer, once hired, is quite literally employed for life. Dismissal for lack of productivity is unheard of. Combine this with a lack of financial inducements to be productive, and it is small wonder that police managers do not see the system as conducive to a commitment to quality. If it makes no difference whether an officer has five self-initiated incidents per tour or five per year, he or she will stay employed and earn the same salary.

The lesson here is that we must be very cautious about the unexamined application of principles from one organizational environment to another.

Limitations on Applying The Second C: Customer Focus

In Houston, Texas, an owner of a retail furniture outlet is ever present in local advertising. Jim McInvale, popularly known as "Mattress Mac," appears nightly on all the Houston television stations. He has done extremely well in his business, is well liked and is known to virtually everyone in the city. Several years ago, McInvale reacted to a presentation by W. Edwards Deming by enthusiastically adopting the principles of TQM. He applied the principles to an already prospering business and found that sales increased substantially. (Interestingly, among other changes that McInvale made was the elimination of sales commissions.) McInvale exhorts his employees on a daily basis to *delight* the customer. And certainly, across corporate America, innumerable organizations would love to not merely satisfy but to literally delight the customer. Can the customer focus of total quality management be applied to policing? Unequivocally, the answer is no. Not only *can't* we delight the customer, we don't even *want* to delight the customer. Several elements of this phenomenon merit elaboration.

One's immediate reaction when the issue of customer satisfaction in policing is raised is to think of those whom we arrest and laugh a little. No, we are not going to delight someone we're taking to jail for booking, no matter how well we treat him or her. But to think of the customer in this context is to fail to recognize the problems with applying this concept to police service. People we arrest are customers in only a very narrow sense of the term. They deserve to be treated with dignity and respect, but the police are hardly there to provide them service. Indeed, from one perspective, they constitute a "defect" that police are eliminating.

The important point is that police agencies are not charged with delighting the average law-abiding citizen, either. Police managers are distributing a scarce government resource, and they are responsible for seeing that the resource is distributed equitably. The average citizen routinely requests, and even demands, more than his or her equitable share of that resource. In residential neighborhoods, everyone wants to see the police drive by more often. Businesses pressure municipal and county governments to provide enhanced police protection. Funeral homes want escort services. Parents want police officers in the schools, both to provide security and to warn children of the dangers of using drugs. The list goes on and on. Further, these are only the very generic demands for police service. Specific cases are even more problematic: the neighborhood complainer who calls the police at the drop of a hat; the eccentric who calls twice a night, every night, to have the police check for strange noises in the attic; merchants who use the police as a substitute for the security service they ought to be providing themselves. Again, the list goes on and on. This leads to a critical point: *Although we may want the police to delight the customer, prudent management of public resources demands that the police leave many customers explicitly unhappy.* If we insist, under the misguided rhetoric of community policing, on delighting the neighborhood complainer, that individual will simply call even more. And, in effect, police managers have misappropriated a precious public resource that should be expended for more important purposes.

Police managers are hardly oblivious to the problem. Using the sanitized terminology *differential response*, agencies across the country have curtailed services. Particularly in urban areas with intense service demands, police managers can no longer afford to send an officer to every request for service. The days when the telephone deployed the patrol force are gone.

Thus, the issue of definition of customer satisfaction for police agencies is far from a simple one. The difficulty arises in trying to give individuals at the level of operations—complaint takers, patrol officers, detectives—reasonable guidelines for responding to the public. While no one expects problematic police customers to be delighted, most administrators don't want them treated with condescending disdain, either. There are countless gray shades of response, depending on the situation. Officers are told, explicitly or implicitly, to exercise discretion and use good judgment. And when a citizen complains, it is not an automatic given that the employee is at fault if the customer is less than delighted. Further, by common experience, police officers know that the job involves dealing with difficult, obstreperous and obnoxious people—not all of whom are offenders. When they receive a lecture consisting of nothing but naive platitudes about how they should be partners with community residents, they are likely to roll their eyes.

Limitations on Applying The Third C: Counting

Police have innumerable interactions with citizens where the calibration of quality service is reasonably straightforward. For example, we expect an officer responding to a traffic accident to be courteous (even caring); efficient, without being officious; and considerate of what, for the citizen, is a traumatic occurrence. For routine complaints for which the police cannot provide any assistance, we expect officers to tell citizens what other help, if any, is available. And so on.

But there are a lot of citizen encounters for which the measurement of quality interaction is open to considerable debate. For example, the findings from the Minneapolis domestic violence experiment suggest that making arrests in such situations is the best course of action. However, subsequent research has suggested that arrests are not necessarily the best response. And regardless of whether various courses of action will prevent future violence, the quality of officer/disputant interaction in these situations is extraordinarily difficult to specify.

Or take a minor-in-possession case. Are the police to arrest a young person for having a beer to celebrate his or her 21st birthday, when it's actually two hours before midnight the day before the birthday? How about 24 hours before? How about a week before? Is an officer who writes numerous traffic citations at an "easy pickings" location doing quality police work or not? Is the officer's counterpart on the next shift, who never writes traffic citations at that location because he or she has decided that his or her judgment is better than traffic engineering when it comes to appropriate signage or speed limits, doing quality police work?

Obviously, this dialogue could go on and on. The point, however, is a relatively simply one. In the manufacturing sector, defects are relatively simple to identify, and quality is defined fundamentally as a lack of defects. For most of the service sector, quality is a bit more difficult to define, but we could still reach close to a consensus on what a quality interaction is about— think of checking into a hotel or receiving service at a restaurant. Not so in policing. Quality in policing is, first of all, situational. Second, even in a given situation, there are varied perceptions of what a quality transaction is. As the homily goes, for every complex situation there are many who will offer simple solutions, and they're always wrong. So it is with this issue.

The use of simplistic tallies of arrests, citations, field interrogations, and even clearances to measure the adequacy of police performance on both an individual and an agency level is frequently criticized. The criticism is certainly justified. Taken by themselves, these types of measures do not adequately represent how well a police department responds to citizens. (One should note as a caution that some police departments that have attempted to abandon these measures found to their dismay that arrests, citations and clearances dropped fairly precipitously. It should more accurately be noted that these measures are inadequate in and of themselves, but they are not irrelevant.) More "sophisticated" measures are almost universally seen as desirable.

For example, a police agency might handle an auto theft for which a recovery never occurs or an arrest is never made, but do so in a manner that provides quality service to the victim. First of all, since the loss is a significant one, whether covered by insurance or not, the agency might consider sending an officer out in person to take the report, rather than doing so by "differential response." The officer, in turn, might treat the citizen with compassion and understanding, take time to complete the report, and even commiserate with the citizen for a while about the "sorry state of affairs" when nothing is safe from theft anymore. There could even be a follow-up phone call one week and then one month later to let the citizen know that the report hadn't been forgotten, but nothing had been found. Most of us would agree that the police agency managing the incident in this manner provided quality police service. The vast majority of citizens don't blame the police department when a car is stolen. Indeed, their likely response is "we need more police." Thus, if the police handle an incident well, the victim is likely to be satisfied. But how do you measure this?

About the only practical way is some sort of survey of complainants/victims. "Were you satisfied with the response time? Did the complaint taker treat you courteously? Was the officer at the scene courteous? Did someone contact you to inform you of progress on the case?" And, indeed, numerous police agencies use such surveys. They are probably a good idea, as they provide some feedback regarding quality of service. But they have serious limitations. The same officer can respond to two citizens in exactly the same way regarding exactly the same type of incident, and receive very different ratings. Remember that one of the characteristics of service Albrecht and Zemke postulated was that "customers' assessments of service quality are subjective and strongly influenced by expectations." Some might argue that if one did sufficiently large sampling, errors would cancel themselves out and one would emerge with a reasonable picture of the average quality of service a given officer or agency provided. But conducting surveys is not cheap. The best information is obtained through personal contact, such as a telephone interview, but that's also the most expensive. Even mail surveys get expensive when the sample is large, not only with regard to printing and postage, but also for tabulating data. With the budget constraints typical in the public sector and, arguably, no critical purpose to which such information is to be put, large expenditures for gathering such data are not likely to be sustainable.

Further, this type of information is subject to systematic bias. Officers who are assigned to certain beats at certain times are very likely to receive higher ratings overall than officers assigned to different beats at different times. There is a lot of difference between the people the police talk to at 10 a.m. and those they talk to at 2 a.m.

Another illustration of the difficulty of transferring TQM measures used in the private sector to policing is the reduction of cycle times. This measure is regarded by both the manufacturing and the service sectors as an important indicator of improved quality. Examples abound:

- the check-out time for a rental car,
- the check-in time at a hotel,
- the turnaround time for insurance claims,
- the rapidity of order fulfillment,
- the rapidity of payment cycles, and
- the rapidity with which phones are answered.

Some of these can be applied to policing. For example, we certainly would take rapidity of telephone answering as one measure of quality. Another might be reduction in the amount of time it took a citizen to receive a copy of a traffic accident report. And then there is, of course, the big one— rapidity of response by patrol. But the final illustration represents the dangers in doing a simplistic transfer of typical TQM measures to police service. It is not that response time doesn't make any difference. It often makes a great deal of difference in terms of citizen satisfaction. Although citizens will tolerate delayed response, particularly if the complaint taker informs them that there will be some delay, they will not be happy with inordinately long response delays. In particular, they will not be happy in instances when they are stressed, e.g., waiting in the parking lot of a mall when their car has been stolen. Or let's be more dramatic. Mom, Dad and the kids go to see Grandma and find her dead on the bedroom floor. No family feels like sitting in the living room for two hours, with Grandma on the bedroom floor, waiting for the police to show up. So response time has some import.

Now let's go back to our earlier scenario on quality handling of an auto theft complaint. In that instance, we dispatched the patrol unit so that our citizen had face-to-face contact with a law enforcement representative to report the very significant loss of property. The officer took his or her time taking the report. And we allocated scarce police resources to a public relations clerk who did routine callbacks. But in doing all that with our scarce police resources, we didn't have officers cruising the streets with uncommitted patrol time, ready to respond rapidly to either the next auto theft complaint or Grandma on the bedroom floor. Which is higher quality police service—taking our time with every complainant, or keeping patrol resources free so that we get to selected complainants more rapidly? There is no answer to this question. Not only is there no unanimity of opinion, but we also aren't even *close* to a consensus. And, ultimately, no matter which opinion any of us hold, we would have to acknowledge that it's exactly that—an opinion, not a fact.

Afterword

Here we get to a point mentioned in the preface to this book. Not all qualitative elements of police work can be quantified. There are too many exigencies, contingencies and intangibles. Private-sector consultants who approach a police department with formula solutions to measure quality are purveyors of snake oil. Offering simplistic measurement solutions is *prima facie* evidence of ignorance of the complexity of the police role.

That is not to say that some common TQM measures cannot be applied to police service. Appendix A lists a number of measures Texas police managers suggested as potentially useful. Some of these measures, as well as others, are discussed in detail in subsequent chapters. Some are relatively easy to tabulate, and some are quite difficult. Some will provide very direct measures of quality, while others will provide only indirect measures. But some measurement is better than none. At the same time, police managers must recognize that we cannot reduce all quality police service to numbers.

References

Albrecht, K., and R. Zemke. 1985. *Service America*. Homewood, Ill.: Dow Jones-Irwin.

ASQC Quality Costs Committee. 1987. *Guide for Reducing Quality Costs*. Milwaukee: ASQC Quality Press.

Brocka, B., and S.M. Brocka. 1992. *Quality Management: Implementing the Best Ideas of the Masters*. Homewood, Ill.: Business One Irwin.

Couper, D.C., and S.H. Lobitz. 1991. *Quality Policing: The Madison Experience*. Washington, D.C.: Police Executive Research Forum.

Crosby, P.B. 1979. *Quality is Free*. New York: McGraw-Hill.

_____. 1984. *Quality Without Tears*. New York: McGraw-Hill.

Deming, W.E. 1986. *Out of the Crisis*. Cambridge, Mass.: MIT Center for Advanced Engineering Study.

Department of Commerce. 1995. *Malcolm Baldrige National Quality Award, 1995 Award Criteria*. Washington, D.C.: Government Printing Office.

Dobyns, L., and C. Crawford-Mason. 1991. *Quality OR ELSE: The Revolution in World Business*. Boston: Houghton Mifflin.

Ernst & Young Quality Improvement Consulting Group. 1990. *Total Quality: An Executive's Guide for the 1990s*. Homewood, Ill.: Business One Irwin.

Gale, B., and R. Buzzell. 1987. *The PIMS Principles: Linking Strategy to Performance*. New York: Free Press.

Garvin, D.A. 1988. *Managing Quality*. New York: Free Press.

Gore, A. 1993. *The Gore Report on Reinventing Government*. New York: Random House.

Grant, E.L., and R.S. Leavenworth. 1980. *Statistical Quality Control*. New York: McGraw-Hill.

Grimm, A.F. (ed.). 1986. *Quality Costs.* Milwaukee: ASQC Quality Press.

Hagan, J.T. (ed.). 1984. *Principles of Quality Costs.* Milwaukee: ASQC Quality Press.

Hatry, H.P., and J.M. Greiner. 1986. *Improving the Use of Quality Circles in Police Departments.* Washington, D.C.: National Institute of Justice.

Hawk, D. 1994. *Total Quality Management: Fact or Fantasy.* Houston: Champion Press.

Herzberg, F. 1966. *Work and the Nature of Man.* Cleveland: World.

Imai, M. 1986. *Kaizen: The Key to Japan's Competitive Success.* New York: Random House Business Division.

Ishikawa, K. 1985. *What is Total Quality Control? The Japanese Way.* Translated by David J. Lu. Englewood Cliffs, N.J.: Prentice-Hall.

Juran, J.M. 1988. *Juran on Planning for Quality.* New York: Free Press.

Kansas City, Mo., Police Department. 1977. *Response Time Analysis.* Washington, D.C.: U.S. Department of Justice, National Institute of Law Enforcement and Criminal Justice.

Kelling, G.L., T. Pate, D. Dieckman, and C.E. Brown. 1974. *The Kansas City Preventive Patrol Experiment: A Technical Report.* Washington, D.C.: Police Foundation.

Lacy, A. 1993. Presentation at Law Enforcement Management Institute's Executive Issues Seminar, Amarillo, Texas.

Lawler, E.E. 1986. *High-Involvement Management.* Washington, D.C.: Jossey-Bass.

McGregor, D. 1960. *The Human Side of Enterprise.* New York: McGraw-Hill.

Miller, L.M. 1984. *American Spirit: Visions of a New Corporate Culture.* William Morrow & Co. Inc.

Ouchi, W.G. 1981. *Theory Z.* Reading, Mass.: Addison-Wesley.

Peters, T.J., and R.H. Waterman. 1982. *In Search of Excellence.* New York: Harper & Row.

Peters, T.J., and N. Austin. 1985. *A Passion for Excellence: The Leadership Difference.* New York: Random House.

Rice, D.A. 1993. *Quality First.* College Station, Texas: Read Center for Distribution Research and Education, Texas A&M University.

Sashkin, M., and K.J. Kiser. 1991. *Total Quality Management.* Seabrook, Md.: Ducochon Press.

_____. 1992. *Total Quality Management Assessment Inventory Trainer Guide.* Seabrook, Md.: Ducochon Press.

Scholtes, P.R. 1988. *The Team Handbook.* Madison, Wis.: Joiner Associates.

Sherman, L.W., and R.A. Berk. 1984. *The Minneapolis Domestic Violence Experiment.* Washington, D.C.: Police Foundation.

Tenner, A.R., and I.J. DeToro. 1992. *Total Quality Management.* Reading, Mass.: Addison/Wesley.

Texas Department of Commerce. 1993. *Quality Texas: Investment for Survival.* Austin, Texas: State of Texas.

Walton, M. 1986. *The Deming Management Method.* New York: Putnam Perigee.

Chapter 2

Defining the Bottom Line in Policing: Organizational Philosophy and Accountability

George L. Kelling

Introduction

It is 8 a.m. Friday, and the second of the twice-weekly meetings of the New York City Police Department (NYPD) precinct commanders is convening in the command center. The 76 commanders are seated at a group of tables arranged in a large U. At the top of the U, a large projection screen hangs from the ceiling. Under the projection screen is a lectern. Directly facing the lectern and screen, at the bottom of the U, the chief of patrol (Louis Anemone) and the chief of detectives (Charles Reuther) sit with Deputy Commissioner for Crime Control Jack Maple. Maple is in the middle. Also present are the eight borough commanders and representatives from the schools, district attorney's offices and parole department. Two issues are under discussion: What are the problems in each precinct, and what are precinct commanders doing about them?

The first precinct commander prepares to speak, taking his place at the lectern. He is accompanied by a detective lieutenant from the precinct. Although the detective is from a centralized unit, it is clear that he, too, will have to account for precinct problems. Data from the precinct commander's district are projected on the screen above his head: the seven index crimes; shooting victims; residents who have felony warrants outstanding, are on parole, and are on parole with parole warrants outstanding; distributions of arrests; and whatever other data are available that reflect the quality of life in the district.

The precinct commander begins his presentation. Within a few minutes, Maple interrupts: "Your rapes are up. What's happening?" The precinct commander shoots back with a description of each rape: how it occurred, where, when, and whether the rapist and victim were acquainted. Maple follows up with a more detailed question about one of the rapes, and the precinct commander turns the lectern over to the detective lieutenant for response. And so the session goes. During this intense questioning, pressure-reducing bantering—typical cop-talk—breaks out. Maple, after checking with the chiefs of patrol and detectives, starts to bring the presentation to a close; however, a precinct commander requests a minute to introduce a neighborhood police officer who has developed a particularly innovative approach to dealing with a quality-of-life problem—hazardous waste—in her beat. The commander describes her work, asks her to stand, and then everyone gives her a hand. The next precinct commander to present, flanked by a detective lieutenant, takes her place at the lectern. The commander who has just completed his presentation knows that he will be back at the lectern in about three months—the time it takes for all the precinct commanders to present, since there are two three-hour meetings a week.

Crime, as measured by the Uniform Crime Reports, is down in New York City, continuing a decline that began about four years ago and is quickening. Between 1993 and 1994, for example, homicides went down 18 percent, with decreases accelerating (down 32% in September from the previous year, 46% in October, 28% in November, and 34% in December) as, in the minds of New York City police, antigun and antiviolence efforts took hold. Likewise, robbery was down 15.5 percent. It was the first year in New York's history that both robberies and homicides declined at a double-digit rate. Overall, felonies were down 12 percent, New York's steepest drop in the last 20 years.

The media have given considerable coverage to these recent declines in New York City's crime rates. The *New York Times* alone provides a good example: starting on New Year's Day, the *Times* began a three-part series by Clifford Kraus that extensively analyzed the decline. By the end of the week, another lengthy story appeared, again reporting the decline. I use the *Times* as an example not because it is the most important newspaper or media outlet in New York City, but because it comes as close to being a newspaper of record as exists in the United States. Nonetheless, similar stories appeared in other New York newspapers, as they do in virtually every city when crime data are released. For media, and for many politicians and the general public, crime data—the Uniform Crime Reports (UCR)—are the ultimate "bottom line" of police functioning.

Several things are striking about such stories. First, many are serious.[1] In the *New York Times'* stories discussed above, for example, fair consideration was given to determine whether the changed strategy and tactics of the NYPD caused the reductions in reported crimes. Second, reporters typically try to get a range of views about the crime rates and how to interpret them. Generally, they turn to known criminologists for comments about the importance of the reported increases or decreases in crime. Responses generally fall into three categories. First, one group dismisses the idea that police activities have anything to do with the crime rate; for them, crime stems from basic structural features of society, and until problems like homelessness, social injustice, economic inequality, and racism are addressed, police impact on crime will be negligible.[2]   Social activists/ academics tend to respond in such terms. A second group tends to respond in somewhat different terms, although their comments are often similarly dismissive of police impact on crime. They tend to respond in demographic terms: crime levels are a function of the age structure of the population and, given the anticipated upturn in the percentage and number of youths in society, their remarks often imply or state, "If you think things are bad now, just wait." The third group generally questions the UCR as a valid and reliable indicator of police productivity. I have been among those in that category. Indeed, in a recent paper titled "Measuring What Matters," using New York City as a case in point, I enumerated many of the shortcomings of UCR statistics and urged the adoption of other measures of success for police departments.[3] More about this later.

This chapter will focus on the third issue, the validity of the UCR as an indicator of police effectiveness, although I will make brief comments about the first two positions. The first, that social injustices must be addressed before police can make a difference in crime rates, is often a political statement intended to advance particular social programs— housing, affirmative action, social welfare, etc. Such programs may or may not be valid, valuable and laudable; however, I expect advocates to support them. Thus, for example, when former New York City Police Commissioner Ray Kelly asked me to help deal with the problem of "squeegeeing" (unsolicited and intimidating washing of car windows at intersections), I was not surprised when libertarian advocates demanded apartments and jobs for window washers. However, when police executives imply that police crime-control activities are futile, or largely so, until basic structural features of society are rectified, it has the trace of a "cop-out": that is, such a position can be used to excuse police agencies for ineffectiveness in dealing with problems or to ignore what can and should be done *today* to improve the lives of people who cannot protect their children, property and quality of life, especially in minority and poor communities. Regarding the second group, a group that posits what I call a "demography as destiny" point of view, they trivialize the impact of social *policy* on disorder, fear and crime. Thus, for example, I have argued elsewhere that the general decline in New York City's subway during the 1970s and 1980s was not just the result of more youths, more drugs, more spray-paint cans, and more libertarians who defined graffiti as folk art and attempted to legally defend the right of youths to use subway trains as their easels. Failed social policy contributed to the subway's decline, and improved social policy led to its reclamation.[4] Simpleminded extrapolations of historical demographic trends that ignore the follies or wisdom of policies inform us about the future only if we do not learn from past policy wins and losses.

The Uniform Crime Reports

Crime statistics became an issue during the early years of the 20th century, when chiefs such as Sylvester in Washington, D.C.; Murphy of Jersey City, N.J.; Hopper of Newark, N.J.; Dietsch of Cincinnati; and others called for the development of crime statistics that would record both offenders and criminal events. Chiefs such as Kizer of Norfolk, Va.; Giffen and Hammil of Kansas City, Mo.; and Beaver of Atlanta kept crime statistics on the agenda of the International Association of Chiefs of Police (IACP) through World War I.[5] In 1929, Bruce Smith, with the support of J. Edgar Hoover and with funds from the Rockefeller Foundation, led in the development of the first edition of *Uniform Crime Reporting: A Complete Manual for Police*. Hoover ultimately assumed responsibility for the administration of crime statistics in the Federal Bureau of Investigation. From the beginning, it was clear that crime statistics would serve at least two purposes. First, as Banas and Trojanowicz have pointed out in their summary of turn-of-the-century chiefs' speeches and papers on the subject, crime statistics would serve the purpose of internal control:

The chiefs frequently conceptualized their mission as a business. Just as they borrowed their imagery from the rapidly industrializing private sector, so they defined their *raison d'etre* as efficiency. Efficiency became synonymous with disciplining the rank and file to the point that officers became viewed as passive entities possessing absolutely no discretion.... By centralizing discretion within the command structure, the chiefs sought an "objective" basis to exercise authority.[6]

But reformers understood that the UCR had a broader function. They were an integral part of the new "science" of policing that would provide the means to shatter the close link between local political leaders and precinct commanders and beat officers. Crime statistics, presented through annual reports, would allow police leaders to go over the heads of local politicians (ward bosses, if you will) to demonstrate police efficiency and effectiveness to the general public. Armed with "scientific" measures of performance, chiefs could worry less about satisfying politicians and their constituencies, at least in early 20th century terms, which included corrupt political collaboration between local leaders and police.[7] Many police reformers became adroit at communicating to the general public through the media, and in the process, both set external expectations about police performance and provided a vision of policing that attracted the organizational allegiance of line officers. Historically, in Los Angeles, William Parker stands out as a master of this art. His 1950s radio and television show, "The Thin Blue Line," shaped a vision of policing that dominated Los Angeles through the administration of Daryl Gates (who was no slouch with the media in his own right): a lean, tough, no-nonsense, militarized "force." Today, probably no one uses the media as skillfully as William Bratton, both in his current job as New York City police commissioner and in his earlier administration of the New York City Transit Police—a skill that has caused Bratton some difficulty with Mayor Rudy Giuliani's staff.[8, 9] To return to earlier times, however, it is little wonder that crime statistics were so important to reformers like Bruce Smith: they were key to both wresting control of police departments from politicians and getting control of officers. And they worked. Along with the other elements of the reform strategy—narrowing function to law enforcement; centralizing factory-like bureaucratic organizations and administrative processes; centralizing control of demand through telephone and, later, one- and two-way radios; and isolating police in automobiles, ostensibly for tactical reasons—reformers, to a greater or lesser extent, were able to get solid control of both their organizations and their personnel. This control was so complete that, as Herman Goldstein noted in 1977, the police had become the least accountable arm of city government.[10]

The Shortcomings of the
Uniform Crime Reports

The idea that UCR statistics were "scientific" measures of either levels of crime or citizen demand for police services, however, was understood to be inaccurate from the earliest days of their formulation. As Banas and Trojanowicz noted, the first volume of *Uniform Crime Reporting* acknowledged the statistical limitations of the Uniform Crime Reports.[11] For example, despite their enthusiasm and, perhaps, unrealistic hopes about the UCR's ultimate scientific value, the authors of the first volume conceded some of the inherent limitations of crime reports: "Attention has also been given to the practical limits of statistics of crimes committed. It will be readily understood that not all crimes are consistently reported to public authorities...."[12]

The UCR's shortcomings as a scientific measure of performance are now so well understood and so universally acknowledged that there is no need to go into detail about them here. Donald Black, in his classic 1970 article, "The Production of Crime Rates," pretty well summed up the problems with the UCR.[13] The issues include whether or not citizens report crime; the police decision to accept a report, modify it or recode it; the relative weighting of the seriousness of crimes and the legitimate and illegitimate factors that can shape such weighting; the limitations in the types of crimes that are recorded (the elimination of white-collar crimes); and, of course, the danger that police can "sharpen their pencils" by discounting legitimate crimes, rejecting complaints, lying, and doing other things to distort self-reported data. To partially eliminate these difficulties, victimization surveys were developed during the 1960s and came to be used to provide more accurate estimates of crime and to evaluate many police and criminal justice programs, practices and innovations. Victimization surveys have their own shortcomings, however. In addition to all the problems of ensuring reliability, victimization surveys are expensive to administer, are available only by region (not cities), and are limited to the same crimes as the UCR. There is little reason to suspect that victimization surveys will routinely be available for cities and police departments to evaluate their activities.

Accountability Redux

The issue of accountability—departmental, unit and officer—however, is no less critical today than it was at the turn of the century. To be sure, the issue of accountability to *whom* is different, given the end of the political machines in cities and the success of police administrators in severing the links between police and politicians, but establishing the terms of accountability for officers, units and departments is no less perplexing and

elusive than it was for early reformers. Take New York City, for example.
There, Bratton is attempting to take a department that is reeling from a
variety of crises and turn it into a high-performing organization. The once-
proud department has suffered from serious corruption scandals; a working
culture has developed that is virulently antimanagement and oriented
toward staying out of trouble, primarily by doing nothing; a management
culture has been oriented around self-protection and lack of accountability;
and a public perception of the police as venal and unproductive has grown,
especially in minority communities. As he did with New York's transit
police during the early 1990s, Bratton has been moving to shift the NYPD to
a new strategy that can be broadly categorized as community policing,
building on the efforts of three previous commissioners. A critical element in
Bratton's approach, perhaps a central one in a department the size of the
NYPD, has been the devolution of authority to precinct commanders. Early,
Bratton sent out the message that the brightest and best mid-managers would
be reassigned to head precincts—a message that precipitated many
resignations. The emphasis on precincts is real. As the director of Harvard's
Program in Criminal Justice, Francis X. Hartman has noted after conducting
focus groups with precinct commanders:

> There is a genuine sense of empowerment among the precinct
> commanders. For the first time in their careers, they have a
> heady sense of being on their own (as one said, "we are drunk
> with power"), of having real responsibility without someone
> constantly telling them what to do. They feel that they are an
> essential part of a momentum that has reduced crime, that
> detectives are working with them in a cooperative fashion, that
> "cops are happy to be cops," and that "more people are aboard
> than ever."[14]

This devolution of authority, as non-New Yorkers may not know, is
taken in the aftermath of a corruption crisis in which several precinct
officers established corrupt liaisons with drug dealers in minority
neighborhoods, taking money and drugs, while brutalizing the community in
the bargain—especially egregious acts given the historical troubles between
police and minority and poor neighborhoods. While the vast majority of
officers remained honest, line officers' blue curtain of silence and mid-
managers' fear of rocking the boat and jeopardizing their careers created an
organizational climate that, while not supportive of rogue officers, tolerated
them. Devolving authority in the aftermath of such revelations, of course,
ran counter to popular wisdom and 70 years of reform administration: when
confronted with corruption, centralize authority. But, convinced that the
worst form of corruption was underutilization of the NYPD in the face of
outrageous levels of disorder, fear and crime, Bratton has opted to push

forward his plan to improve the quality and increase the aggressiveness (read "proactivity," not "combativeness") by devolving authority to precinct commanders. The crucial question, of course, in a large department like New York's, is how to increase and improve the accountability, especially of precinct commanders. As is apparent from the opening anecdote, UCR data are a significant element in holding precinct commanders accountable.

A Slight Diversion

I have often wondered how much different policing would be today if the results of the Kansas City Preventive Patrol Study had been different.[15] That is, suppose that on the basis of the UCR and victimization surveys, crime had been reduced by statistically significant but otherwise minimal amounts in areas in which we increased uncommitted patrol time, and that it had risen in areas where we decreased patrol time. Moreover, suppose that nothing else was different: recognition of increases or decreases in patrol levels was still absent, fear levels remained the same, citizen satisfaction with police services remained the same, and police attitudes about citizens and citizen attitudes about police remained the same. (Police attitudes toward citizens were not measured in the Kansas City study, but they were in both the Newark Foot Patrol Study and the Evaluation of the Neighborhood Foot Patrol Program in Flint.[16] Both police officer and citizen estimations of each other were markedly improved by the introduction of foot patrol.) Suppose, as well, that the response time studies showed similar results: that is, they did not affect levels of citizen satisfaction or fear, but had an impact on on-view crimes that exceeded the reported 3 percent—say by 200 percent, up to 9 percent.[17] The question I am posing is, of course, whether or not policing would still be going through the changes of today if traditional reform tactics had proved to be marginally effective in dealing with crime. The fact that we will never know makes the question no less relevant.

What brings this question to mind in this context is an interesting short piece by Larry Hoover, the editor of this book, and Tori Caeti, in the *TELESMAP Bulletin:* "Crime-Specific Policing in Houston."[18] The article is noteworthy because of Houston's history: its pioneering role in the development of community policing, and the subsequent rejection of community policing—at least as it was defined and implemented in Houston—by a newly elected mayor. Hoover and Caeti describe Houston's new approach and label it "crime-specific policing." They emphasize that "crime-specific policing" is not a return to "traditional policing" (what I would call "reform" policing), and their description of the philosophy, strategies and programs would certainly warrant their claim. Clearly, rapid response to calls for service, a reform strategy mainstay, continues to be a major priority in Houston. This is the case in many other cities that emphasize community or problem-oriented policing, as well, so it is hard to fault the Houston Police Department or Hoover and Caeti on this point.

The statement of the Houston Police Department's philosophy, however, contains an especially important point, a point clearly emphasized in New York and apparent in my opening anecdote, as well. To quote the authors: "Police agencies can impact the level of crime and disorder in a community. The police *do* make a difference. Saying that crime and disorder are a product of social and economic forces the police cannot and should not affect is rejected."[19] This is an important statement. It is a cornerstone of Bratton's administration in New York. It is a point that I have tried to make elsewhere and that must be reinforced.[20] A basic purpose of police is crime prevention. The idea that police cannot do anything about crime and that they stand helpless in the face of demographics, drugs, gangs, or whatever is unacceptable—often, as I have mentioned above, a "cop-out" that covers lack of strategic commitment and absence of planning and implementation.

Having put forward this philosophy, the article goes on to document Houston's strategies and programs, and to analyze Houston's UCR statistics and compare them with data from four other Texas cities. The conclusions include the following: as reflected in the UCR, crime has dropped in all of urban Texas; Houston's drop has been greater than the other cities' (27.8% vs. 20.7% in combined robbery, burglary and auto theft); Part II offenses have risen as a result of more proactive policing (officer-initiated arrests); proactive policing has increased. Throughout the article, Hoover and Caeti carefully acknowledge the problems with UCR data, the possibility of "cooking the books," and the difficulties inherent in using crime statistics. The article closes with a note that "this is not a commentary on the efficiency of policing strategy among the five comparison cities," and "'writing off' crime-specific approaches in favor of community policing is assuredly premature."[21] One could disagree with some of the issues and assumptions presented in the article and sidebars—the issues of whether community policing lacks a definition and whether problem-oriented policing runs a distant second to community policing, and the assumption that somehow crime-specific approaches are outside of community or problem-oriented policing (after all, are not specific crimes problems that yield to proper analysis and response?). But these are not the issues here. The point I wish to make is that Hoover and Caeti's analysis may well be accurate: the crime-specific activities described could be yielding significant results. After all, I do believe that the reenergized activities of the NYPD are reducing crime. In both places, the philosophy that police *can* make a difference and the implementation of that philosophy by holding officers, units and the department accountable for suppressible crimes in their areas might explain the differences. But I am still reminded of my questions about the consequences if traditional patrol had made a difference on crime statistics and victimization in Kansas City during the 1970s.

Police Serve Many Values

Organizations serve many values. Indeed, even in the private sector, the bottom line—profit—while an important value, is but one of many values that organizations serve. For example, my friend and colleague Robert Johnson is president and chairman of the board of First Security—a large regional private security firm. For Johnson, profit clearly is an important issue. But First Security's values and goals include quality service that exceeds client expectations, integrity, confidentiality, instant response to service complaints, and employee satisfaction. A basic philosophy of First Security is that it can both do *good* and do *well*. Its values are promulgated for both external marketing purposes and internal guidance and control. Externally, they tell prospective clients about the kinds of services they can expect, and they identify for current clients the kinds of services they should be receiving. Internally, such values put forward the terms of accountability for units, managers and employees. Moreover, these values have teeth in the organization: managers are held strictly accountable for achieving *all* the goals of the organization, not just profit.

This point, that organizations have multiple goals, is not all that profound; however, it has often been lost in policing and police departments. It explains my concerns about the preventive patrol experiment: measuring police performance solely by crime statistics simply ignores consequential values. These values include justice, integrity, fear reduction, citizen satisfaction, protection and help for those who cannot protect or help themselves, and many others. Judging a tactic or set of tactics solely by one measure—crime—regardless of how it is measured, and even if the measurement is accurate—is inadequate. It fails to communicate to the general public what they have a right to expect from police. Likewise, measuring the impact of police departments solely by their impact on crime fails to inform managers, units and line personnel what is expected from them. Preventive patrol by automobile, even if it had made a significant but minimal impact on crime, simply failed in too many other respects— maintaining order, collaborating with citizens and community institutions, gathering information, reducing fear, fully exploiting the talents of police officers and providing them with rich occupational experiences, etc.—to be a sustainable or dominant police tactic.

The consequences of not communicating externally and internally all the values organizations serve and enforcing their pursuit can be grave. The recent collapse of England's Baring Bank was an example of what happens when profit is overemphasized and rewards, financial and other, get linked to that goal. Deviance resulting from the pursuit of narrow goals has been seen time and time again in policing: special units gone awry in their pursuits of arrests; zealotry in pursuit of drug dealers; organizational denigration of units and personnel pursuing other legitimate and important goals; undue recognition for those in the organization who use improper means but, nonetheless, achieve high numbers of arrests; and "cooking the books." "Cooking the books," by the way, is hardly restricted to police: in the interests of making a company look good for stockholders or potential investors, employees can manipulate profit levels in a variety of ways, including underreporting income, overreporting expenses and depreciation and/or distributing income, depreciation and operating costs over longer or shorter periods.

The point is, crime, as reflected by the UCR—and, for that matter, by victimization surveys—is one element of the bottom line of policing; it is not *the* bottom line. Like profit in the public sector, crime levels communicate to community stakeholders and to police units and personnel partial information about how the organization is doing. Moreover, crime data allow managers like Jack Maple and his many colleagues in departments throughout the United States to determine how well personnel understand some of the problems that afflict their areas and to hold personnel accountable for such understanding. Although not made explicit, it is probably the case that similar mechanisms of accountability are being used in Houston.

In sum, early 20th century police leaders such as Bruce Smith, who helped develop the original UCR, contributed enormously to the development of policing in the United States. They wanted to shift from an accountability structure that held policing hostage to ward political machines to one that documented important organizational goals—police performance in dealing with crime. They were keenly aware of both the external and the internal value of doing so. Unfortunately, just as narrow preoccupation with citizen and political satisfaction corrupted and distorted policing during its earlier stages, narrow preoccupation with crime corrupted and distorted mid-20th century policing.[22] (Preoccupation with citizen satisfaction to the exclusion of other measures has the same corrupting and distorting potential now.) Consequently, police practitioners, scholars and city officials will have to be extraordinarily careful to develop measures of accountability that fully reflect the values that police departments serve— indicators of justice, integrity, wise use of force, citizen satisfaction, efficiency, and so on. Maple's approach in New York has helped immeasurably to invigorate NYPD mid-managers. There is ongoing work in the NYPD to develop additional indicators of managerial performance that reflect other values, especially integrity and quality of performance. Something akin may well be happening in Houston. The wonder of this era in policing is that so many experiments are being conducted. The need to develop multiple measures of police performance that reflect the multiplicity of police achievements, however, has never been so acute.

Notes

[1]Some may be serious, but they are so cynical that it is hard to take them seriously. Sydney H. Schanberg, for example, wrote an op-ed piece titled "If Crime is Dropping, Who Can Be Sure," in *New York Newsday* (Feb. 21, 1995). While the op-ed piece contains some interesting points, its pervasive cynicism is apparent in statements such as "Am I suggesting that Commissioner Bratton ... has diddled with the crime statistics? Yes, he almost certainly has. Most commissioners do, though perhaps not with his level of artistry," and "To sum up, since anything in the world is possible, it may be that there *has* actually been a drop in crime in New York City. But we will never have any way of knowing, as long as we have to rely on the dubious figures that are fed to us now."

[2]Some academic ideologists do not let research interfere with their conclusions. Richard Moran, for example, constantly misuses the Kansas City Preventive Patrol Experiment to justify his belief that police have no impact on crime. Whether he knows better or not, the preventive patrol study was a study of a tactic—preventive patrol by automobile to create a feeling of police omnipresence—not a study of the impact of either the number of police or policing in general on crime. Likewise, his dismissive attitude toward fear reduction that results from foot patrol stems from a naive view of the relationship between disorder, fear and serious crime. For the most recent example of such ideology in print, see his op-ed piece, "More Police, Less Crime, Right? Wrong," *New York Times*, Feb. 27, 1995.

[3]George L. Kelling, "Measuring What Matters: A New Way of Thinking About Crime and Public Order," *City Journal*, Spring 1992, pp. 21-32.

[4]See George L. Kelling, *Fixing Broken Windows: Restoring Order in American Cities*, Free Press, New York, forthcoming, Spring 1996.

[5]Dennis W. Banas and Robert C. Trojanowicz, *Uniform Crime Reporting and Community: An Historical Perspective, National Neighborhood Foot Patrol Center*, East Lansing, Mich., Michigan State University, 1985.

[6]*Ibid*, p. 11.

[7]See, for example, L.S. Timmerman, "The Annual Police Report," *The Annals* 146, November 1929. See also, George L. Kelling and James K. Stewart, "The Evolution of Contemporary Policing," in William A. Geller, ed., *Local Government Police Management*, 3rd ed., International City Management Association, Washington, D.C., 1991, pp. 3-21.

[8]Kelling, *Fixing Broken Windows*.

[9]*New York Times*, Feb. 16, 1995.

[10]Herman Goldstein, *Policing a Free Society*, Ballinger, Cambridge, Mass., 1977.

[11]Banas and Trojanowicz, p. 11.

[12]*Uniform Crime Reporting: A Complete Manual for Police, Committee on Uniform Crime Records*, International Association of Chiefs of Police, New York City, 1929.

[13]Donald J. Black, "The Production of Crime Rates," *American Sociological Review* 35, August 1970, pp. 733-748.

[14]Francis X. Hartmann, memo to Commissioner William Bratton, Feb. 22, 1995, "Learning from the Precincts."

[15]George L. Kelling et al., *The Kansas City Preventive Patrol Experiment*, Police Foundation, Washington, D.C., 1975.

[16]*The Newark Foot Patrol Study*, Police Foundation, Washington, D.C., 1981, and Robert C. Trojanowicz, *An Evaluation of the Neighborhood Foot Patrol Program in Flint*, Michigan State University, East Lansing, Mich., 1982.

[17]See William Spelman and Dale K. Brown, *Calling the Police: Citizen Reporting of Serious Crime*, Police Executive Research Forum, Washington, D.C., 1981, for a summary of the response time studies.

[18]Larry Hoover and Tory Caeti, "Crime-Specific Policing in Houston," *Texas Law Enforcement Management and Administrative Statistics Program Bulletin*, Vol. 1, No. 9, December 1994. Bill Blackwood Law Enforcement Management Institute of Texas, Huntsville, Texas.

[19]*Ibid*, p. 1.

[20]Kelling, *Fixing Broken Windows.*

[21]Hoover and Caeti, p. 11.

[22]I thank David Kennedy, a research fellow in the Program of Criminal Justice, Kennedy School of Government, Harvard University, for helping me to fully understand the consequences of citizen and political satisfaction as a sole goal of policing.

Chapter 3

Measuring Overall Effectiveness
or, Police-Force Show and Tell

David H. Bayley

Introduction

This chapter addresses what might be called "the chief's question," namely, How do we know when a police department is performing satisfactorily? This is the same question David Couper tried to answer in his 1983 report, "How to Rate Your Local Police," published by the Police Executive Research Forum. The question is central to police politics, for which chiefs are primarily responsible. Unless it can be answered to the satisfaction of the public and its elected and appointed representatives, the police are unlikely to get the resources they say they need. People want to be assured that the money given to the police produces the safety they so earnestly desire. Although providing information about police performance is a critical task for chiefs, most evaluations of policing do not assess the institution's overall effectiveness. Instead, they focus on particular programs and activities, such as drug-market disruption, foot patrols or emergency response. Scholars and other professional evaluators shy away from global assessments, perhaps because they seem too broad-gauged and unwieldy. Judging the performance of a police force in general is more than a technical matter of choosing appropriate measurement criteria and methodologies; it involves controversial decisions about what the police should do and how they should do it.

Despite the lack of attention to evaluating the general performance of police forces, I believe that the institutional effectiveness of the police will increasingly become an issue. Indeed, the pressures for an institutional evaluation of policing are becoming so intense that the question is not, in my opinion, whether police will engage in performance evaluation, but when. I say this for four reasons.

First, the general public seems to believe that crime is rising and that there is little that the police or the criminal justice system can do about it. Recent polls show that crime is Americans' number one concern (*New York Times*, Feb. 23, 1994). People not only are frightened, but their faith in law enforcement has also been eroding (Reiner 1992; Shearing 1993; Grabosky 1992). Another indication of a decline in confidence in the police is that the number of private security personnel is increasing sharply. Public-sector police are losing "market share." Similarly, people are increasingly doing things to protect themselves, such as hardening the defenses of their homes and forming block watches and citizen patrols. Although the police pledge that they will control crime if they are given more resources, the public is not accepting their promises as trustingly as they used to. Public opinion about the police almost seems contradictory. People voice strong support for increasing the number of police, but they act as if they no longer think that the police are doing an adequate job.

Second, governments at all levels are under mounting pressure to economize. "Doing more with less" has become the watchword among all levels of American government. As a result, governments are establishing new auditing and oversight procedures to ensure that they spend money more efficiently and effectively. One device has been to ask police to develop "performance indicators" by which their activities may be judged.

Third, police leaders themselves are gradually becoming convinced that good management involves program evaluation. Two decades ago, evaluations of police work were very rare. Now they are commonplace, often undertaken by outside scholars, consultants and experts. Management training for senior officers, itself a relatively recent development, almost always stresses the critical importance of performance appraisal. Whether they be "total quality management" or "management by objective," today's managerial philosophies all emphasize performance measurement. The grants for projects and programs for which departments now compete usually require some evaluation of both the process of implementation and the results. Finally, police departments are expanding their own research and planning units, transforming them from go-fers for the chief to offices where strategic planning and program evaluation can take place.

Indeed, although the public is so far unaware of it, the police have become one of the most open bureaucracies in government. They are second only, I submit, to public schools. American police, especially, should be given more credit for this climate of openness and visibility than they have been. They are setting the standard for the rest of the world.

Fourth, the police's technical capacity to collect, manage and analyze operational information has risen dramatically in the last decade. Until quite recently, police managers did not immediately know how many officers were on duty, where they were assigned or what they were doing. Now, police managers have current information at their fingertips about calls for service and crime occurrences, personnel availability, resource deployment, workload activity, and actions taken. Using census data, many departments can now match the projected needs of beats, precincts or entire jurisdictions to the resources available to them.

The point is that police are being pushed, from both within and without, to demonstrate that they are managing effectively—achieving what the public wants. Since the intellectual know-how and the technical capacity have now been created to make this demonstration, the genie of performance measurement is out of the bottle. Thus, the pressing question is, How should the police go about demonstrating that they are effective?

This chapter attempts to answer this question. First, it examines the sorts of performance measures now being used. They include rates of crime and victimization, assessments of the fear of crime, and various measures of police activity. Second, it examines the tradeoffs among performance measures, and the effects that adopting different ones has on police operation as well as police accountability. Third, it recommends several principles that police and the public should follow to ensure that police performance is responsibly demonstrated.

The Choices

The most popular measure of police effectiveness is crime rates. People want to know whether the risk of being a victim of crime is increasing or decreasing. The police promise to "serve and protect," and that means protection from crime. Crime rates are the heart of the matter, both for police and for the public. In the United States, crime rates are determined by information local police departments give the FBI as part of the Uniform Crime Reporting (UCR) system. Information is collected systematically about eight types of serious crime, known as Part I or Index crimes: murder and non-negligent manslaughter, rape, robbery, aggravated assault, burglary, larceny-theft, auto theft, and arson. Other developed democratic countries have similar national crime-reporting systems. Because participation in the UCR system has become universal in the United States, the public gets quarterly updates through the media about changes in local as well as national crime rates, broken down by offense categories. The UCR reports are undoubtedly the most visible police performance measure.

Unfortunately, the UCR crime figures are not as good as they look as an indicator of police effectiveness. While they are valid and general, reflecting what people want to know about the police across the country, they have two major shortcomings.

First, they are unpredictably unreliable (Sherman 1982). Their accuracy depends on what the public is willing to report to the police and on the honesty, as well as the assiduousness, of the police in recording what is reported.

To avoid these problems, the U.S. government began conducting victimization surveys in 1973, in an effort to find out what crimes are happening to people without the mediation of police reports. In these surveys, a large sample of households (42,000) are asked every three months whether members have been the victims of crime, regardless of whether or not they have reported the crimes to the police (*Sourcebook of Criminal Justice Statistics* 1992). The picture of crime that emerges from the National Crime Survey (NCS) is substantially different from that obtained through UCR methodology. For example, UCR figures show that violent crime (murder, rape, robbery, aggravated assault) has risen steadily since 1973. NCS figures, however, show that violent crime against persons (murder not included) peaked in 1981 (*Sourcebook* 1992, t 3.4) and that the victimization rate for violent crimes declined by 13.2 percent between 1973 and 1989.

So the problem police departments face is that different methodologies for assessing the incidence of crime lead to different conclusions about the effectiveness of the police. The UCR measures will continue to dominate local police performance evaluation because they are cheaper than victimization surveys. The system is now universal, and the costs of participating in it are small. The UCR has become so well established that a police department would need to explain why it does not contribute data to it. The NCS's information, however, is not built from the bottom up, taking advantage of what localities are already doing. It is a national sample survey that cannot be broken down by particular jurisdictions. To obtain local victimization data, localities would have to commission their own surveys. The costs of doing this are substantial, and they are difficult to justify when the superiority of victimization surveys over police reports of crime is debatable.

Second, all data on the incidence of crime, whether obtained from police records or victimization surveys, suffer from a fundamental defect as a measure of police performance. Crime is not something the police can really control. Sad to say, crime is not determined by what the police do, or by how many of them there are. Criminologists have shown again and again that the best predictors of crime—among police forces, cities, states, and countries, as opposed to individuals—are economic and social factors, notably income, unemployment, education, prevalence of minorities, households headed by single women, household size, and home ownership (Walker 1989). Crime rates in large cities can be predicted accurately 80 to 90 percent of the time when these factors are taken into account. The principle seems to be that the larger the unit of analysis, the greater the variance predicted. This finding may surprise the public, but it does not surprise the police. On the basis of their own experience, police often ruefully observe that law enforcement is little more than a Band-Aid on the cancer of crime.

From a political point of view, therefore, reliance on reported crime rates as a police performance measure would seem to be risky for the police. It makes them responsible for circumstances they cannot control. They do not deserve praise when crime rates fall, or blame when they rise. Until recently, however, the political risk has been slight. Given a choice between reported crime rates that are rising and victimization rates that are falling, police chiefs have preferred the rising reported rates. Their reasoning seems to be that if crime is out of their control, it is better to have rising rates than falling ones because they can then argue that they need more resources. Police chiefs fear public complacency that may result from falling rates more than they do public criticism that results from rising rates. So far, rising rates have not been considered signs of inadequate police performance; rather, they have been considered indications of inadequate numbers of police officers.

At the grassroots, however, disillusion with the police may be setting in, as I indicated at the beginning of this chapter. This may undermine the historically uncritical support the public has given the police. If it does, police leaders can be expected to say publicly what they have been saying privately for many years, namely, that reported crime rates are invalid as a measure of police performance.

In sum, because reported crime is related very tenuously to police performance, police may increasingly be put at political risk when they use it as an evaluation indicator. Victimization surveys are not the solution for local departments. They, too, are unresponsive to policing, and they are also costly for local departments to undertake. From the police point of view, therefore, both of these common measures of crime are largely out of their control, with victimization surveys having the added disadvantage of being more costly.

Fear of Crime

The inadequacies of both reported and victimization survey crime rates as measures of general police performance are not news to either the police or criminologists. In fact, extensive discussion about their inadequacies during the 1980s led to the introduction of a new performance measure—the fear of crime. The reasoning was that while the police might not be able to overcome the power of social circumstances in generating crime, they could at least minimize the fear, especially exaggerated fear, that accompanied it (Skogan 1990). It was assumed that the police might have more leverage over crime subjectively than objectively. This was not a cynical ploy designed to make people feel secure even when they were not. The fear of crime directly affects the quality of life, independent of actual victimizations (Skogan 1988, 1990). Moreover, fear itself may be criminogenic because it causes people to act in ways that encourage crime (Kelling 1985). An example of this is when people stop using public places and accommodations, thereby removing the critical mass of noncriminal people who deter crime by their presence.

Surveys assessing the fear of crime are now common. In the United States, commercial polling companies regularly report national as well as city results (*Sourcebook* 1992). Fear items are also part of the periodic British crime survey, as well as of national surveys conducted by the prime minister's office in Japan. Elsewhere in the world, a few local governments or local police departments commission annual surveys about crime, the fear of crime, and police performance (e.g., in New South Wales, Australia; the Kent Constabulary, Great Britain; Reno, Nev.; and Fort Stockton, Texas). The practice appears to be spreading. Furthermore, evaluations of the effectiveness of particular police programs or strategies usually incorporate surveys of the public's fear of crime (Kelling et al. 1974; Police Foundation 1981; Skogan 1990; Rosenbaum 1986; Hornick et al. 1989).

Subjective assessments of police performance now go beyond the fear of crime. They include confidence in the police, satisfaction with specific police contacts, perceptions of police misbehavior, commitment to community action against crime, and trust in one's neighbors. A few police chiefs, dismayed by the complexities of linking objective changes to police practices, have explicitly adopted a completely subjective test of police performance, arguing that police forces are as good as the public thinks they are, and that public opinion is the best measure of performance.

Although the fear of crime is a problem in its own right, shaping public behavior and impacting the quality of life, there are significant problems with making it a measure of police performance. Like crime, fear cannot be controlled by the police. Media presentations of crime may be as powerful in shaping public perceptions as any police actions. In Winnipeg, Canada, for example, local radio talk shows were deluged with complaints about rising crime immediately after the city got cable news service from Detroit, even though the local crime rates had remained stable.[1] In a careful study of the news-making process, Steve Chermak showed that when dramatic local crime stories are lacking, newspapers and television stations fill in with crime stories from around the country imported from the wire services (Chermak 1993; Ericson n.d.). If this is generally true, then the fear of crime may not only be unrelated to what local police are doing, but may also be unrelated to local crime conditions.

Making the reduction of fear a priority may conflict with other, equally valuable objectives in policing. One certainly would not want the police to emphasize public opinion about crime at the cost of preventing actual crime. Similarly, shaping police actions according to the distribution of fear in a community could produce some questionable allocations of resources. Senior citizens, for example, have the greatest fear of crime, but they are the least likely to be victimized (*Sourcebook* 1992, t 3.17). Young males are least fearful but most at risk. If a choice has to be made, which of these crime "problems" should be considered the more serious?

The point is that protection from crime is what the public wants most from the police. In attempting to determine whether the police are succeeding at it, researchers use both hard and soft—objective and subjective—measures. Neither of them may be under police control, at least when measured across areas that are not very small. To go beyond reported crime measures raises the cost of evaluation. Costs also rise when crime evaluation focuses on small geographical areas, which it must to show the effects of police programs. All in all, judging the effectiveness of a police force against crime involves a choice between an objective measure that is cheap but unresponsive to policing, or a subjective measure that is costly and also likely to be unresponsive to policing.

Police Activities

Along with crime measures, the second most widely used group of performance indicators are those that reflect the activities of the police. These typically include the number of arrests made, the number of traffic citations issued, the response times to calls for service, and the amount of illegal drugs seized. Some police departments have also counted the number of Neighborhood Watch groups established, the number of community crime-prevention meetings held, the number of victim-assistance contacts made, and the racial diversity of police personnel. In addition, there are qualitative measures of police activity, such as the adoption of department value-statements, policy guidelines in problematic areas of police conduct, and procedures for handling citizen complaints.

Activity measures are very attractive to the police for two reasons: they use information already at hand, which minimizes costs, and they are almost completely under police control, which reduces risk. Most of the standards currently employed in the United States by accreditation agencies, as well as by management consultants, relate to police activity rather than impact.

At present, Great Britain is the leader among developed democracies in evaluating police performance systematically (Bayley 1994). By and large, its efforts rely on measures of police activity. For example, the Audit Commission for Local Authorities and the National Health Service collect information annually on the performance of all 43 British police forces. The information was made public for the first time in December 1994. The Audit Commission's performance measures are as follows.

Management of Calls and Incident Response
(1)   Time in which 99 percent of 999 calls are picked up
(2)   Percentage of time the target for response times for emergencies is achieved

Crime Management
(3)   Reported crime rate/detected crime rate (per 1,000 population)
(4)   Dwellings burglary rate/detection rate (per 1,000 dwellings)
(5)   Violent crime rate (aggravated assault, sexual assault, robbery)/detection rate (per 1,000 population)
(6)   Serious crime detected/total number of police officers

Traffic Management
(7)   Number of breath tests/number of positive breath tests
(8)   Number of prosecutions for speeding and dangerous driving per 1,000 km of road
(9)   Number of Vehicle Defect Rectification Scheme (VDRS) notices per 1,000 km of road

Public Reassurance and the Maintenance of Public Order
(10) Percentage of total officer-time spent on foot or bicycle patrols
(11) Percentage of arrests not resulting in a charge
(12) Number of working days lost as a result of assaults on officers

Community Relations
(13) Percentage of officer strength, female
(14) Percentage of officers, ethnic minorities/percentage of ethnic minorities in the force area
(15) Complaint rate/substantiated complaint rate (per 1,000 population)

Resources and Efficiency
(16) Expenditure on policing per head of population

(17) Pay costs of all ranks above constable/pay costs of all constables (i.e., costs of supervisory overhead)
(18) Percentage of total staff that is civilian
(19) Percentage of local government revenue spent on police
(20) Yearly police expenditure/number of police officers

Possible Public Opinion Items
(21) Percentage of telephone calls surveyed where citizen expressed satisfaction with police handling
(22) Percentage of people calling for police assistance who, when surveyed, were satisfied with police response

Of the 20 measures, 18 represent things that the police do, as opposed to the effects that the police have on society. Only items 12 and 15 depend on actions initiated by the public rather than the police.

Also in Britain, the Kent Constabulary draws up a yearly Citizens' Charter that publicly commits it to specific levels of performance under various headings. Citizens' Charters are an initiative of John Major's Conservative government that is being expanded to all departments and public-sector undertakings. The Kent Constabulary uses nine performance measures, and they are updated and published monthly:

(1) public satisfaction with police service;
(2) adequacy of police coverage for calls for service, i.e., availability of dispatch units;
(3) crime-victims' satisfaction with police handling;
(4) ratios of crimes detected to crimes reported;
(5) speed in answering telephone calls;
(6) caller satisfaction;
(7) speed of emergency response;
(8) satisfaction of all people having contact of any sort with police; and
(9) public criticism of the police.

Although activity measures are cheap and responsive to police initiative, they, like crime measures, are questionable as measures of performance. Their primary defect is that they are presumptive. They measure what the police are doing rather than what the police are accomplishing.

In evaluation jargon, police activities are outputs of police organizations, rather than outcomes. Using activities to measure police effectiveness assumes that these activities actually make communities safer. This is often very doubtful. For example, does increasing the number of police in a community deter crime? Most politicians seem to think so. Yet there is no evidence that increasing the number of police reduces crime rates (Loftin and McDowall 1982; Krahn and Kennedy 1985; Gurr 1979; Silberman 1988; Walker 1989).

Similarly, high numbers of arrests do not automatically make communities safer. It depends on why the arrests are made. Arresting someone for riding a defective bicycle has a different effect than arresting a serial rapist. Moreover, communities with high arrest rates may not, in fact, be safer than others; they may simply have more crime. Drug seizures, too, measured in either weight or street value, are more reflective of supply costs and demand levels than of police effectiveness in interdicting drug activity (Eck 1989; Nadelman 1988; Reuter and Kleiman 1986).

Finally, police departments frequently speak with pride about the speed with which they respond on average to 911 calls for service. Yet research has shown that reductions in the average speed of response have no effect on crime, arrests or even citizen satisfaction (Bieck and Kessler 1977).

Gauging police effectiveness by counting their actions is appealing because activities are under police control, but it is unsatisfactory because the actions may not contribute to community safety. It seems, therefore, that the enterprise of police performance evaluation is caught between a rock and a hard place: what people most want to know about—safety—is hard to measure and weakly related to what the police do, while what the police do is easy to measure but may not make any difference to the public's concerns.

Measurement Trade-offs

Table 1 lists indicators that are being used, or that are recommended to be used, to measure police performance in Australia, Britain, Canada, and the United States. The indicators fall into two groups—direct and indirect. Performance is measured directly when the indicators reflect what police achieve by way of public benefits. Performance is measured indirectly when indicators show what the police are doing in terms of actions. The rationale for using indirect measures is that if police perform well, the social objectives of policing will be achieved. In other words, direct measures evaluate the ends of policing; indirect measures evaluate the means of policing.

Both direct and indirect measures can be further divided between hard and soft indicators. Hard indicators are objective, reflecting concrete events; soft indicators are subjective, reflecting people's impressions of events.

These distinctions allow us to understand more easily the trade-offs that must be confronted in measuring police performance. Police, as well as those who supervise them, should use the chart to categorize the measures they are using in their localities. This will allow them to determine whether they are getting full value from performance measurement, according to the principles that I shall now set forth.

Table 1

Performance Measures

I.   Direct

    A.   Hard   Crime rates
                     Criminal victimizations
                     Real estate values
                     Public utilization of common space
                     Commercial activity
                     Number of disorder situations pacified
                     Number of community problems solved
                     Substantiated complaints about police behavior

    B.   Soft   Fear of crime
                     Public confidence in police
                     People's commitment to neighborhoods
                     Satisfaction with police action
                     Complaints about police service
                     Willingness to assist police
                     Perceptions of police rectitude

II. Indirect

    A.   Hard   Number of police
                     Number of patrol officers
                     Ratio of administrators to police officers
                     Response times
                     Arrests
                     Clearance rates
                     Number of community crime-prevention meetings
                     Number of Neighborhood Watch meetings
                     Speed in answering telephones
                     Number of follow-up contacts with crime victims
                     Value of drugs seized
                     Strength of internal affairs units
                     Written policies in problematic areas
                     Departmental value statements
                     Recruitment diversity

    B.   Soft   Morale
                     Officer self-esteem
                     Police perceptions of their public reputation
                     Police knowledge of communities

1. Direct measures are better than indirect measures for determining the police's social value. Only direct measures show whether the police are being effective.
2. Police can be more responsible for performance measured indirectly than directly.
3. Performance measurement is easier and cheaper when indirect indicators are used.
4. The greater the pressure on police to be cost-effective, the more likely they are to substitute indirect for direct performance measures. This occurs because bureaucratic self-interest tends to shift measurement from things that cannot be controlled to things that can. It is easier for police managers to demonstrate that they have kept a requisite number of police officers on the street, have responded within a minimum amount of time to calls for service, or have answered telephones promptly than to demonstrate that they have used their resources so that public safety has been improved. Borrowing from Gresham's law, which says that bad currency drives out good currency, I propose Bayley's corollary of performance measurement: the greater the insistence on efficiency, the less the attention to effectiveness (Bayley 1994).
5. Soft indicators are important supplements to hard ones because perceptions contribute to the quality of life and also affect behavior.
6. Direct soft measures are probably no more responsive to police initiatives than direct hard measures. Indirect soft indicators, however, are probably less under police control than indirect hard indicators. In other words, it is easier to influence police behavior than police attitudes, but it is equally difficult to affect either the public's behavior or its attitudes.
7. Substitution of soft for hard measures encourages police to become managers of opinion rather than of circumstances.
8. To make the police accountable, performance evaluation must involve direct as well as indirect measures. Police action without beneficial results is irresponsible. Efficiency without effectiveness is a false economy. At the same time, the assessment of effectiveness necessarily involves studying police actions because actions are the means to ends. Indirect measures cannot be avoided when evaluating effectiveness. It follows that direct measures should not be viewed as preferable to indirect measures. Indirect measures are

unsatisfactory only when they are used exclusively to determine whether police performance is satisfactory.

Principles of Responsible Performance Measurement

Can the evaluation of police performance be done so as to demonstrate both effectiveness and efficiency? Can the trade-offs of performance measurement be minimized? Most importantly, can the police be evaluated in terms that reflect public needs as well as in terms that they can reasonably be expected to achieve? The answer to these questions is yes, provided the police adhere to the following precepts.

First, police must give up the pretense of being the first line of defense against crime. The true first lines of defense are families and churches, teachers, employers, workmates, friends, community groups, and peers. The police represent only the first line of deployment by government against crime. By themselves, the police can do little to prevent crime, at least as long as they continue to use traditional strategies. If they continue to acquiesce to, and sometimes insist on, being evaluated in terms of crime control, they are in danger of losing the public's support because they are pretending to be able to do something that they cannot. Recognizing this predicament, police tend to pass off indirect measures for direct ones. They would be much less politically exposed, however, as well as more useful in developing more powerful solutions to the crime problem, if they would be more honest with the public about what they can and cannot do.

Second, police efforts to prevent crime should be evaluated only when they are targeted on specific sorts of crime in specific locations. The major lesson from the community-policing initiatives of the 1980s and 1990s is that police cannot prevent crime across the board, but can have a demonstrable effect only when they focus on particular kinds of crime at particular places and times. For example, they can be successful in reducing auto theft around a naval dockyard in Norfolk, Va.; drug dealing in a downtown park in Hartford, Conn.; thefts from autos around Tiger Stadium in Detroit; prostitution in a residential area in Edmonton, Canada; and drive-by shootings near a high school in south-central Los Angeles (Eck et al. 1987; Trojanowicz and Bucqueroux 1990; Goldstein 1990; Sparrow et al. 1990).

In other words, the police contribution to crime prevention should be evaluated only when it has a reasonable chance of succeeding and of being seen to succeed. To demonstrate their effectiveness, the police have to target their shots. This proposition has an important implication. Because the police cannot do everything, they will have to negotiate with communities on what they are going to do. This is necessary to make crime prevention by the police politically acceptable. It is also important as a crime-prevention technique, because consultation from the police can educate the public about the realities of crime causation and can enlist them in meaningful preventive efforts. Herman Goldstein is right when he argues that the police have no chance of controlling or preventing crime unless they become a problem-solving institution that takes the public into its confidence in doing so (Goldstein 1990).

Third, the police must take credit for all that they do, not simply for their attempts at crime control. The search for police effectiveness has been hamstrung by being measured too narrowly. Police make a larger contribution to society than simply controlling crime, one that is easier to demonstrate. This occurs in three areas particularly, all of which critically impact the quality of life: (1) authoritative intervention in disorderly, dangerous and unpredictable situations; (2) investigation of crime, arrest of criminals and collection of evidence required to obtain convictions; and (3) assumption of a leadership role in teaching communities what they need to know to prevent crime and enhance safety.   Police are already doing the first two—authoritative intervention and criminal investigation—and they are beginning to learn to do the third—community crime prevention. Prompt and fair-minded intervention by the police at individuals' request is a substantial achievement of modern democratic societies.   It marks a qualitative improvement in government responsiveness.   Likewise, demonstrating the existence of a legal and moral order is essential for developing a humane and orderly civic culture.   Criminals and other miscreants cannot "get away with it" with impunity. Finally, the police are best situated to educate people about what they can do to protect themselves against crime.

The police also perform other valuable functions that they may take additional credit for, such as providing emergency rescue services, controlling large crowds and collective disorder, and developing information about serious crimes that may occur.

Fourth, the police must be evaluated in terms of the type of organization they create, specifically, whether it can do focused crime prevention as well as authoritative intervention and criminal investigation. Experience with community- and problem-oriented policing during the past decade shows clearly that for the police to prevent crime, they must develop the capability to analyze community needs, to formulate multilateral strategies, to mobilize all of a community's resources, to coordinate efforts across agencies, to adapt the delivery of their services to varied social circumstances, and to evaluate the effectiveness of what is done (Bayley 1994).

Earlier, I argued that police performance should not be measured solely by levels of activity.   Measurement should reflect what the police accomplish in society.   But the problem with activity measures—indirect, hard—is not just that they are presumptive; they tend to be mechanistic, more attentive to what an organization does than to what it is capable of doing. To close the gap between outputs and outcomes, new output measures must be devised. These should reflect the capabilities of police organizations to adapt, to consult, to mobilize, to diagnose, to strategize, to solve problems, and to evaluate. The best indicators of what a police organization can do are not response times, arrest rates and drug seizures. The best measures are program budgets, decentralization of command, systematic searches for "best practices," bottom-up problem-solving, supervisors who facilitate rather than just audit, appointing for skills rather than rank, and information systems that are management-driven. In short, the quality of management is the missing element in most assessments of the performance of police organizations.

Conclusion

Performance evaluation is more than an academic exercise, a matter of methodology and numbers. How performance is measured affects not only what the public knows about the police, but also the character of police operations and the management climate. Because performance evaluations establish priorities, incentives and requirements, they are much too important to leave to technicians. Performance measurement should be viewed as an integral, ongoing part of the management of policing.

For the police to be responsible to the public's trust, performance evaluation must emphasize outcomes. The way around the difficulties of measuring the accomplishments of policing (direct, hard indicators) is not by substituting public opinion surveys (direct, soft indicators) or tallies of police activities (indirect, hard indicators); rather, it is by making qualitative appraisals of the organizational capability of the police to perform as effective crime prevention requires. Output measures become less presumptuous when they describe capabilities rather than activity. By evaluating the character of police management, indirect hard measurement is nudged closer to direct hard measurement. Organizational character is the bridge between outputs and outcomes. It follows, therefore, that both qualitative and quantitative appraisals must be part of responsible performance measurement.

In summary, performance measurement is essential to responsible democratic policing. Police have nothing to fear from it as long as they are honest about their objectives, evaluate separately and appropriately the various contributions they make to society, focus their crime-prevention activities on specific problems, and endeavor at all times to build a smarter organization. If police play the evaluation game by these rules, then they and the public will both win.

Notes

[1]This story is often told in Winnipeg but has not been confirmed by research. It reflects a theory about the media's impact on crime perceptions that people appear willing to believe despite the lack of confirming evidence.

References

Bayley, D.H. 1994. *Police for the Future.* New York: Oxford University Press.

Bieck, W., and D.A. Kessler. 1977. *Response Time Analysis.* Kansas City, Mo.: Board of Police Commissioners.

Chermak, S. 1993. "Interested Bystanders: An Examination of the Effect of Crime on Newsmaking and Newsmaking on Crime." Ph.D. diss., School of Criminal Justice, State University of New York.

Couper, D.E. 1982. *How to Rate Your Local Police.* Washington, D.C.: Police Executive Research Forum.

Eck, J.E. 1989. *Police and Drug Control: A Home Field Advantage.* Washington, D.C.: Police Executive Research Forum.

Eck, J.E., et al. 1987. *Problem Solving: Problem-Oriented Policing in Newport News.* Washington, D.C.: Police Executive Research Forum.

Ericson, R.V. N.d. "Patrolling the Facts: Secrecy and Publicity in Police Work." *British Journal of Sociology* 40, 2:205-226.

Goldstein, H. 1990. *Problem-Oriented Policing.* Philadelphia: Temple University Press.

Grabosky, P. 1992. "Crime Control and the Citizen: Non-Governmental Participants in the Criminal Justice System." *Policing and Society* 2, 4:249-72.

Gurr, T.R. 1979. "On the History of Violent Crime in Europe and America." *Violence in America: Historical and Comparative Perspectives.* Edited by H.D. Graham and Ted R. Gurr. Beverly Hills, Calif.: Sage Publications.

Hornick, J.P., et al. 1989. *An Evaluation of the Neighbourhood Foot Patrol Program of Edmonton Police Service.* Ottawa, Canada: Ministry of the Solicitor General.

Kelling, G.L. 1985. "Order Maintenance, the Quality of Urban Life and the Police: A Line of Argument." *Police Leadership in America: Crisis and Opportunities.* Edited by William A. Geller. Chicago: American Bar Foundation and Praeger Publishers. Pp. 296-308.

Kelling, G.L., et al. 1974. *The Kansas City Preventive Patrol Experiment: A Summary Report.* Washington, D.C.: Police Foundation.

Krahn, H., and L. Kennedy. 1985. "Producing Personal Safety: The Effects of Crime Rates, Police Force Size and Fear of Crime." *Criminology* 23, 4:697-710.

Loftin, C., and D. McDowall. 1982. "The Police, Crime and Economic Theory: An Assessment." *The American Sociological Review* (June) 47:393-401.

Nadelman, E.A. 1988. "The Great Drug Debate: The Case for Legalization." *The Public Interest* 92:3-31.

New York Times. February-March 1994.

Police Foundation. 1981. *The Newark Foot Patrol Experiment.* Washington, D.C.: Police Foundation.

Reiner, R. 1992. "Fin de Siecle Blues: The Police Face the Millenium." *Political Quarterly* (page proofs, n.d.).

Reuter, P., and M.A.R. Kleiman. 1986. "Risks and Prices: An Economic Analysis of Drug Enforcement." *Crime and Justice: An Annual Review of Research.* Edited by Norval Morris and Michael Tonry. Chicago: University of Chicago Press.

Rosenbaum, D.P. 1986. *Community Crime Prevention: Does It Work?* Beverly Hills, Calif.: Sage Publishing Co.

Shearing, C.D. 1993. "The Relation Between Public and Private Policing." *Modern Policing.* Edited by Michael Tonry and Norval Morris. Chicago: University of Chicago Press. Pp. 399-434.

Sherman, L.W., and B. Glick. "The Regulation of Arrest Rates" (paper for the American Sociological Association, September 1982).

Silberman, C. 1978. *Criminal Violence, Criminal Justice.* New York: Random House.

Skogan, W.G. 1988. "Community Organizations and Crime." *Crime and Justice: A Review of Research.* Vol. 10. Edited by Michael Tonry and Norval Morris. Chicago: University of Chicago Press.

_____. 1990. *Disorder and Decline: Crime and the Spiral of Decay in America's Neighborhoods.* New York: The Free Press.

Sourcebook of Criminal Justice Statistics. 1992. Washington, D.C.: Bureau of Justice Statistics.

Sparrow, M., et al. 1990. *Beyond 911: A New Era for Policing.* New York: Basic Books.

Trojanowicz, R., and B. Bucqueroux. 1990. *Community Policing: A Contemporary Perspective.* Cincinnati: Anderson Publishing Co.

Walker, S. 1989. *Sense and Nonsense About Crime.* Monterey, Calif.: Brooks/Cole Publishing Co.

Chapter 4

Developing the Capacity for Crime and Operations Analysis

Dennis J. Kenney

Introduction

There are no technological problems remaining for crime analysis. Despite the concerns of many, during the past five to 10 years the needs of law enforcement have driven significant advances in systems designed to aid in crime fighting, operations analysis and general information management. At times, the areas of development have addressed unique concerns such as the need for automated suspect sketches, age enhancements of suspect or missing-persons photos, or analysis of ballistic or forensic evidence. More often, however, police developers have become more proficient at paralleling project and personnel management tasks long used by their counterparts in private industry. As a result, tasks as diverse as tracking investigative caseloads, scheduling and deploying personnel, and building and using case solvability factors are now possible. And finally, the merger of mainframes and microcomputers now permits the construction of large-scale databases to support applications as complex as expert knowledge systems (artificial intelligence) or as simple as on-line queries of suspect and MO files for tactical analysis of offenders and their crimes (Gramlich and Kenney 1993).

While the technological concerns may be greatly diminished, unfortunately, problems of commitment and concept in crime analysis continue to trouble even today's most advanced police organizations. While some observers have noted the frequent failures resulting in unnecessary cost and dashed expectations and have attributed the failures to varying factors (see Layne 1993, for example), the reality is one of priorities. Traditionally, the police have always placed a much higher priority on their crime fighting functions than on order maintenance and nonemergency public services. As a result, most agencies are relatively well-equipped with weapons, vehicles, surveillance technology, and so forth, while remaining underequipped in the support fields involving information management and analysis. Similarly, where an emphasis in these latter areas has resulted, too often agencies have been content to accept off-the-shelf applications generically designed to outdated specifications.

Of equal concern are agencies that fail to understand what analysis can add to their operations and impact. Not uncommon are those that become content with systems' producing their UCR, budgets and speeches as a primary focus. In such cases, little actual analysis takes place. While many may go a step further to produce *crime reports* that summarize previous activities, few are actively involved in efforts to *forecast crime potentials*, *detect patterns* to guide operations, or develop *crime-suspect correlations*. This may be because, even today, too few police managers are convinced that information-driven operations can be beneficial. Good cops, they often suggest, should intuitively know what to do and where to do it. Thus, to improve crime analysis, we should turn our focus from technology and look instead at the conceptual issues—the fundamentals.

The Functions of Crime Analysis

Recently, in an effort to explain the role of crime analysis in the private sector, a loss-prevention specialist told of a poster contest for a security association. Among the finalists was an entry that read, "Premises patrolled by guard with shotgun and attack dog, three nights per week. You guess the nights" (D'Addario 1989:4). In fact, in crime analysis, the roles are reversed—it's the offender who chooses the night and the analyst who does the guessing. There are, however, a few factors working in the analyst's favor.

The first is the now well-established idea that a disproportionately large share of crime is committed by relatively few offenders. During the late 1960s, Marvin Wolfgang and his colleagues (1972) first noticed the uneven distribution of crime among criminals. After tracing the records of all males born in Philadelphia in 1945, Wolfgang discovered that while nearly 35 percent of the group had had an officially recorded contact with the police, only 6 percent had committed more than half (52%) of the group's known crimes. Even worse, these offenders tended to commit the more serious offenses. For example, this small group of chronic offenders was responsible for nearly 71 percent of the cohort's murders, 73 percent of the rapes, and 82 percent of the known robberies. A decade later, these findings were supported by a much larger follow-up study of juveniles born in 1958 (Tracy et al. 1985). Since then, others (Greenwood 1982; Blumstein and Cohen 1979; Elliott et al. 1983) have estimated from interviews with incarcerated high-rate offenders that their actual rates of offending varied from only a few crimes per year to as many as 50 or more. Whatever the actual number, it appears clear that the police are fortunate to be dealing with a fairly small pool of repeat customers.

A second and equally important advantage arises from criminals' tendency to be creatures of habit. Like most of us, those who commit crimes seldom like to work harder than they have to. Thus, their decisions about where to travel and what to expect are often unconscious ones based on knowledge of an area and previous experiences. This means that while the criminal may have a particular target in mind, equally often, the selection process is either spontaneous or undirected. Brantingham and Brantingham (1984:338-39) compare this offender to the motorist searching for a gas station in an unknown or poorly known area of the city.

> As experiential knowledge grows, an individual motivated to commit an offense learns which individual cues are associated with "good" victims or targets. The cues, cue clusters and cue sequences (spatial, physical, social, temporal, and so on) can be considered a template [that] is used in victim or target selection. Potential victims or targets are compared to the template and either rejected or accepted, depending upon the consequence...
>
> Once the template is established, it becomes relatively fixed and influences future searching behavior, thereby becoming self-reinforcing.

They go on to note that since most victims tend to live lives of predictable patterns, it is easy to expect offenders to do likewise. It is that predictability, especially when coupled with the repetition of the high-rate offender, that gives crime analysis its real potential. For agencies willing to support efforts to discover such patterns, the benefits can be immeasurable.

Crime Analysis for Prevention

Given the potentials for predictability, by focusing on the location, time or situation in which crimes take place, along with the methods of offending used, efforts to harden potential targets from a variety of threats can be enhanced. For example, in 1975, the Southland Corp. worked with the Western Behavioral Sciences Institute to examine their often-robbed 7-Eleven stores. From that analysis, preventive measures to improve lighting, visibility, employee training, and cash handling were developed (Crow and Bull 1975). Similar efforts at prevention can be developed for other settings as well—

neighborhoods, housing complexes and business districts. In Jacksonville, Fla., an analysis of rapes in one neighborhood found that they occurred in conjunction with burglaries. When those burglaries were examined, analysts found that the burglar most often entered through an unlocked door (Spelman 1988). Simple precautions helped neighborhood residents to reduce their risks until the rapist was eventually caught. Finally, even crimes such as employee theft and fraud can be effectively addressed with help from analysis (see D'Addario 1989).

Now obviously, success at directed crime prevention may also tend to make offenders work harder and travel farther to commit their work. Even here, however, we know that *crime displacement* is rarely at a one-to-one ratio. In fact, although displacement is an often-offered theoretical possibility, recent reviews of research into enforcement and crime prevention tactics suggest that there may be less to fear than we might assume. For example, from the recent literature, Eck (1994:106) reports that 33 studies covering a wide range of criminal behavior (violent predatory crime, consensual offenses, thefts, property destruction, and suicide) actually looked for displacement effects. Surprisingly, only three found evidence that much had occurred. Of the remaining 30 studies, 12 found some displacement present, while 18 found none at all. Based on this evidence, he concludes, "there is more reason to expect no displacement than a great deal." Thus, while it is reasonable to recognize the threat of displacement, such a threat is unlikely to seriously negate the gains from analysis-directed prevention efforts. And even where displacement does occur, the effort may still be successful if the offender has been forced out of his familiar surroundings where he is more likely to be noticed and make mistakes.

Crime prevention efforts may also focus on victim patterns. For example, during the mid-1980s, police in Newport News, Va., noticed that thefts from vehicles near the shipyard area occurred disproportionately in seven parking lots during the evening shift. With that knowledge, police used directed patrol and general crime prevention tactics. Equally important, however, were steps taken to reduce the vulnerability of victims who often left their cars unlocked, parked in remote areas, and with much-sought-after items in view for the taking (Eck and Spelman 1985).

More generally, criminologists have long suspected that the most crime-prone areas are those with the least social cohesion (Harries 1990). In neighborhoods where resident supervision is present, for example, offenders (especially young ones) have reduced opportunities and an increased likelihood of being observed. Where there is less cohesion, however, where neighbors seldom interact and are not comfortable helping each other, the kinds of surveillance and cooperation necessary for informal control are less likely to take place. It is just this awareness that has led police to their community-oriented focus today—a focus that makes intensive use of analysis-driven prevention efforts.

Crime Analysis for Tactical Deployment

Far more common than crime prevention are tactical deployment efforts using crime analysis. Beginning with the early directed patrol operations, task force efforts and split-force projects, agencies came to realize that if patterns could be detected and crime potentials could be forecast, the effectiveness of surveillance and stakeouts could be enhanced. Similarly, saturation of an area with officers could increase apprehensions as well as offender risk and deterrence.

More recently, as agencies have adopted team policing strategies, problem-focused policing and community policing models, quality information has allowed for an even broader range of interventions. For example, in Garden Grove, Calif., analysts found a single bar that was the site of 75 crimes a year. In Boston, researchers examining crime calls over a five-year period discovered several addresses with more than 100 dispatches a year (Spelman 1988). And in Minneapolis, where the pioneering "hot spots" research took place, analysis showed that only 3 percent of that city's addresses were the subject of 50 percent of all calls for police service (Sherman 1989). Five percent of the addresses accounted for all of the stranger crimes known to police (Gaines 1994).

Findings such as these have led to projects such as RECAP (Repeat Call Address Policing), where police focus on solving problems to both better provide services and reduce overall calls from such troubled locations. Where the crime or disorder problem occurs primarily in a public area, other agencies have returned to the directed patrol D-runs, foot beats and field interrogations for suppression. And finally, where repeat offenders can be identified, targeted efforts that focus on them and their crimes have been widely used for years. With each method, of course, analysis must play the central role in the delicate process of matching resources with the specific problem of concern.

Crime Analysis as Investigation

Usually overlooked is the third role for crime analysis—the identification of crime-suspect correlations to assist investigations. Since offenders tend to be creatures of habit, their methods or descriptions can often give their identities away. By matching suspect and MO files, police can often develop leads. If so, *more* arrests can result.

Less obvious, however, is the ability of analysis to contribute to *better* arrests. We know from research in Britain that the distinguishing feature between good and not-as-good police agencies has less to do with the number of offenders arrested than with the number of charges per arrest. For example, when Burrows (1989) matched six police areas (each from different police forces) to compare burglary clearance rates, he found tremendous disparity among them. However, when he focused on the numbers of *offenders* handled by each agency, the differences closed considerably. The distinction, of course, can be found in the "secondary" clearances—the clearing of multiple crimes with one arrest. While some might argue that such differences are little more than matters of accounting, Burrows goes on to note that improved clearance rates can go far to improve confidence in police generally, while giving added peace of mind to victims whose offenders have been caught. Further, with multiple crimes at their disposal, prosecutors are in a far stronger bargaining position and courts can more easily hand down stiffer sentences. And remember, the analysis that produces secondary clearances is considerably less costly than the effort required for the original arrest.

Even better, from our own repeat offender (ROP) research, we know that targeted investigations can significantly increase the probability of apprehension and prosecution, and the severity of the sentence assigned. As part of their proactive, perpetrator-oriented unit, the Washington, D.C., police (and many others since) began assigning special teams of investigators to habitual offenders believed to be committing five or more Part 1 offenses per week. Identified through a variety of officer-initiated analyses, these offenders were then targeted by the investigators, who had 72 hours to make their case. After six months' experimentation, the results showed some promise.

While the ROP effort was expensive, the project's evaluation "clearly showed that ROP increased the likelihood of arrest of targeted repeat offenders" (Martin and Sherman 1989:143). Further, the arrestees had twice as many prior arrests as did offenders arrested by other means. In fact, perhaps the primary weakness in the approach was in the methods available to identify and select appropriate targets. Most jurisdictions simply lack the ability to pursue adequate analysis to support such proactive strategies.

Crime Analysis as Evaluation

Finally, crime analysis should be—but seldom is—used by police agencies for operational evaluation. In its simplest terms, operational evaluation involves posing a sequence of basic questions following a program or intervention:

1. Was there a real change, as intended?
2. What proportion of that change resulted from the initiative attempted as opposed to coincidental events?
3. What were the unintended consequences?
4. Were the results cost-effective?

Unfortunately, obtaining answers to these questions is often a difficult, at times impossible, goal. It may not be possible to distinguish between real change and random fluctuations, especially if the data collected are poor. Thus, it is usually hard to move from demonstrating a *correlation* between an initiative and its outcome to a firm conclusion of *causation*. Nonetheless, with the careful use of crime analysis, managers can usually examine the potential benefits of a program or effort with a reasonable degree of safety from mistaken assumptions of either success or failure.

Understanding the Goals of Crime and Operations Analysis

The bottom line is that to have an effective crime analysis program, an agency must first reach an organizational consensus on what its goals are to be. Information-driven crime prevention, tactical deployment, investigations, and evaluations can each be accomplished quite easily—none requires expensive technology. What is necessary, however, is commitment to the basic elements on which good analysis is built.

Data Collection

It should be obvious that the quality of analysis depends on the quality of the data one has to analyze. While virtually all police departments are awash with data, not all collect the same kinds of information, nor do they collect their data in the same ways. Some are systematic, so as to produce reliable results. Some care less and are haphazard. Those in the latter group will be far less effective, as important pieces of the crime puzzle will not be available because some officers fail to record them. And even if information is collected, because it will be recorded differently by each officer, important clues might not be recognized. To compare the two methods, we should look at a data collection example that is more intuitive to policing—the case of fingerprints.

While searches for latent fingerprints can be time-consuming and expensive, they can also be invaluable to crime solving. Obviously, since latents are not at all useful until they are collected and categorized, some departments spend a good deal of effort collecting and processing them at each scene, in order to link related crimes to an offender. Some agencies, however, collect prints but do little with them. While these prints may be useful once an offender is caught, they will not be much help in catching him. Still other agencies do little to collect latent fingerprints at all.

Crime analysis information works much the same way; you get out of it only what you put into it. To say that the police should collect data, however, is not to advocate overwhelming officers with paperwork. In other words, all data are not the same—nor are all data even useful. Almost without exception, police departments everywhere record large amounts of information.

Unfortunately, most of it is never used for anything, which makes the collection effort wasted. In one large East Coast department, for example, officers are routinely pressed to conduct field interrogation (FI) contacts with individuals found on the streets late at night. The FI cards completed by these officers, however, are then forwarded to crime analysis, where they are stacked neatly on top of file cabinets for storage. Using the fingerprint analogy, if you are not going to process or compare them, then why dust for them in the first place? For crime analysis, you need not collect more information—just better information, more systematically. The end result is almost always less effort but better output.

The Sources of Information

As almost everyone knows from the community and problem-oriented literature, information that is useful to police should come from many different sources, both internal and external. For example, in addition to police reports, good analysts will also use insurance reports, parole and probation reports, city and county planning data, school records, and census tract data to include information on households, employment and other demographic factors. While most of us have accepted the need for such diverse information by now, we have not given much thought to the methodology needed to collect it. Without such consideration, the data we do collect are likely to be haphazard and may even interfere with the analytic process.

Collecting Information From External Sources

Most agencies probably have few choices for external information, since they have little control over the sources. Still, agreements can be reached so that specific information is provided in a usable format on a regular basis. School disciplinary actions are an example.

In the mid-1980s, after recognizing that a number of serious habitual juvenile offenders were among local students, Jacksonville, Fla., school officials entered into a partnership with the Duval County Sheriff and local state's attorney to track the "worst of the worst." The idea was to develop policies and procedures to manage the offenders' impact on classroom order. The result was the creation of an interagency database that allowed each agency, along with the juvenile courts, probation office and several service agencies, to share "offender-oriented" information. In a short time, information about truancy, referral rates for absence, tardiness, behavior problems, student conduct violations, and academic history was made available for the purpose of creating a multiagency supervision and intervention plan. As a result, a clear picture of disruptive incidents and trends became possible, along with additional knowledge of how youths network with other students. From such analysis, troubled youths could more quickly be identified and intervention more broadly applied. Such efforts had not been previously possible because the participating agencies had long believed that information could not or should not be shared. The result, of course, was the maintenance of separate and usually incomplete files (Higgins 1987). Fortunately, most jurisdictions have provisions similar to those available to Jacksonville to allow interagency sharing of even juvenile information (Patterson and Houlihan 1983).

Collecting Information From Internal Sources

Internally, the police have complete control, though they often fail to exercise it. As they construct a process for the collection of data from their own sources, there are two caveats for them to keep in mind. First is that whatever the process, it must be kept *systematic*. Typically, analysts today must read narrative reports by officers, taking from them the data they need. Not only is such a process time-consuming in that it usually requires multiple computer entries, but also, the resulting data is often incomplete. Incomplete data decrease what researchers refer to as *measurement reliability*. Without clear guidelines, officers pressed to return to service will often overlook important bits of information that may be readily available. And they are not entirely to blame, since their primary goal in report taking is to satisfy basic recording requirements having little to do with analysis. So common is this problem that, during the 1970s, investigators' and prosecutors' complaints about the poor quality of police reports prompted departments throughout the country to establish checklists.

Of equal concern are the inexact results such methods produce. Since the information collected must pass through several interpretive stages, each conducted by a different person or unit, subtle but significant changes can occur. As the facts of the incident move from the victim to the officer, to data entry and, finally, to the analyst, the introduction of error (and bias) should be expected. And indeed, the differences between accidental damage and vandalism, or even trespassing and burglary, can be exceedingly fine. A systematic process, however, can remove much of the after-scene interpretation, while offering a routine framework for the recording officer to follow in gathering and reporting the facts of each case.

The second requirement of data collection is that it be *simple*. Most administrators regularly express concern about the paperwork demands on their officers. Many refuse to improve their methods, out of fear of adding even more requirements. As already noted, however, much of the information that many agencies already collect goes unused. Much of the current collection is also inefficient.

Invariably, when departments do review their existing methods, they find that good data collection takes less time and effort than what they currently do. As a result, with little effort but some thought toward analysis, they can eliminate unnecessary efforts, while simplifying those that remain. Simplicity is important for accuracy, as well. If officers don't understand the data they are collecting, they certainly can't be expected to collect them well. Finally, the data that are collected should be easily transferred to a form suitable for analysis. If coding is a separate step (as it is with narratives), time is consumed and errors are introduced. Simplicity is the key.

Most agencies find that some form of forced-choice checklist works best. Among the advantages checklists offer over narratives are the following:

1. They can be all one form or multiple form.
2. They offer guidelines to officers as they conduct their investigations.
3. They are quicker to use, since officers check boxes rather than write paragraphs.
4. They require no interpretation.
5. They need no coding.
6. Data entry is simplified. In fact, computer scanning and portable computers can be easily modified, though caution should be taken to ensure quality.

Table 1 offers a few functional categories as examples.

Data Collation

Once an agency's data sources are available, the next concern is to put them to work in analysis. For most, this means the creation of databases so that automated searches and comparisons can be made. Though an automated approach is preferable, many agencies are misled with the notion that expensive computer applications are the answer. Unfortunately, they are not a substitution for analytic creativity, and they certainly do not ensure success.

During the mid-1970s, the Dallas Police Department created the Real-Time Pattern Detection (RTPD) system on the city's mainframe computer. Each day, the system compared each of the characteristics of the previous day's crimes (about 200) with those of the past month (N=6000). Matches were reported so that closer comparisons could be made.

It was a nice idea that required considerable programming to determine what constituted a sufficient match for consideration. In the end, however, what they produced at great cost was a system that labored to produce 10 matches a day—nine of which were typically discarded by the analysts, who could tell at a glance that the matched offenses could not possibly be related. After five years of work and much money spent, the best the system ever did was to link one-half of 1 percent of the city's crimes. In other words, this

Table 1

Data Elements From Crime Reports and Supplements

Events	Modus Operandi	Persons	Vehicles	Property
Identifies	*Identifies*	*Identifies*	*Identifies*	*Identifies*
Report Number	Report Number	Report Number	Report Number	Report Number
Event Classification		Person Classification	Vehicle Classification	Type
Geography	*Burglary Offenses*	*History*	*General Descriptors*	*General*
Street Address	Point of Entry	Reason for Contact	Make	Narrative
Large (District/Zone)	Method of Entry	Date of Contact	Model	
Medium (Sector/Beat)	Suspect's Actions	Address of Contact	Style	
Small (Grid)	Victim's Location	Area of Contact (LG)	Year	
	Elements	Area of Contact (MED)		
	Tools Used	Area of Contact (SM)		
Temporal	*Robbery Offenses*	*General Descriptors*	*Specific Descriptors*	*Specific*
Beginning Date	Suspect's Actions	Name	Tag/License	Brand
Beginning Time	Threats	Alias	State of Tag	Model
Ending Date	Force	Home Address	Color	Style
Ending Time	Pretext	DOB	Features	Serial #
Shift	Knowledge	SSN #	Recovery Address	Size
	Movement	ID #	Recovery Date	
	Victim Location	Race	Recovery Area (LG)	
		Sex	Recovery Area (MED)	
		Age	Recovery Area (SM)	
		Height		
		Weight		
General	*Theft From Auto*	*Specific Descriptors*		
Case Status	Point of Entry	Build		
Prints	Method of Entry	Facial Hair		
Method of Escape		Complexion		
Location Type		Clothing		
Property Attacked		Tattoo Type		
Narrative	*Sex Offenses*	Tattoo Location		
	Victim Location	Scars		
	Solicited	Teeth		
	Use of Telephone	Speech		
	Suspect Characteristics	Hair Length		
	Suspect Actions	Hair Style		
	Force	Weapon Used		
	Victim Type	Weapon Features		

Source: Simmons, J. (1994)

sophisticated computer program had declared that 99.5 percent of Dallas crimes were unrelated to each other. Obviously, this was not likely, since the findings from the earlier research into criminal careers showed that a small number of offenders were responsible for a majority of all crimes and nearly two-thirds of all violent crimes (Walker 1989).

Though they had undertaken a pioneering effort, the Dallas police had relied too heavily on technology. A more creative analyst uses the computer only to supplement his or her own investigative skills. By searching databases, for example, he or she might learn the following:

- Two street robberies were committed by a tall blond man with black sneakers.
- No other crimes match. However, both crimes did occur on Main Street in the evening.
- Another search finds 100 robberies in this area—12 of which were committed by blond men.
- Of those 12, six had similar MOs—a fact discovered in still another search.

In this case, it was the analyst's skill, experience and creativity that determined what to look for. The computer only made it possible to do so faster. On its own, technology might have linked the initial two robberies. It was the analyst, however, who turned it into an eight- or even 14-crime series.

The question, then, is, What kind of technology is most useful? To some, only the largest cities should be served by computers. In smaller jurisdictions, they say, manual systems are fine. And at one time, they were probably right, although primarily because of the limits of the systems. In fact, unwieldy management information systems probably drain more energy than they are worth. They also greatly restrict the searches that are possible, making the above scenario unlikely. To avoid this concern, each agency has a series of issues to resolve.

The first is the mainframe vs. microcomputer debate. As we all know, mainframe computers are faster in their searching ability and can store far more data than their microcomputing counterparts. They are also far more difficult to learn and much less flexible and convenient. Thus, most are agreed that while *crime information*—summary reports and the like—can be produced on mainframes, *crime analysis* cannot. Mainframes can be valuable, however, for storing and archiving data, so long as they can be readily accessed by the smaller machines. Such transfers are no longer difficult.

Also at issue is the software that can be used. Here, most departments have at least three choices. One option is to develop an analysis system in-house. This assumes, of course, that the agency has access to a programmer who is sufficiently skilled in both analysis techniques and computer programming to bring the two together. On the upside, this approach results in a customized system that is tailored to the developing department's individual needs. On the downside, it can be an expensive and very lengthy process. And often, agencies do not actually know what their needs are until the system is in use, and even then, they learn of its deficiencies and other possibilities quite slowly. As a result, the in-house system usually goes through several generations of improvements before it becomes truly useful. Unfortunately, that can take several years.

The second approach is to contract with an independent firm. While they, too, could custom design a system, that option would be prohibitively expensive in most cases. And even if expense were of less concern, the problem of needs assessment would remain. As a result, most agencies using this approach select a "canned" package instead. This, too, has advantages and disadvantages.

Since the system being installed is already in use elsewhere, most vendors can set their systems up and get them running quickly. The trade-off, however, is that what gets installed is usually generic in its approach and often dated in its design. Unfortunately, this usually means that in the effort to satisfy every need, these systems usually master none. Of course, some customized modifications may be possible, though they are frequently expensive and quite restricted in what they can do. In the end, most users tend to be limited by their program designer's creativity, and few of them have any police analytic experience.

The third approach is a system transfer. Here, an agency obtains an application developed for or by another agency, a transfer that can occur at one of three levels:

- *Concept transfers*—only the ideas or processes are passed along. Included here are file types and general reports.
- *Design transfers*—refer to the system's programming specifications, data collection procedures and data element definitions.
- *Operational transfers*—pass along actual computer programs, forms and reports.

As microcomputers become the preferred analysis platforms, transfers will undoubtedly become more prevalent. In fact, that is the approach that most agencies should probably follow.

A Summary of Ideas

So far, this chapter has stressed the need to develop routine procedures to support crime analysis operations—routines from data collection to analysis. That said, some caution is in order to avoid an overreliance on those very routines. It is, of course, true that such procedures can be important if the complex tasks of analysis are to become more efficient. We saw this in San Diego when they put crime analysis to work in their career-criminal program. In the beginning, their success rate at identifying serious offenders was only 17 percent. Two years later, after much practice, the success rate rose to 39 percent.

Still, routines can also stifle a crime analysis unit's creativity and flexibility. In fact, the more proceduralized the actual analysis becomes, the more it usually becomes restricted to only standardized methods. When this occurs, analysts tend to give less and less thought to what is needed to test and widen each crime series. What works then is to use routine procedures (such as data collection and collation) while conducting varied types of analyses. With the following thoughts in mind, such balance is far easier to reach.

There Is More Than One Kind of Bad Guy

It is almost always better to plan a unique analysis for each crime series than to rely on the usual techniques for every series that comes along. This is especially important when we remember the complexity of most crime matches. Indeed, even the most careful offenders will have some variation, and even the most accurate descriptions will contain inaccuracies. Of course, this means that the analyst is in a difficult position.

On the one hand, analysts must use caution in pronouncing patterns, since nothing will destroy credibility faster than sending officers to track down false leads. At the same time, however, most analysts are probably too cautious. All of the particulars in a crime pattern are unlikely to match exactly. To ask that they do is to ensure that only the most obvious patterns will be found. And, of course, the officers have probably already discovered the obvious patterns on their own.

To manage this balancing act, many agencies with crime analysis systems that work prefer to use analysts who are experienced officers on whose judgment they can depend. These analysts, in turn, know how to vary their approach as needed.

Use the Computer—Don't Let It Use You

It is easy to blame lack of creativity on the computer. Managers should remember, however, that it is their agency's processes and lack of imagination that provide the real limitations.

Beyond that, managers should also be cautious of the overly sophisticated methods frequently promoted. Time-series analysis, deseasonalization, complex patrol and investigator allocation schemes, and most recently, expert systems that attempt to combine textbook knowledge with established procedure in an effort to mimic the decision-making logic of humans may each look promising. To the agency lacking the basics, however, these methods will seldom be very useful. Unfortunately, they will consume large amounts of resources, especially time and confidence, for very marginal results.

Perhaps one exception to this rule involves the development of mapping techniques to visually display crime-related information. Maps, of course, provide a means to deal with complex data so as to reduce their complexity and increase understandability. Most of us are familiar with the old pin maps used earlier, though we should remember that their primary disadvantage was the time required to create and update them. With the easy-to-use mapping programs available today, however, that problem is no longer a concern. Recently, in addition to plotting crime incidents, accident locations and the like, some agencies have gone even further with their use of maps in an effort to show officers other conditions relevant to their planning and problem-solving. Examples here might include the plotting of demographic information such as employment patterns, school attendance and the presence of single-parent families. Others might display factors important in offender decision-making, such as areas with easy access, low-security housing, and the availability of bushes and other means of cover (Harries 1990).

Remember the Bottom Line of Analysis

While good routines are important in finding patterns, they say little about what to do with them. The primary goal of crime analysis is to help operational units in dealing with problems. Discovering those problems is only part of the process. Understanding them and finding solutions are equally important.

In developing a crime analysis capability, managers should always be careful not to confuse techniques with goals. Regardless of all considerations about career criminals, frequent victims and physical locations of incidents, the real purpose of an analysis unit's efforts is to more effectively and/or efficiently pursue police operations. It is not possible to do so without good relations with operational personnel, both officers and supervisors. While this may seem obvious, it is amazing how many crime analysis units fail to establish a working relationship with front-line personnel. To foster a working reliance, there is no substitute for person-to-person contact.

Additionally, for the analyst's part, the question should always be, So what? Probably the most common complaint about analysts and their work is that they are not specific enough, that the products they produce are too seldom much help. Most officers are not analysts, and they probably do not want to be. To them, it is an imposition to receive a report—especially a lengthy one—that tells a lot about individual crimes but little about what to do about them. While the officer's primary intent should be to find out what can be done, the analyst's goal should be to produce results that suggest options. In that light, remember that the more statistically oriented an analysis report is, the less useful it will be. If crime analysis is to be successful, analysts must also intently market their findings with products that are easy to read and understand, while contributing information useful to an officer's decision-making. In short, they must make their users dependent on them. When that occurs, crime analysis may, at last, realize its full potential to contribute to police processes.

Conclusions

Taylor (1989) recently noted that with the computer age upon us, the technological trend for law enforcement has brought tremendous change in police personnel, roles and services that has, for the most part, resulted in increased efficiency and effectiveness. Information systems are no longer the expensive, one-time investments of the past. With the systems currently available, even the smallest police departments have the capacity to become automated at a cost they can afford. Even better, the small, inexpensive systems available today have greater memory and processing capacity than what was available on the large, complex systems of the recent past.

And the timing could not be better. Until only recently, many treated police work in terms of physical security and reactive response, which led to a lopsided use of technology. More simply put, as in all endeavors, the technology can be found where the priorities are. Since the police have generally placed a much higher priority on their crime-fighting functions than on order maintenance and nonemergency services, they may be well-equipped with weapons, vehicles and surveillance technology, but they are generally underequipped in the support fields.

More recently, however, the tools of these areas have become more available and in demand as agencies have felt budgetary and political pressure to streamline operations, cut administrative overhead and allow better oversight of resources. The adoption of new goals and procedures, such as the focus on problem- and community-oriented efforts that require better access to diverse sources of information, has also introduced the need for more responsive information systems. Fortunately, technology is no longer a problem.

References

Brantingham, P., and P. Brantingham. 1984. *Patterns in Crime*. New York: Macmillan Publishers.

Burrows, J. 1989. "Investigating Burglary: The Measurement of Police Performance." *Police and Policing: Contemporary Issues*. Edited by D. Kenney. New York: Praeger.

Crow, W., and J. Bull. 1975. *Robbery Deterrence: An Applied Behavioral Science Demonstration*. La Jolla, Calif.: Western Behavioral Science Institute.

D'Addario, F. 1989. *Loss Prevention Through Crime Analysis*. Stoneham, Mass.: Butterworth Publishers.

Eck, J. 1994. "The Threat of Crime Displacement." *Crime Displacement: The Other Side of Prevention.* Edited by R. McNamara. East Rockaway, N.Y.: Cummings and Hathaway Publishers.

Eck. J., and W. Spelman. 1985. *Crime Analysis Project Interim Report: Accomplishments During Phase One and Plans for Phase Two.* Washington, D.C.: Police Executive Research Forum.

Gaines, L. 1994. "Persons, Places and Activities: Crime Analysis as an Enforcement Tool." *Police Computer Review* 3(2).

Gramlich, C., and D. Kenney. 1993. "We're Already in the Future." *Police Computer Review* 2(4):1.

Greenwood, P. 1982. *Selective Incapacitation.* Santa Monica, Calif.: Rand Corp.

Harries, K. 1990. *Geographic Factors in Policing.* Washington, D.C.: Police Executive Research Forum.

Higgins, G. 1987. "Serious Habitual Offenders—The Bad Apples." *School Safety* 11 (Winter).

Layne, K. 1993. "Back to the Future." *Police Computer Review* 2(1):1.

Martin, S., and L. Sherman. 1989. "ROP: Catching Career Criminals." *Police and Policing: Contemporary Issues.* Edited by D. Kenney. New York: Praeger.

Patterson, J., and K. Houlihan. 1983. *Confidentiality of Juvenile Offense Histories: A Statutory Review.* Washington, D.C.: Office of Juvenile Justice and Delinquency Prevention.

Sherman, L. 1989. "Repeat Calls for Service: Policing the 'Hot Spots.'" *Police and Policing: Contemporary Issues.* Edited by D. Kenney. New York: Praeger.

Simmons, J. 1994. *A Concept for a Crime Analysis Model.* Washington, D.C.: Police Executive Research Forum.

Spelman, W. 1988. *Beyond Bean Counting: New Approaches for Managing Crime Data.* Washington, D.C.: Bureau of Justice Statistics.

Taylor, R. 1989. "Managing Police Information." *Police and Policing: Contemporary Issues.* Edited by D. Kenney. New York: Praeger.

Tracy, P., M. Wolfgang, and R. Figlio. 1985. *Delinquency in Two Birth Cohorts*. Chicago: University of Chicago Press.

Walker, S. 1989. *Sense and Nonsense About Crime: A Policy Guide*. Pacific Grove, Calif.: Brooks/Cole Publishing.

Wolfgang, M., R. Figlio, and T. Sellin. 1972. *Delinquency in a Birth Cohort*. Chicago: University of Chicago Press.

Chapter 5

Measuring Quality: The Scope of Community Policing

David L. Carter

In Lansing, Mich., citizens throw a police officer a surprise party to thank him for making their neighborhood safer. In McAllen, Texas, a police officer regularly walks by herself down the streets of a "barrio" that was previously so dangerous that officers did not even patrol it by car. In San Diego, a burglary victim waits two days to report the crime because she only wants to report it to "her police officer." In Aurora, Colo., officers form a rock band and help build a race car in order to work with youth. In Reno, Nev., a police officer decides what community problems to solve after surveying the residents of his beat area. And in Fort Wayne, Ind., a patrol officer of 18 years says his career "has been saved" and his lethargic attitude changed as a result of a new approach to policing. What is happening to the cynical, authoritative, isolationist police officer who only seeks to put "scumbags" in jail?

The emergence of community policing as "cutting edge" law enforcement is visible everywhere—in textbooks, scholarly journals, police trade magazines, law enforcement professional meetings, political pronouncements, and, increasingly, the media. Based on the groundbreaking work of the late Robert Trojanowicz through his research on neighborhood foot patrol in Flint, Mich. (Trojanowicz n.d.), and the work of Herman Goldstein on problem-oriented policing (Goldstein 1990; see also Eck and Spelman 1987), the concept's specter has piqued interests in both the professional and the academic communities. This interest has been further propelled by the Harvard University executive sessions on community policing, the research and technical assistance from the National Center for Community Policing at Michigan State University, and a series of research grants (many still in progress) from the National Institute of Justice (NIJ) to investigate issues of community policing with respect to its operational effects, extent of adoption, alternate models, and relationship to accreditation. Based on this foundation, the Bureau of Justice Assistance (BJA) began a comprehensive Training and Technical Assistance (T/TA) program to help police departments nationwide in organizing and implementing community policing initiatives. Moreover, the concept has become an integral part of the Clinton administration's "war on crime," as well as the watchword for crime control for both police and politicians across the United States.

Despite this breadth of information and resources, a great deal of confusion remains about various aspects of the concept. Questions routinely arise: Should it first be tested on a small scale? What types of new responsibilities should the police embrace? Where do the police draw the line in responding to community needs? How are traditional responsibilities and practices reconciled with changes required for community policing? How does the relationship between the police and other government departments change with a broadened police role? How will management and labor relations change within the police department? How can a resistant community be motivated? How do the police reconcile 911 call demands with community policing deployment?

These are among the issues that have been raised—and remain largely unanswered—with respect to implementing community-based policing. Embodied under the title of "Program Scope" as part of the Law Enforcement Management Institute's Executive Issues Seminars, this chapter explores these issues, offering thoughts, experiences and food for thought.

Program Scope as a Matter of Philosophy

Questions to consider...

1. *If community policing is a philosophy of policing, can it be implemented on a partial basis within a police department?*
2. *Can one philosophy (e.g., "reform" policing) apply to a certain assignment, shift or geographical location, while community policing applies to another assignment?*
3. *Is community policing a philosophy of police management? Police operations? Both?*

At the outset, a fundamental issue that must be addressed is the inherent nature of the community policing movement. Many would argue that to even discuss it as a "program" is to miss its essence. Community policing, as defined by leaders in the field, is not a programmatic activity at all. Rather, it is a *philosophy* of police management and operations. For example, Trojanowicz and Bucqueroux define it as

> a new *philosophy* of policing, based on the concept that police officers and private citizens working together in creative ways can help solve contemporary community problems related to crime, fear of crime, social and physical disorder, and neighborhood decay. The *philosophy* is predicated on the belief that achieving these goals requires that police departments develop a new relationship with the law-abiding people in the community, allowing them a greater voice in setting local priorities, and involving them in efforts to improve the overall quality of life in their neighborhoods. It shifts the focus of police work from handling random calls to solving problems [emphasis added] (1990:5).

This perspective incorporates a new way of looking at the business of policing that has ramifications for goals, operations and management. Substantial shifts in what are defined as police responsibilities and how those are accomplished are inherently an element of a philosophical change of depth, not the superficiality of traditional programmatic shifts. In this vein, Kelling and Moore, in discussing the evolution of policing in America, observed that the movement toward community-based policing "represent[s] a new organizational approach, properly called a community strategy" that "operates from organizational assumptions different from those of reform policing" (1988:11).

This new organizational approach embodies different management methods, different operational responsibilities, and redefined relationships between officers and managers, police and citizens, and police departments and other government agencies. The actual structure of this movement remains static. For example, some discussions in both literature and practice argue that there are notable differences between community-based policing and problem-oriented policing. If so, is this a philosophical conflict that will limit program scope? On this point, Moore and Trojanowicz observed,

> If there is a difference between the strategy of problem solving and the strategy of community policing,... it lies in a different view of the status and role of the community institutions, and in the organization and arrangements constructed to enhance community involvement (1988:8).

Taken further, it may also be argued that differences similarly lie in program scope. Problem-oriented policing is somewhat more narrow, focusing more on readily defined—or discernible—problems that can be addressed from a strategic approach. Community policing, however, views problems more broadly and includes a focus on "quality of life" issues as well as distinguishable problems that generate calls for service. Both, however, employ management styles that differ from traditional styles, both seek to establish a more efficient and effective police service, and both take a proactive approach to police operations.

Thus, the essential difference is in the way the concepts are operationalized, not in the inherent philosophical goals. Even considering this debate, on the matter of philosophy, Herman Goldstein has described problem-oriented policing by noting,

> In its broadest context, it is a whole new way of thinking about policing that has implications for every police organization, its personnel and its operations. With an ever-present concern about the end product of policing as its central theme, it seeks to tie together the many elements involved in effecting change in the police so that these changes are coordinated and mutually supportive. It connects with the current move to redefine relationships between the police and the community. Fully implemented, it has the potential to reshape the way in which police services are delivered (1990:3).

Implicitly, Goldstein also appears to view this movement as a philosophical shift in policing. If it involves a "whole new way of thinking" about the police function, and if it can "reshape the way police services are delivered," then the philosophical elements are in place. Interestingly, Goldstein infers that, despite its philosophical elements, it does not explicitly have to be "fully implemented."

The author also subscribes to the position that community policing is a philosophy, and that it can have some effect if only partially employed. Viewed pragmatically, community policing is a philosophical shift in the way police officers practice their profession, but it is operationally difficult for most police departments to completely change their philosophical underpinnings in one comprehensive initiative. Incremental change is a much more manageable approach, offering experimentation, time for transition and political safety as options.

Different attempts at community policing have brought different labels as a means to tailor the philosophy to the specific needs of communities. Among those labels are (in no particular order) the following:

- Flint, Mich.—*Neighborhood Foot Patrol*
- Newport News, Va.—*Problem-Oriented Policing*
- Baltimore County, Md.—*Citizen-Oriented Policing Experiment (COPE)*
- Kansas City, Mo.—*Target-Oriented Policing*
- Madison, Wis.—*Quality Policing*
- Houston—*Neighborhood-Oriented Policing*
- Aurora, Ill.—*Resident Officer*
- Detroit—*Mini-Station*
- Lewiston, Maine—*Community-Oriented Policing*
- Fort Worth, Texas—*Code Blue*
- Aurora, Colo.—*Police Area Representatives*

Many other departments have developed their own labels or simply refer to their approach as "community policing." Regardless of how it is labeled or explicitly implemented, each of these initiatives is attempting to deliver police service in a different manner, and they all subscribe to the consistent philosophical elements of proactive, service-driven policing.

In sum, if we accept that community policing is indeed a philosophy, can it be effectively introduced as the basis for a long-term organizational commitment on a piecemeal basis? This will largely depend on the commitment given to the change, the willingness to reallocate resources, and the amount of procedural flexibility management is willing to permit. If the department can permit—and absorb—these changes for a sufficient time to evaluate their effects, then an incremental approach will have value, with the *caveat* that full implementation of the philosophy will likely be much slower in coming. Resocialization of personnel and restructuring of organizational processes are time-consuming changes that simply cannot be rushed.

Program Scope as a Matter of Management Orientation

Questions to consider…

1. *Traditional "reform" police management…*
   - *Can community policing work in a predominantly bureaucratic and scientific management environment?*
   - *What managerial reforms have to be made?*
2. *Contemporary trends in management…*
   - *What are the implications of "total quality management" and "value-added management" for community policing initiatives?*
   - *Relying on the concept of "reengineering the organization," consider the question, If we blew this place up and started over, what would we do differently?*

- *What should we eliminate entirely?*
- *What can we do that would make things easier for our customers?*

Traditional police management is referred to as "reform" policing because of strides taken over the past 50 years to improve the quality of police service, as well as efforts made to gain greater organizational control and accountability, which had been lost through the spoils system of politics. The reform doctrine postulated that the police had to "professionalize," to become more accountable and effective in dealing with crime, while at the same time reducing corruption and malfeasance among police officers. Based on the work of former Berkeley, Calif., Police Chief August Vollmer, "the father of American policing," emphasis was given to (1) officers' training needs, (2) reforms that enhanced police accountability for actions and misconduct, and (3) the ability to provide the most efficient and effective police service.

As the reform movement grew, police management principles increasingly adopted popular management philosophies of the day, including the bureaucratic model (*vis-a-vis* Max Weber) and premises related to scientific management (*vis-a-vis* Frederick Winslow Taylor). These developments are exemplified in the books and management practices of former Chicago Police Superintendent O.W. Wilson, who heightened reform efforts and increased this "professional" vision throughout the law enforcement community. His national leadership changed the face of American policing, raising the reform movement to a higher plateau in pursuit of August Vollmer's—Wilson's mentor's—vision.

Reform policing is characterized by rigid organizational controls, limited discretion, personnel specialization, centralization of authority, organizational inflexibility, and clearly defined lines of authority, responsibility and communications (i.e., chain of command). In addition, the authoritarianism and cynicism often found among line-level officers is also reflected in organizational relationships and processes. This is aggravated by the near obsessive-compulsive behavior found among police personnel and reflected in organizational procedures. These characteristics beg the question of whether community-based efforts and creative problem solving can be effectively implemented within this "reform" environment. The author would argue that the answer is no, which supports the need for inculcating a revised philosophy of policing.

Given the responsibilities resulting from a broadened mandate and the activities required of officers to fulfill those responsibilities, it appears that reform-era police management is inconsistent with community-based organizational needs. As one illustration, a concern police executives increasingly express relates to the compatibility of law enforcement accreditation and community policing (see Carter and Sapp 1994). Accreditation was conceived and implemented within the parameters of reform-era policing. Consequently, operational, management and policy standards largely reflect the traditions of reform. Yet, as accreditation became a reality, the community-based era of policing was emerging. A number of chiefs, as well as the leaders of the International Association of Chiefs of Police (IACP), expressed concern that the reform-based accreditation standards and community policing were in conflict. While this does not appear to be inherently true, there are reasonable concerns that need to be addressed. Community policing, it appears, can be used in an accredited agency with some "tinkering" to policies and processes related to the accreditation standards (see chapter 12). Going back to the issue of philosophy, this would seem to support the notion that community policing can be implemented on a limited basis within the department. However, this option has limitations and may not be the most efficient methodology.

Community policing seems to be most compatible with contemporary management philosophies such as total quality management (TQM), value-added management and corporate reengineering. Both community policing and contemporary management philosophies are driven by "customer" demands and are concerned with providing the best service possible. Both are concerned with resolving problems as comprehensively as possible, just as both are concerned with motivating employees and increasing employee job satisfaction. Indeed, we may consider viewing community policing simply as the application of quality management to police organizations.

Relying on contemporary management principles, several elements for improving a police department become apparent. Expanding on the work of Couper and Lobitz (1993), one may summarize these elements as follows:

1. A police executive should create and nurture a *vision* that gives clear long-range direction for the department.
2. An executive's life and leadership style should be in tune with community expectations and his or her personal beliefs and values.
3. An executive must be able to listen to both employees and community members to understand desires, expectations and problems. Listening should be an ongoing process, which includes providing feedback on these concerns.
4. Personnel recruitment and selection should be done with an eye toward tomorrow to get the best possible employees to help meet the executive's vision. Police departments should avoid hiring people simply to "fill positions."
5. It's "turf," not time, in policing—that is, concern should be focused on neighborhoods and citizens' problems, not on time management and officer deployment schemes.
6. Community *perceptions* regarding crime, police performance and quality-of-life problems are as important as actual problems and should not be ignored.

7. An executive should practice the quality improvement method to give the best possible service and value to the community in relation to the expenditure of police resources.

The movement toward community policing requires significant organizational change—change that does not come easily for any organization. For police departments—which are paramilitary, bureaucratic structures with members who have been somewhat socially isolated from the community as a result of their occupation—attempts at change are particularly challenging. A common response in humans is to resist change; to say that a new approach will not work. Thus, most attempts to introduce change, regardless of the rationale, will be met with a natural defensiveness.

Our history of policing has shown, however, that many previously sacred beliefs about law enforcement were forced to give way to new ideas after research suggested that there might be flaws in the traditional logic (Radelet and Carter 1994). Based on that knowledge, law enforcement leaders explored new police responsibilities and different operational tactics. Within this framework, community policing evolved and grew as research and experimentation pointed the way. Pundits have begun to look at the concept anew. They have witnessed how it flourishes in numerous departments, and though some still will not concede that it can work, at least they are willing to take a fresh look at the possibilities.

How does this change occur? While not definite, a general transition process appears to emerge. First, leaders realize that traditional police approaches have not succeeded. Second, attitudes about the police function among administrators, line personnel and citizens begin to change. Third, community assessments are performed to identify redefined police responsibilities. Fourth, new organizational and operational approaches are conceived to meet the newly defined police responsibilities. Fifth, the community is enlisted to work cooperatively with the police to achieve the desired results. Finally, both law enforcement and the community commit to continuing and expanding on the initiative.

One contemporary line of management thought that seems particularly compatible to community policing and implementating change is "reengineering the corporation." The initial premise of this concept requires that leaders consider the question, If we blew this place up and started over, what would we do differently? They must then consider these questions: What should we eliminate entirely? and What can we do that would make things easier for our customers? (Hammer and Champy 1993).

A fundamental element of the reengineering premise is to organize around *processes* rather than *departments*. Applying this to community policing has important ramifications for program scope. That is, to what extent can the police organization's structure, deployment practices and personnel assignments be altered to accommodate a community policing initiative where the scope of that initiative is limited? Using this approach, deployment practices would focus on changing officers' shift schedules so they could meet with citizens and community groups who could help solve problems, rather than organizing the department around traditional schedules for comprehensive 24-hour coverage. This, of course, would have important implications for call management. Similarly, departments might consider disbanding or reducing criminal investigation divisions to have more uniformed officers with broader responsibilities—including investigations—to fully implement community policing. Needless to say, an effort to organize around processes will generate some negative reactions from many involved. Some will view it as an inordinate expansion of program scope, but it may be one that is required to fully (and effectively) see the benefits of this initiative.

Program Scope as a Matter of Mandate

Questions to consider...
1. *How far can (or should) the police mandate be broadened?*
2. *How do we determine this breadth of the mandate?*
3. *What is "quality of life," and how is this the business of law enforcement?*
4. *If the public mandates broader police activities, how does a police executive know where to draw the line?*

An important goal of community policing is to improve the quality of life in a community. Implicitly, this includes a range of factors traditionally related to the police function, including reducing victimization, apprehending criminals, reducing fear of crime, and resolving conflicts (such as domestic disturbances). Similarly, regulatory activities such as controlling traffic, having abandoned cars towed, and enforcing laws related to alcohol, health and safety have been viewed as police responsibilities, but those activities have been considered less important than the crime-related functions. Working with youths has historically been viewed as a collateral area where the police frequently act, but not so much as an inherent responsibility, although this has slowly changed with programs such as Drug Abuse Resistance Education (DARE). Conversely, dealing with problems of neighborhood decay, unsightliness, street maintenance, parks, and the like has rarely been viewed as a police responsibility.

The priorities of law enforcement are beginning to change with the advent of community policing, which attempts to balance traditional foci with those activities historically viewed as being peripheral to law enforcement. As officers begin performing diverse tasks that produce a better quality of life for citizens, they build broader expectations in the public's mind about "what the police should do." These broadened—and heightened—expectations have important ramifications for the department's management.

One of the most obvious issues is the budget. When the public demands broader services, government is "persuaded" to respond. It is difficult for elected officials, in particular, to deny the mandates of their constituency. Thus, funding support may have to be increased to deal with broadening police activities. It is important to note that community policing advocates argue that additional police officers and funds are not always needed because officers are used in different, more efficient ways. Indeed, there is evidence to support this (Radelet and Carter 1994; Trojanowicz and Bucqueroux 1990). However, in the political environment, public support for popular programming will frequently translate into more funding and "empire building."

This leads to another problem: disenfranchisement of other government departments. At the first level of disenfranchisement, when government leaders decide to increase the police budget, it typically must come at some expense to other government departments. Thus, even if outright cuts do not occur in other departments, growth and/or current levels of staffing or programming may not be maintained. Reducing funding support for one entity to build support for another is a sure way to build resentment. Thus, budgeting disenfranchisement not only reduces a department's ability to perform its work, but it may also diminish the quality of the relationship between the police and other departments. This poses an interesting paradox—as other government departments lose their funding and programming ability, they also lose their ability to effectively work with the police department to solve community problems. Moreover, as resentment builds, other departments may be less inclined to help the police department. The police must respond to their community's quality-of-life "mandate" in some manner; thus, they become more aggressive and, as a result, more politically empowered. Disenfranchisement, therefore, can broaden in a spiral.

One method to deal with this disenfranchisement can be found in Fort Worth, Texas. The city has developed an initiative called "Code Blue" in an effort to provide the best possible service to all citizens. While community policing is an important element of Code Blue, the concept goes beyond the police department. Each element of city government is committed to providing the best service to citizens, which means that some departments' efforts must be coordinated with and supportive of other departments' work.

The movement toward "quality-of-life programming" also brings with it new models of government accountability. If the police are providing broader services to the community, what can other government departments do? In essence, as police responsibilities broaden and they become more responsive to community demands, citizens may begin to ask how other government departments should change. Should parks and recreation be more aggressive and promote public health activities? Should the street department be more aggressive in developing safe and aesthetic roads and rights-of-way, rather than focus on maintenance of roadway surfaces? Should the solid waste department aggressively promote a recycling program?

With these changes in accountability, perhaps police administrators should look for interdisciplinary alliances with other departments to help develop programming—in other words, executive team building. For example, it may be feasible for fire inspectors to also perform crime prevention "target hardening." Similarly, the public health service may help with programs directed toward reducing violent crime, building inspectors may be trained in "crime prevention through environmental design," and social workers may work more closely with the police to identify people who are victims or perpetrators of such crimes as domestic violence, sexual assault, drug trafficking, or theft.

Police executives must avoid an inwardly directed myopic view of change to the exclusion of understanding the systemic effects that community policing initiatives pose. Enlightened police leaders must develop (and practice) sound political acumen in order to enlist cooperation from other departments, sharing the vision of a broadened "quality of life" for which all elements of government must contribute.

Given the movement toward enriching the community's quality of life, it seems self-evident that community policing broadens the police mandate (c.f. Manning 1978). Unfortunately, when this type of growth occurs, it will likely either tread on the responsibilities of others or be viewed as an inappropriate exercise of police authority. In either case, if police actions are viewed as a trespass on others' "turf," then conflict will emerge, thereby displacing initiatives and goals. For example, the Portland, Ore., police provide training for landlords in such areas as tenant selection, eviction processes and other "tenant management" strategies to keep "undesirables" out of rental buildings (notably, public housing). If community members or civil libertarians interpret this training as an inappropriate use of police authority, systemic damage could be done to other programs in the community policing initiative.

In another example, some police departments are seeking to expand DARE instruction in the public schools so that it starts before the fifth grade and continues for several years. This could conceivably be viewed by teachers and school officials as a political trespass on their responsibilities, implying that "anyone can teach" and that "the schools are doing an inadequate job" in preparing children to be good citizens. Such a reaction could undermine the program altogether.

There is little debate that community policing expands the traditional vision of law enforcement. Ethically, the police have the obligation to articulate reasoning for this expansion and reach only into those areas that are legitimized by the community and public institutions. Politically, the police must be able to defend their position based on sound reasoning and community needs, not emotion or simple beliefs that they are doing "what's right." Make no mistake, broadening the police mandate is an important decision that can have a wide-ranging impact on police budgeting, staffing and operations, both now and in the future. As such, it is an endeavor fraught with risk, receiving tenuous support within both the community and the government structure. To not recognize and prepare for this expanding scope is politically and functionally dangerous.

The thorny questions that must be answered regarding this expansion center around the types of programming the police undertake, whose responsibilities they may encroach on, the extent to which the public wants them to pursue nontraditional activities, and the intent or reasoning behind the broadened mandate. If the rationale is strong and politically palatable, then this broadened scope will be accepted, with the proviso that some successes must be seen on the horizon. If not, resources will be wasted and potentially enhanced public service may be lost.

Program Scope as a Matter of Operations

Questions to consider...

1. *By broadening the scope of duties, are we making police officers more professional or more like "craftsmen"?*
2. *How do we reconcile the differences between "community policing" and "problem-solving"?*
3. *To what extent is it reasonable to respond to community demands that are on the periphery or outside the statutory mandate of the police (i.e., noncriminal problems)?*
4. *To what point can we let go of traditional police activities (e.g., responding to nearly all calls, preventive patrol or fast response times) to replace this with other work such as problem-solving or being community organizers?*

Inherent in any community policing endeavor is the *operational* impact of "program scope." Defining the actual activities for which officers are responsible and facilitating those activities pose significant problems the department must handle. For example, if community police officers are permitted to use "flextime" in their shifts, this may pose both coverage problems for calls and animosity among officers who do not have the flextime option. However, alternating shift times may be important for the community police officer to accomplish his or her tasks. To resolve this operational paradox, police administrators tend to follow the easy path—forbid the controversial activity, in this case, flextime. Yet operational complexities must be addressed and resolved if community policing successes are to be realized.

There is no doubt that some abuses will occur. For example, in Houston, some officers were assigned to focus their efforts on "beat integrity." They were to use their own initiative to define problems, contact citizens and perform whatever tasks deemed necessary to reduce crime and manage public concerns in the beat. In many cases, officers were essentially "out of service" for the entire shift, and therefore unavailable to handle calls. Similarly, because officers were "out of touch," they often had no contact with supervisors during the shift, leading to some abuse of their discretionary "free time." One legend was that some officers would report to work, drive to San Antonio, have their picture taken in front of the Alamo, and return to Houston before the end of their shift. These officers obviously were professionally irresponsible and showed this by abusing their autonomy. (Regarding whether this legend is true, one police official said, "I've seen several pictures of HPD cars in front of the Alamo.") An important lesson from this experience is that flexibility and creativity can occur, but that does not absolve the need for accountability and supervision.

The police department's operational scope is inextricably related to the executive's interpretation of the community policing philosophy and the management philosophy and values the executive practices. These are put into practice via the department's corporate strategy. "Defining a corporate strategy helps an organization, its employees and its executives [understand the police department's mission]. An explicit corporate strategy tells outsiders who invest in the organization what the organization proposes to do and how it proposes to do it" (Moore and Trojanowicz 1988:2).

Ideally the corporate strategy will be developed through a multistage approach, described as

> [an] iterative process that examines how the organization's capabilities fit the current and future environment.... A strategy is defined when the executive discovers the best way to use his organization to meet the challenges or exploit the opportunities in the environment (Moore and Trojanowicz 1988:2).

Unfortunately, this has all too frequently been done on an *ad hoc* basis as a reaction to changing trends in policing and changing community demands. This "catch-up" approach lacks vision, planning and thoughtfulness, thereby limiting the police organization's efficiency and effectiveness.

How are operations broadened? By examining what the police department needs to accomplish and the manner in which this will be done (i.e., the corporate strategy). To illustrate this, figure 1 describes various police responsibilities (shaded areas). Some of the activities required to accomplish these responsibilities are shown next to them. Sometimes these activities are "traditional," sometimes not. In the latter cases, they reflect the broadened scope. As an example, to increase criminal apprehension, the police department may perform traditional activities such as crime and intelligence analysis. Moreover, beyond developing traditional criminal informants, they may also establish stronger ties with law-abiding citizens who can also serve as important sources of information on crime and criminals. Similarly, the police department may further explore a nontraditional approach such as having a formal citizen patrol program, as done in Houston and Fort Worth.

The operational activities in figure 1 are not meant to be exhaustive; rather they illustrate how the scope of activities may be broadened, blending tradition with innovation. Expanding the scope and accomplishing these tasks can only be effectively accomplished if the department's corporate strategy is in place.

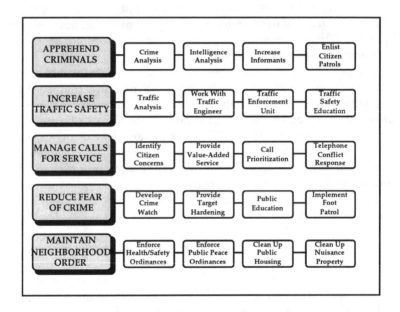

Fig. 1. Examples of community-based police operations

Program Scope as a Matter of Political Issues

Questions to consider...
   1. *Internal...*
        • *How do we overcome dogmatism?*
        • *How much can reasonably be done as a starting point?*
        • *Does community policing threaten the status quo among officers? That is, if implemented as a broad perspective, will it threaten officers who have invested their energies in the traditional career path?*

2. External...
   - If community policing is successful, will this create conflict with other government departments? If so, what effects will this have on intergovernmental relations and cooperation?
   - With community policing successes, what problems may arise if the chief's political influence is increased?
   - If community policing is broadly implemented and immediate results are not demonstrated, will this threaten political support for the police?
3. Community...
   - How do we handle increasing (and broadening) problem-solving demands from the community?
   - If the community is empowered by community policing, what are the ramifications for police management?

The scope of community policing will inextricably be related to threats toward the initiative that are generated from the political environment. Political threats are factors that may undermine organizational control or impede successful implementation of the community policing philosophy. These threats may be characterized in four basic forms (figure 2).

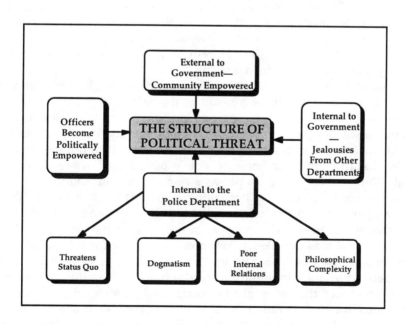

Fig. 2. The structure of political threat

The first are threats *external to government.* These are political influences the community exerts that can place police administrators in confounding managerial positions. For example, community police officers who develop a strong, substantive rapport with a neighborhood may find community members flexing their political muscles if an officer is to be reassigned. A protest from community members stating that they "don't want to lose their police officer" places unusual demands on the department—particularly if community demands are voiced to political leaders. A community empowered in this manner places limits on the department's administrative flexibility and may even impede the officer's career development. Police organizations must be prepared to rationally respond to this pressure in order to maintain organizational control, while at the same time avoiding alienation of the community or political leaders. As the scope of the initiative is broadened, the political pressure will become more omnipresent. How does one manage this, and where must one draw the line?

From an entirely different perspective, external political threats can also be an undermining influence when the community's perceptions of "success" are not met. Given the nature of community policing activities—preventing crime, resolving quality-of-life issues, influencing long-term social change, solving problems—results are difficult to see, or just as importantly, hard to quantify. How do the police demonstrate such things as "prevented crime" or "changed values"? Moreover, American society wants to see immediate results from a new initiative—something that will not happen with community policing. When no successes are obvious, political support from the community will begin to erode. Moreover, as the scope is broadened, "failures" will become even more damaging.

A second type of political threat occurs when the *officer is politically empowered* by the community as a result of the relationship he or she has established with citizens. As an example, in Flint, Mich., the residents of a neighborhood were opposed to pending action by the city council to rezone a portion of the area for commercial use. Unsure of what to do, the citizens sought advice from their community police officer on how to fight this proposal. Rather than acting simply as a *resource* for the community, the officer began acting as an *advocate*, taking actions that were essentially a political campaign to oppose the proposal. Acting as both an organizer and a catalyst, the officer even led a protest, in uniform, at the city hall. (The rezoning proposal was defeated.) When called to task for this action, the officer maintained he was "doing his job" by trying to solve a "quality of life" problem defined by the community he was serving. When the department informed the officer that he might be disciplined (simply with a letter of reprimand), the community raised its voice in support of "their officer." Thus, the officer and citizens influenced political decisions and intervened in organizational control practices.

A third threat exists *internal to the government entity*. That is, as the police department establishes a stronger relationship with the community, garnering political support from that constituency, it also gains political leverage within the broader government structure. If the police department finds itself in the position of being the most prominent among equals in its relation with other government departments, problems may arise. As discussed previously, other department heads may feel somewhat disenfranchised in the political structure if they feel their departments are being devalued. Conflicts may occur, leading to poor interdepartmental cooperation on activities that are designed to provide better service to the community. Consequently, police executives need to give special attention to team building, noting that any successes that enhance the quality of life in the community are a result of combined efforts, not just those of the police department.

The final political threat exists *within the police department*. This can surface in four basic ways. First, community policing threatens the *status quo*. People who have invested their energies in a certain career path may find the path to professional development has changed. Consequently, they have an incentive to not support, or perhaps even undermine, any new initiative. Second, the natural tendency of dogmatism emerges when any new initiative is proposed. Generally, the more expansive the change, the greater the resistance will be. Despite the presence of a well-intentioned and well-devised plan for implementing the community policing philosophy, if an effective educational effort is not made to convince all organizational members—sworn and nonsworn alike—of the need and the benefits that can be achieved, then community policing will not be successful. In particular, line-level officers hold the keys to success and consequently hold important political power, on which experimentation with the philosophy rests.

Third, because community policing is a philosophical change in law enforcement, it cannot be explained or demonstrated as easily as a new program, such as Neighborhood Watch, saturation patrol, physical crime prevention, or street sweeps. Essentially, the concept is difficult to understand, particularly in the short term. Stereotypes of community policing—for example, that it is the same as the foot patrols of years past—are assumed to be the sum and substance of the philosophy; thus, new community-based operational initiatives may be attempted in the traditional philosophical manner. Without understanding the breadth of community policing as a philosophy, organizational members may become misdirected in their efforts.

The final element, poor internal relations, exists all too frequently and is often more intense in community policing. Such organizational conflict occurs when emphasis is given to new initiatives that replace traditional activities and individuals in the "spotlight" (such as highlighting community policing officers instead of SWAT officers). Typically, inadequate attempts are made to incorporate all employees into the new initiative, which only aggravates the problem. Those employees who feel disenfranchised by the situation may not participate or support the initiative; in the worst case, the employees may sabotage the effort. These internal problems are usually evident, for example, when community police officers are referred to as the "Wave-and-Grin-Squad" or "Lollipop Cops."

The political dynamics associated with community policing are substantial factors that must be anticipated in the scope of any initiative. If one's management or operational plans fail to take the political threats into account, the scope will become irrelevant because the initiatives will likely be doomed for failure.

Program Scope as a Matter of the Future

Questions to consider...
1. *How can ongoing evaluation direct future program scope?*
2. *What is the relationship between program scope and long-range planning?*
3. *How can the "R^3 (R-Cubed) Model"—refocusing, refining and reallocating—be applied to direct change for the police department?*

With an evolving philosophy of policing, changing demographics in society, greater economic constraints, and diverse political mandates, the police will find it necessary to explore important—sometimes radical—new directions in police management and operations. Moreover, increased prevalence of multi-jurisdictional crimes and generally increased police officer responsibilities add more emphasis to the need to reexamine the structure and processes of police organizations. In preparing for the future, the police must engage in a comprehensive self-assessment of their current status— managerially and operationally—to explore the directions that are needed to best face the future. This self-assessment might take the approach of *refocusing*, *refining* and *reallocating*—what the author refers to as the R^3 (R-cubed) approach.

Refocusing refers to defining—in written form—what activities and services the police department will perform in the future. It requires a reexamination of the mission, goals and objectives and a restatement of them as they fit the department's future. As has been discussed, police departments tend to be moving toward a community-based policing model that increases and broadens services. Moreover, police officers are increasingly urged to use their discretion in proactively solving problems. These factors need to be articulated in the department's guiding principles.

The new five-year *Corporate Strategy of the London Metropolitan Police* provides an illustration of a plan with a focus on the future. This plan is a "future-oriented" document developed over a several-year period with the specific intent to refocus the Met's direction—an exercise that has obvious implications for refining and reallocating initiatives. To illustrate this, the revised "strategic intention" of the London Metropolitan Police is as follows:

1. ...to remain a visible, predominantly unarmed, approachable police service in order to provide a reassuring presence across London. This, the Met's overriding policing style, has its roots deep in the community.
2. ...to increase consultation with the public and their representatives; to inform and respond to their views and their particular and changing needs, as far as we can; and to improve our internal communications. We intend to maintain our place as leaders in policing philosophy and practice.
3. ...to establish a clear view of the relative importance of policing tasks and improve our performance in those areas of police activity [that] are identified for priority attention. It may be necessary deliberately to divert manpower away from some areas of work to address these priorities.
4. ...to maintain a range of specialist services [that], in support of our general policing style, reflect the changing and dynamic needs of those living and working in London. Such specialisms must also encompass those national responsibilities we presently bear.
5. ...to achieve a sufficiency and disposition of personnel—both police and civilian support staff—to make us more effective in the delivery of our service and to realize the full potential of all individuals within the Service, promoting professionalism together with high standards of personal conduct. All personnel must be well-trained, led and managed.
6. ...to ensure adequate technical and other appropriate support for our workforce. Investment here must be sustained and have as its twin goals the greater effectiveness of staff and the provision of better working conditions for them.
7. ...to give a high-quality service to all our customers, particularly the public, delivered in a way that represents good value for money. This requires exacting self-scrutiny of our performance, against agreed standards, through inspection and review procedures. We will continue to promote good practice and correct errors; if we are wrong and grievances are justified, we will accept our mistakes (1992:3).

Refining refers to fine-tuning the department's infrastructure. Once the department's direction has been formally refocused, then policies, procedures, job descriptions, personnel evaluations, and training must be adjusted to match the refocused mission. This is a time-consuming process that requires creative thinking and reflection on the executive's vision. It should not be taken lightly, for it is the currency of organizational change. If the infrastructure does not functionally support the mission, goals and objectives, then little forward progress can be made.

As one example, many police departments are realizing that traditional employee-performance-appraisal systems really do not measure officers' work as related to departmental goals. Instead, the measures amount to little more than "bean counting," documenting such things as miles driven, traffic citations issued or reports written—all of which the officer can manipulate. Alternatively, some departments—such as those in Lewiston, Maine; McAllen, Texas; and Aurora, Colo.—are using narrative, qualitative evaluations that are goal-directed measures focused on substantive officer activities. Arlington, Texas, uses a mixture of qualitative and quantitative measures that "scale" an officer's performance based on work traits and "critical success factors" anchored to specific job duties. In another approach, as part of their personnel assessment, the Richardson, Texas, Police Department sends out two "customer surveys" per officer, per month, to rate officer behavior and performance from the view of the citizens with whom they have directly interacted. Thus, refinements in one aspect of a department's infrastructure provide important adjustments to departmental direction for the future.

The final element of R^3 is *reallocating*. New organizational directions will most likely require a reallocation of resources (i.e., people, budget, equipment). For example, community policing is a labor-intensive activity for the patrol force. Thus, officers working on other assignments may have to be transferred back to patrol from a desk assignment or the traffic unit, for example. Similarly, as problem-solving strategies become the *rigor du jour*, new demands may be placed on the support staff—such as the records unit or the clerical personnel who assist with correspondence and message taking—requiring appropriate resources to respond.

The application of R^3 is essential for implementing plans for the next generation of policing. Important areas that must receive particular attention in the R^3 process are

- personnel recruitment, evaluation and development;
- special programs currently in use;
- use and allocation of facilities;
- matters of collaboration and cooperation among the police department, other government agencies and civic groups;
- characteristics and operations of support services; and
- budget-planning processes and priorities.

Future problems can only be addressed and future goals achieved if a proper foundation is laid. The relationship between the R^3 approach and program scope is inescapable. Because of the systemic nature of the process, as each element of R^3 is addressed, the parameters of program scope will change. There are no formulas to guide one through this regeneration. It is an intellectual exercise that requires commitment, vigilance and patience.

Epilogue

While community policing has become commonly accepted as the direction for the future, it remains an amorphous and fragile concept. In some locales where it had a strong start, progress has slowed and even reversed (for example, in Alexandria, Va., and in Houston). In other locations, community policing has become institutionalized as the accepted practice, even after leadership changes in the departments (e.g., in Madison, Wis., and in Baltimore County, Md.). Many other departments are just now exploring the concept and are finding that understanding and communicating the philosophical nature of it is as difficult as grasping smoke. This inherently leads to confusion and uncertainty, which retards maturation of any programmatic activities until the "players"—officers, supervisors, citizens, politicians—can clearly see their role and the direction in which this change will take them. A strong foundation of thought, planning and vision is essential to begin the change process. Without that, failure will be on the horizon.

References

Carter, D.L. 1994. "Politics and Community Policing: Variables of Change in the Political Environment." *Public Administration Review* (Summer).

Carter, D.L., and A.D. Sapp. 1994. "Issues and Perspective of Law Enforcement Accreditation: A National Study of Police Chiefs." *Journal of Criminal Justice* (forthcoming).

Couper, D., and S. Lobitz. 1993. "Leadership for Change: A National Agenda." *The Police Chief* (December):15-19.

Eck, J.E., and W. Spelman. 1987. *Problem-Solving*. Washington, D.C.: Police Executive Research Forum.

Goldstein, H. 1990. *Problem-Oriented Policing*. New York: McGraw-Hill.

Kelling, G.L., and M.H. Moore. 1988. "The Evolving Strategy of Policing." *Perspectives on Policing, No. 4.* Washington, D.C.: Harvard University and National Institute of Justice.

London Metropolitan Police. 1992. *Corporate Strategy of the London Metropolitan Police: 1992-1997.* London: London Metropolitan Police.

Manning, P. 1978. "The Police Mandate." *Policing: A View From the Street.* Edited by P. Manning and J. Van Maanen. Santa Monica, Calif.: Goodyear Publishing Co.

Moore, M.H., and R.C. Trojanowicz. 1988. "Corporate Strategies for Policing." *Perspectives on Policing, No. 6.* Washington, D.C.: Harvard University and National Institute of Justice.

Radelet, L., and D.L. Carter. 1994. *The Police and the Community.* 5th ed. New York: Macmillan Publishing Co.

Trojanowicz, R.C. N.d. "Neighborhood Foot Patrol In Flint, Michigan." East Lansing, Mich.: National Neighborhood Foot Patrol Center, Michigan State University.

Trojanowicz, R.C., and B. Bucqueroux. 1990. *Community Policing.* Cincinnati: Anderson Publishing Co.

Chapter 6

Community Problem-Oriented Policing: Measuring Impacts

Darrel W. Stephens

Mayor, members of council. As your police chief, I appreciate the opportunity to share with you the police department's accomplishments over the past year. We had a good year. Reported Part 1 crime declined by more than 10 percent. All eight Part 1 crime classifications declined—with the sharpest reductions in violence. We are very pleased with these numbers because we had experienced several years of increased reported violent crime in the community, which had been a major source of concern to everyone. At the same time, our overall workload increased by over 10,000 calls for service. We answered 183,000 calls last year, but we were able to maintain our goal of a less-than-five-minute response time for emergency calls. Arrests declined slightly, and Part 1 crimes solved by investigators increased from 20 to 22 percent. We also completed our second year of community policing and are pleased with the progress made so far. Although it is very difficult to explain fluctuations in reported crime, we believe some of the decline over the past year is attributable to this new program. We have dedicated 10 officers to this effort who are working full time in two of our high-crime neighborhoods. If our budget request for 10 additional officers is approved, those officers will be dedicated to community policing as well. Thank you. Are there any questions?

Mrs. Martin glanced nervously at her watch. It was almost 9:30 a.m., and the Midtown bus was 30 minutes late. She thought that if it were not there in the next 10 minutes, she would cancel her trip and try again tomorrow. She had to complete her shopping and be back in her house before 2 p.m., when the drug dealers began to show up on the corner by the bus stop. It was just about two years ago—almost six months after the death of her husband—that a young man knocked her down and stole her purse. It was dusk, about 5:30 p.m., and she was only three houses away from the safety of her home. She was lucky, she thought—she had suffered no serious injuries and she had only lost about 10 dollars. But she was afraid to be on the street when the drug dealers were out. Although they had never really bothered her directly, she was certain that the young man who stole her purse was a drug addict. My, how the neighborhood had changed, she thought. She and her husband had moved there 35 years ago. At that time, all of the houses were well cared for, flowers always bordered neatly mowed lawns, and every three or four years, fresh coats of paint were applied to the outsides of the houses. Most of the neighbors had moved on after their children had graduated from high school. It had just been in the past 10 years that the neighborhood had declined. There were several vacant houses now, and all of her friends were gone. She stayed locked in her house, afraid to leave except for her weekly shopping trip. The bus arrived, and as she got aboard, she thought she would have just enough time to safely complete her errands, if she hurried.

Introduction

The police chief reports to the city council that the department had a very good year. But Mrs. Martin is confined to her house in fear, except for during a narrow time frame when the streets are free of the drug dealers who have taken over her neighborhood. This contrast represents the fundamental dilemma with which the police have had to wrestle for many years. By standard measures, the police did have a good year. Yet Mrs. Martin and many other citizens have altered their way of life for fear of becoming a victim of crime. In fact, a recent poll reported in *USA Today* indicated that 43 percent of Americans no longer shop at night because of the fear of crime. How can the police have a good year while a significant portion of the citizens in their city are living in fear?

Over the past 20 years, it has become clear to many in policing that both the traditional approaches to addressing crime, fear and other problems and the measures of effectiveness have fallen short of many people's expectations. This has caused a significant number of police departments to seek new approaches to addressing old problems. It has also caused many police departments to ask whether their work really makes a difference beyond dealing with the immediate incident.

Community problem-oriented policing has attracted considerable attention as a way of enhancing effectiveness as measured by crime and workload statistics, as well as by citizen satisfaction with police services. A recent survey indicates that 42 percent of the police departments serving populations of over 50,000 reported having some type of community policing program in place (Trojanowicz 1994). In spite of the apparent interest in community policing, there is considerable skepticism about the concept and its potential for improving police effectiveness (Manning 1988; Greene and Mastrofski 1988; Klockars 1988; Kaminer 1994).

The debate over the value of community policing takes many forms. Skeptics argue that it is primarily a public relations gimmick that attempts to make citizens feel good, with little real substantive contribution to dealing with crime. They are also critical because of the difficulty police departments have had with providing a clear definition of what they mean by community policing. They point to several cities where departments claim to be doing community policing, yet the activities vary significantly from one to another. In one city, community policing is framed as a return to foot patrol; in another, it is extra officers dedicated to public housing; in another, it is a special bicycle patrol unit; and in yet another, it is several storefront police offices with whom citizens can interact. Another department may claim that every officer is doing community policing because such policing is really a philosophy or attitude. In addition, skeptics may point out with great smugness that there are no empirical studies that show that community policing is more effective than traditional policing.

Community policing advocates argue that history and research demand a change in the way the police handle their responsibilities.[1] They point to the research of the 1970s and 1980s that raised serious questions about the assumptions police have made concerning the value of preventive patrol, rapid response and follow-up investigations. They raise troubling questions about the large increases in the numbers of people arrested, prosecuted and incarcerated over the past three decades, although crime has generally increased. When, they ask, can we expect the deterrent effect of arrest, prosecution and incarceration to take hold?

Both the skeptics and the advocates of community policing raise important and valid questions. Much of the debate and disagreement lies in fundamental questions about what the police should be doing, what should be measured and how. Although these are seemingly simple questions, determining police effectiveness turns out to be a very complex enterprise. In fact, it may be impossible for the police to ever say with certainty that their work resulted in a specific outcome, because there are simply too many variables that may have influenced the results. Moreover, police departments may not be able to use measures that may be helpful because of the cost and level of sophistication required to collect and analyze the data.

This chapter addresses the issues involved in measuring the impact of community problem-oriented policing. To do that, a definition of this concept is offered, along with an explanation of how it differs from and builds on traditional policing practices. Also discussed are measures that have been used for many years to support investments in traditional policing, with a view toward their value and limitations. That section is followed by a discussion of community problem-oriented policing measures, using for examples the experiences of several agencies over the past several years, including the St. Petersburg, Fla., Police Department.

The chapter then focuses on the integration of some of the traditional measures used in policing with problem solving. Much of the discussion and debate about community policing acknowledges the difficulty of implementation but generally does not recognize that some traditional activities (reacting to calls for service, retrospective investigations, etc.) must coexist with the new ideas being proposed. The final section addresses the importance of the police's placing a greater emphasis on outcomes than they have in the past.

Community Problem-Oriented Policing

A continuing issue in the community policing debate that relates directly to measuring impacts has been the lack of a clear definition that provides a sense of the concept's key aspects. Another issue has been the ongoing debate between advocates of problem-oriented policing, who see "solving problems" as the primary work of the police, and advocates of community policing, who have tended to emphasize the improvement of police-community relations as the primary goal. Although this is clearly an oversimplification of a debate that has been going on for at least 10 years, the discussion has been valuable because it has produced a definition that provides a better sense of what this change in policing is all about. The following definition was first offered by John Eck as Police Executive Research Forum (PERF) staff members worked with other national police organizations in the development of documents to facilitate their work in advancing community policing.[2]

> *Community problem-oriented policing is defined by its two key components: community engagement and problem solving.*

Community engagement is an ongoing dialog between the police and members of the public. It takes place in a variety of ways. It occurs in formal meetings with the police, as well as in routine contacts that take place on street corners. Any contact between police employees and a member of the public is an opportunity for community engagement.

Problem solving is the principal service of the police. Problem solving involves identifying problems in the neighborhood, understanding the conditions that give rise to these problems, developing and implementing solutions tailored to relieve the problems, and determining the impact of the solutions on the problems.

These two components are inseparable. Engaging the community without problem solving provides no meaningful service to the public. Problem solving without engagement risks overlooking the most pressing community concerns and tackling problems that are of little concern to the community with tactics that the community may find objectionable. Further, since community members know a great deal about what goes on in their neighborhood and have access to resources important to addressing problems, their engagement in problem solving is vital to gaining valuable information and mobilizing coordinated responses to problems. Through community engagement, police accountability is enhanced because of the need to determine the effectiveness of collaborative problem-solving efforts.

Many of those involved in the debates and discussions regarding community policing and problem solving have adopted Eck's definition because it recognizes the importance of both working with members of the community and solving problems (see Lurgio and Rosenbaum 1994; Bennett 1994; Trojanowicz and Bucqueroux 1989). The St. Petersburg Police Department has adopted this definition in their efforts to implement community problem-oriented policing on a citywide basis. It has been helpful in clarifying the concept for both officers and members of the community. It emphasizes that a good working relationship with the community is important for addressing many of the problems they look to the police to solve. The definition also serves to underscore the idea that a safe neighborhood requires much more than just the police's and the community's liking each other—problems of concern to both must be handled in a more effective manner than they have been in traditional policing.

There are two key differences between community problem-oriented policing and traditional policing. The first, and perhaps most critical, entails recognizing that the work of the police is to help solve the problems of concern to the public, which contributes to creating a safer environment and is within the scope of their authority. Traditionally, the police have invested the greatest portion of their resources in reacting to incidents—calls for service, crime reports and the like. To be sure, the police will always invest resources in handling incidents. In time, however, as experience and sophistication grow with problem solving, more problems will be resolved and a shift in how officers spend their time will take place. Rather than spend the majority of their time reacting to calls for service, officers will invest most of their time in working with members of the community to solve problems.

The second key difference is the structure of the relationship with the community. In traditional policing, citizen roles are usually narrowly confined to being the "eyes and ears" of the police, mindless supporters, victims, or financiers of the enterprise. In community problem-oriented policing, community members are viewed as important players in understanding the problem and framing solutions, thus contributing more than just tax dollars to resolving the problem. Police officers are expected to listen to community members as one way of identifying problems of concern. Officers are expected to consult with community members affected by or involved in the problem to gain a better understanding of both the nature of the problem and its impact. Officers are expected to work with community members to identify and implement solutions to problems. Without real community participation, it is unlikely that safe neighborhoods can be created and maintained.

Traditional Policing Measures

Perhaps the most important source of police frustration, and the most severe limitation under which they operate, is the conflicting roles and demands involved in the order-maintenance, community-service and crime-fighting responsibilities of the police. Here, both the individual police officer and the police community as a whole find not only inconsistent public expectations and public reactions, but also inner conflict growing out of the interaction of the policeman's values, customs and traditions with his intimate experience with the criminal element of the population. The policeman lives on the grinding edge of social conflict, without a well-defined, well-understood notion of what he is supposed to be doing there (Campbell 1970).

The debate over what the police should be doing and how to measure it is not new. It was particularly heated in the late 1960s and early 1970s, as Americans came to grips with what seemed at the time to be unprecedented levels of crime, violence, drug abuse, and civil disobedience. The public's fear turned these problems into major national political issues. In the space of about five years, several national commissions examined issues related to these problems. These commissions, particularly the 1967 President's Commission on Law Enforcement and the Administration of Justice, prompted the federal government to create the Law Enforcement Assistance Administration (LEAA), which launched an effort to conduct research and aimed to improve police effectiveness in America. The President's Commission report on the police was also instrumental in the Ford Foundation's establishment of the Police Foundation in 1970. Although LEAA saw its demise in 1978, during the Carter administration, and the Police Foundation stopped funding research by the late 1970s, the work of these institutions made contributions to policing that continue to have an impact today. Among their greatest contributions was the early research that examined some of the most basic assumptions the police made about their impact on crime.[3]

A 1972 experiment conducted by the Police Foundation and the Kansas City, Mo., Police Department questioned the impact of random preventive patrol on crime (Kelling et al. 1974). Response time studies by the Kansas City, Mo., Police Department and PERF found that the relationship between response time, arrests and citizen satisfaction was not as strong as the police believed (KCPD 1976; Spelman and Brown 1981). Research on criminal investigations by Rand Corp., Stanford Research Institute and PERF indicated that follow-up investigations by detectives did not contribute as much as most people believed to solving crimes—the most important predictors of whether a crime would be solved were the quality and quantity of information obtained by the patrol officer initially responding to the scene (Greenwood and Petersilia 1975; Greenberg 1972; Eck 1985).

In addition, other researchers began to document that much of the police's work involved activities that were not directly related to crime (see Misner 1969; Black and Reiss 1967; Webster 1970; Bercal 1970; Goldstein 1968). This work was significant, as well, because it began to indicate that policing was a much more complex enterprise than many believed. It also started the process of documenting that community members looked to police for help in dealing with a wide range of issues and that the police were expending considerable resources responding to them. Although it was not until computer-aided dispatch systems became affordable for most police agencies in the mid-1980s that data on these activities became routinely available, the research served as an important catalyst for some to begin looking at what the police contributed to the community in a different way.

Before then, the police had generally confined the measurement of their work to reported crimes, arrests, clearance rates, and response times.[4]

While many departments continue to emphasize these measurements today, some have expanded the measures they use to include other aspects of their work. Traditional measures include:

- Reported Crime
- Response Time
- Arrests
- Crime Clearance Rates
- Workload
     Calls for Service
     Self-Initiated Activity
- Citizen Contacts
- Citizen Complaints
- Major Events

Each of these measures provides some information on police activity and conditions in the community. The value of each of the measures varies. Many of the measures are indications of input or what police do—not of outcomes or impact. Most of the measures have limitations related to the difficulty of collecting data and data accuracy. The measures are discussed in more detail below, from the perspective of their use in traditional policing, their limitations and their value.

Reported Crime

An annual ritual that takes place in cities across America is the issuance of a press release comparing the latest FBI Uniform Crime Report statistics with those of the previous year. Police chiefs, sheriffs or their press officers dutifully inform the public about whether reported crime has increased or decreased. In keeping with the ritual, reporters ask why reported crime has taken the turn that it has. The police generally respond that they don't know for sure, since so many factors influence community crime levels. The crime statistics quickly move to the background as daily stories of crime, violence and drug abuse take their place, stories that ultimately have a much more powerful effect on the public's view of neighborhood safety.

The level of reported crime is an important factor that community members and politicians take into account when thinking about police effectiveness. Over the years, the police have also emphasized reported crime as a measure of effectiveness. Police have often credited new programs or initiatives with reductions in reported crime. For years that reported crime increases, police point to drugs, guns, declines in family values, lack of jail space, or a host of other reasons to account for the change. The challenge remains for the police to put crime statistics in the proper perspective for both themselves and the public.

To do so, they must acknowledge their limitations. They must understand that not all crime is reported to the police and that changes in the statistics from one year to the next—up or down—may not reflect real changes in crime rates. The police must be more honest with the public about what they can and cannot do about crime. The police are obviously limited in their ability to affect community conditions that create an environment where crime will thrive. Crime is a much more complex phenomenon than either the police or the public is willing to acknowledge. That is why it is so important that the police begin to recognize this complexity and help the public understand it as well.

The police can have an impact on crime. While that impact may not be fully reflected in annual reported crime statistics, it is important that police make a much more concentrated effort to ensure the community is aware of the contribution they do make. The police contribute by investigating a specific crime, pattern or citywide problem using traditional and nontraditional responses. These approaches can and do make a difference. Part of the problem, however, is that arrests and criminal justice responses have been emphasized over prevention strategies.

Response Time

Since the 1930s, when radio-controlled patrol cars were introduced, response time has become an important measure of police efficiency and effectiveness in the minds of many. It is often viewed as an outcome—as if arriving at the scene of a call in three minutes is an accomplishment of some meaning in and of itself. Response time was given a boost as an important measure in 1967 with the publication of *Police*, a report from the President's Commission on Law Enforcement and Administration of Justice. The report indicated that response times of two minutes or less resulted in a significant increase in arrests. A few years later, the National Commission on Standards and Goals' report on the police indicated that police departments in urban areas should respond to all emergency calls within three minutes. The report stated:

> FBI studies indicate that the clearance rate of crime goes up as response time of patrol units is reduced. The figures show that police solve two-thirds of the crimes they respond to in less than two minutes, but only one out of five when response time is five minutes or longer. Therefore, unsolved crime is reduced when

agencies [e]nsure that patrol officers are available and respond
immediately to serious incidents (*Police Report* 1973).

It was argued that rapid response would not only increase the chances
of arrests, but would also serve as a deterrent to criminals and improve citizen
satisfaction with the police.   These beliefs resulted in significant
investments in 911 telephone reporting systems, computer-aided dispatching
and patrol resources to maintain the lowest possible response time. By the
time empirical research on response time suggested that it was important in
only a small number of cases, the police were overwhelmed with 911 calls
(most for nonemergencies) and found themselves running from call to call,
with little time to properly handle the call or do anything else. In addition,
the public thought that a "good" police department responded to all calls
immediately.

Rapid response is an important aspect of police service in those limited
circumstances where a true emergency exists.   Beyond that, working to
achieve a quick response is a drain on public resources that could be more
effectively directed toward activities that might have an impact on the
problem prompting the call.   The challenge that police face is to manage
resources in a way that ensures officers are available for emergency calls,
while allowing them time to work on problems.

Response time measurements should be focused on emergency calls. It
should not be forgotten that even with sophisticated computers, police
response time is very difficult to measure with any precision. Traditionally,
response time has been measured from three benchmarks. The first is when
the call is received; the second, when the police unit is dispatched; and the
third, when the unit reports arrival at the scene. Obviously, response time
factors are much more complex.

The traditional benchmarks do not address the time that elapsed
between when the crime occurred and when it was discovered. Nor do they
take into account the time from discovery of the crime to notification of the
police.   The call processing time is relatively accurate, but the third
benchmark is troublesome. Officers may report arrival when they are a
couple of blocks away from the scene, depending on radio traffic. Moreover,
even if an officer reports arrival when he or she arrives at the address, it
takes time to actually contact the caller. If the call came from an apartment
complex, for example, it may take the officer another three or four minutes to
make contact with the caller and begin gathering information on what has
occurred.

Arrests

When police report they have arrested someone for a highly visible violent crime, one can almost sense a collective sigh of relief in the community. Both the police and the public have long viewed arrests as a solid police performance measure. An arrest indicates that the police have solved a crime or a series of crimes. It demonstrates that something has been done. The police regularly report arrests in major cases and include arrest totals in statistical reports they prepare to justify budgets. Arrests have been an important part of individual officer performance assessments, with better marks given for arrests for more serious crimes and for higher overall numbers.

Arrests do indeed measure police activity, and they are important performance indicators for individual officers. Unfortunately, arrests have also been overemphasized as a performance indicator for both police officers and departments. In many cases, making an arrest has become the objective, rather than solving the crime problem the arrest is supposed to address. This has been particularly true for areas like narcotics or traffic enforcement.

As a measure of individual performance, arrests have generally been emphasized over other activities because they seem to be easy to count. However, there are some difficulties. One has to do with measuring the quality of the arrest. Few police departments routinely track arrest outcomes, so it is difficult to determine whether the prosecutor filed charges or obtained a conviction. Even if the arrest is tracked, in most cases it is very difficult to determine whether the outcome—conviction, plea bargain, dismissal—was related to the officer's performance.

Another problem is arrest counts. In most cases, there are two or more officers present when an arrest is made. Two or more officers may take credit for arresting one person on activity logs. As a result, police department numbers on arrests are often very different from the number of people actually booked into jail.

An additional problem with arrests as a performance measure has emerged in recent years. The arrest itself has become, in some instances, a means of exercising control over particular problems, without any real intent to prosecute. In 1987, the Washington Metropolitan Police Department conducted massive narcotics sweeps and made over 45,000 arrests. The much-heralded Minneapolis domestic violence research indicating that an arrest alone was a deterrent to future violence encouraged police agencies to make arrests on all of those calls. Arrest has also been used as a solution for the homeless problem, and it continues to be the primary response to prostitution. In most cases, prosecutors and the courts have little interest in these types of arrests and do what they can to dispose of them as quickly as possible. The police frequently find themselves being called upon to deal with a wide range of problems for which arrest or the threat of arrest is the primary response.

Crime Clearance Rates

Clearance rates have become an important measure of performance for individual detectives and the police organization as a whole. The "clearance" concept comes from the FBI Uniform Crime Reports initiated in the 1930s in concert with the International Association of Chiefs of Police. A clearance indicates a crime has been solved. Police are allowed to clear a case when someone has been arrested (not charged) for the crime. In some cases, police are allowed to take "exceptional clearances" when they have probable cause to make an arrest, but are unable to do so because, for example, the person is in prison or is dead. Nationally, clearance rates have remained in the area of 20 percent for many years. In spite of this relatively low figure, clearance rates have still prompted criticism and concern. In some cases, clearance, rather than arrest and prosecution for the crime, has become the objective. It is not unusual for people who have been arrested for one crime to confess to dozens of others, because they are on their way to jail anyway and they know they will not be charged with them. These cases have raised questions, and in some instances, investigations have shown that the individuals could not have possibly committed the crimes to which they have confessed. Although most police departments have developed procedures for monitoring clearances, a shadow has been cast over their use as a performance measure.

Patrol Workload

With the introduction of computer-aided dispatch systems, police workload statistics have become an important measure of police performance. The numbers of calls for service have become a key statistic in police performance reports. Police departments routinely share call information with the community to indicate how hard they are working and how they are using resources. They often supplement call information with reports of officers' self-initiated activity. These reports include the number of cars stopped, traffic tickets issued, suspicious subjects checked, buildings checked, field interview reports completed, and similar activities that officers generally initiate on their own.

These measures have value to the extent that they provide the community with an indication of how the police are using resources. The statistics say nothing about the impact of these activities or whether some other use of time would better benefit the community.

Citizen Contacts

Over the past 10 to 15 years, police departments have frequently included citizen contacts as a part of their performance measures. Such measures have largely emerged from police efforts to emphasize crime prevention. Recognizing the difficulty with establishing a clear relationship between prevention and victimization, prevention programs have focused on measures that can be counted fairly easily. As a result, citizen contacts have been counted as a key measure of performance. The numbers of crime watch meetings, citizens attending the meetings, home or business security surveys, Operation ID participants, and the like have become important measures of police activity.

Like the other measures of police activity, these indicate activity levels but provide no indication of impact. Rarely do police follow up to see whether recommendations on a home or business security survey are implemented. Even more rare is an effort to determine whether there is a relationship between these activities and victimization levels.

Citizen Complaints

An emerging police performance measure is the number and disposition of citizen complaints against police officers. As calls for citizen review boards increased during the late 1980s, some police departments began routinely sharing information on citizen complaints with the community to demonstrate that the police took these matters seriously. Generally, departments report the number of complaints, their nature and their disposition. Dispositions usually are reported as sustained, not sustained, exhonorated, or unfounded.

Citizen complaints are an important measure of how police departments go about their work, but like other measures, they are not free of difficulty. One of the most trying aspects of making sense of citizen complaints is what they really mean for the police and community. Does a high number of complaints reflect a police department that places little emphasis on how citizens are treated? Or does it indicate that citizens are confident their complaints will be taken seriously? What does a sustained rate of 15 or 20 percent mean? That police are not good at investigating their own, or that most complaints are the result of a misunderstanding of complex legal procedures?

As long as the police make a good-faith effort to capture citizen complaint information and accurately report it to the community, it should be a useful measure that will serve them well. It will convey a sense of openness to the community that should ultimately serve to strengthen the relationship—even if some view the information reported as negative.

Major Events

For adults over 45, the Chicago police's performance at the 1968 Democratic National Convention is a firmly entrenched memory. Almost everyone today has opinions about the Los Angeles Police Department based on the way they handled the 1988 Summer Olympics, the riots following the first trial of the officers involved in the Rodney King incident, and the Nicole Simpson/Ronald Goldman murders. The way the Philadelphia police handled the MOVE incident continues to influence the views of many in that community. Citizens in Dade County, Fla., have lasting impressions of the police based on their response to the aftermath of Hurricane Andrew.

Clearly, an important measure of police performance from a citizen's perspective is their ability to handle major events. How police handle major events in their community can inspire great confidence or can be an albatross around their necks that becomes entwined with almost everything they do.

Inputs—Process—Outcomes

What is the bottom line for the police? Is the bottom line the absence of crime? Is it a sense of safety in the community? Is it an immediate response to a call for service, or citizen satisfaction with police service? The private-sector bottom line—a profit—is not nearly as difficult to measure, and stockholders all agree that it is an important purpose. It is a lot more complicated for the police and government in general to determine the appropriate bottom line. Not only do the police encounter a wide range of views on what the bottom line should be, but it is also very difficult to determine whether what they do has an impact. If the bottom line is safety or the absence of crime, how is the police contribution toward that outcome determined? In a neighborhood that is free of reported crime, can the police take credit? The complications of measuring police performance are obvious when one begins to think about them. In the place of profit as a bottom line, the police, and government in general, have substituted a variety of proxy measures. As James Q. Wilson notes in "The Problem of Defining Agency Success,"

> There are no "real" measures of overall success; what is measurable about the level of public order, safety and amenity in a given large city can only partially, if at all, be affected by police behavior. (For example, if the murder or robbery rates go up, one cannot assume that this is the fault of the police; if they go down, one should not necessarily allow the police to take credit for it.) Proxy measures almost always turn out to be process measures—response time, arrest rates or clearance rates—that

may or may not have any relationship to crime rates or levels of
public order (Wilson 1993).

Given the difficulty of measuring outcomes, the fact that most
traditional measures are proxies should not be a source of great concern as long
as there is a clear understanding of what the measures represent. Moreover,
process measures provide some indication of what the police are doing,
which is important to determining outcomes to the degree that is possible.
What is most important is that the police make a greater effort to measure
outcomes.

As police departments have gained more experience with community
problem-oriented policing, outcomes have received greater attention.
Problem solving requires that officers try to assess the results of the solution
they have implemented. Clearly, there are difficulties with determining
the impact of an officer's problem-solving effort, but at least three important
results occur. First, focusing on a specific problem—drug-selling location,
repeat calls, neighborhood burglaries—makes it a little less complicated to
relate police and community actions to outcomes. Second, problem solving
identifies outcomes as an important aspect of the process. And third, because
solutions are tailored to the problems, the door is opened for a wider range of
measurements that may provide a better sense of the police contribution to
the outcome. Problem solving does not resolve the measurement issues for the
police, but it helps place the police in a better position to relate what they
do to outcomes.

Community Problem-Oriented Policing Measures

Within professional policing circles, it is now widely accepted
that a commitment to substantial change in direction or
strategies carries with it a commitment to learning from the
process of change and evaluating its impact. In contrast with the
past, there is a welcome readiness to subject innovative programs
to evaluation. But one of the many consequences of the
widespread popular interest in community policing is that it has
generated its own intense pressures for a quick evaluation of
impact. Mayors, city managers, local legislators, budget officers,
the public, and veteran police officers—among others—ask:
"Does it work?" They want some assurance that the changes they
are being asked to endorse and finance will meet the claims made
for them (Goldstein 1994).

Competing pressures have caused the police to place a great deal more
emphasis on developing meaningful measures of their performance. These

pressures come in part from the continuing difficulty that local government faces in financing the services police provide. They come from the public's demands that the police do something about the crime that has contributed to a general loss in their sense of safety. They come from police executives' and others' growing understanding of the shortcomings of the more traditional police performance measures. They come as well from demands in various quarters that the police provide some indication that their proposals for community problem-oriented policing will have an impact on crime, fear and violence. The result has been the emergence of a wider range of police performance measures and a greater willingness to invest resources in gathering the data to use these measures.

This willingness to look at police performance from a broader perspective has produced measures that are more focused on outcomes than traditional measures. Listed below are measures that are being considered by police departments around the nation that are involved with community policing and problem solving.

- Problem Solving
- Citizen Satisfaction
- Repeat Business
- Displacement
- Neighborhood Indicators

Obviously, these measures are not unique to community problem-oriented policing, but they are generally not a part of the routine thinking in police departments committed to traditional policing approaches. Like traditional policing measures, they have strengths and limitations. They are discussed in greater detail below.

Problem Solving

According to Eck's definition of community policing, problem solving is the principal service the police should provide. Goldstein (1979, 1990), Eck and Spelman (1987) and others have made a convincing case that police should shift their focus from "incidents" to problems to improve their effectiveness. Building on the idea of a problem focus espoused by Goldstein and tested initially in Madison, Wis., and Baltimore County in the early 1980s (see Goldstein 1979, 1990; Taft 1986; Cordner 1985), the Newport News, Va., Police Department developed and tested a problem-solving process that many agencies have since adopted (Eck and Spelman 1987).

This problem-solving process contains four stages, each important to measuring police problem-solving performance. The stages are scanning,

analysis, response, and assessment, and the process has come to be known as
SARA (Eck and Spelman 1987).

Scanning represents the part of the process where problems are
identified. Rather than focusing exclusively on a specific call or
crime, officers are expected to group these incidents together and
attempt to define the problem in a more precise manner.

Analysis is the stage of the process where begins the process of
gathering information on the problem in order to gain a much
better understanding of the underlying conditions. The analysis
includes searching for information from a variety of sources,
including the community.

Response is the part of the process where solutions are developed
and implemented. The solutions are tailored to the specific
problem, based on knowledge gained from the analysis stage.

Assessment is the stage where officers are expected to determine
if the solution that was implemented had any impact on the
problem.

This four-part process has been adopted by police departments throughout
the country and has contributed to the increasing focus on the outcomes of
problem-solving efforts.

Eck and Spelman also suggest five outcomes from problem-solving
efforts.

The first is the elimination of the problem.   Depending on the
seriousness or nature of the problem, complete elimination is not something
that one can normally expect from problem-solving efforts. More often,
success is found in one of the other possible outcomes.

The second outcome is a reduction of the number of incidents. Clearly,
the police have used a reduction in the number of incidents as a performance
indicator for some time. In problem solving, the relationship between a
change in the number of incidents and what the police are doing should be
more clear because the responses are tailored to the specific problem. Rather
than simply increase police presence in a neighborhood where there has been
an increase in auto thefts, the police might focus on residents who own the
particular type of car being stolen to encourage target-hardening measures. A
reduction in the number of thefts of that type of vehicle might suggest a
relationship between the tactic and the outcome.

*The third outcome is a reduction in the seriousness of the incidents or
the amount of harm.* A reduction in the amount of loss from convenience store
robberies based on a change in cash-management techniques is an example of

this outcome. Or if stores with two clerks show no injuries or deaths from robberies, that might indicate a reduction in harm based on a strategy arising from an improved understanding of the problem.

The fourth outcome is an improved response to the problem. In Newport News, through a problem-solving effort aimed at domestic violence homicides, procedures were changed for the way the police, the rest of the criminal justice system and the service providers responded to domestic violence. The result was a more comprehensive and coordinated way of dealing with the problem, providing better service to the victims. Another example of an improved response might be greater efficiency in dealing with the problem.

The fifth outcome is shifting responsibility for handling the problem to a more appropriate agency. In some communities, police have seen significant reductions in calls for service as services have been established to handle the needs of homeless people. Police now direct individuals in need of help to shelters rather than rely on arrest and jail to address the problem.

Although there are process measures in problem solving, and they are important, the focus is directed more toward outcomes. Generally, the problems have been defined with enough clarity and the response focused so that outcome measures are not quite as difficult to determine as traditional policing measures.

Citizen Satisfaction

In the past 10 years, as the private sector has placed more emphasis on customer satisfaction as an important measure of their work, the government and the police have done the same. In the private sector, the basic assumption is that a satisfied customer will more likely patronize the business or use the product in the future, as well as recommend it to friends, which—it is believed—will help increase profits. For the police, citizen satisfaction is an important measure as well. But the reasons are different, and it is a much more complicated concept.

Citizens who are generally satisfied with services are thought to be more likely to work cooperatively with the police when needed, and they are probably less resentful of investing tax dollars in safety and security. Moreover, citizens cannot easily take their business elsewhere.[5] Citizens also have a voice that is somewhat akin to a stockholder's, with a wide range of options to express their point of view about police services. So the police must think about citizen satisfaction a little differently from how business thinks about customer satisfaction, and they must look for every opportunity to measure it.

One way of gauging citizen satisfaction is through the number and type of complaints and commendations the police receive about service.

Complaints were discussed earlier as one of the traditional measures, and despite limitations, they do have value as one indicator of the quality of police service. Other useful indicators are the letters and telephone calls the police department receives from citizens who believe the police handled an incident particularly well. As with complaints, it takes a special effort on the part of a citizen to write or call with compliments about an interaction with the police department. Most departments acknowledge compliments and note them in officers' personnel files. Few departments analyze them to gain a sense of how the information might be helpful—simply as an indication of the degree of satisfaction with the service, or perhaps to identify behaviors that the department might encourage in some formal way.

Some police departments have established formal mechanisms for ongoing citizen assessments of the quality of police response by using brief postcard or letter questionnaires—much like those one finds in restaurants and motels. Madison, Wis., Chief David Couper began mailing questionnaires to every 50th person who filed a report with the department in early 1987. That amounted to about 160 surveys mailed each month. They received a return of 35 to 40 percent. The survey asked citizens to rate the police response on a scale of one (poor) to five (excellent) on seven areas, including concern, knowledge, quality of service, solving the problem, putting citizens at ease, and professional conduct. An open-ended question, How can the police improve?, was also included in the survey. The responses were routed back to the chief, who read them all. The results were also periodically published in the department's newsletter, along with basic demographic information about citizens responding. In addition, the surveys were available to any officer interested in reading them (Couper and Lobitz 1991).

Police might also want to track news stories, editorials and letters to the editor as indications of satisfaction with police service. As with other measures, these have limitations, as they are influenced by the interests of the media and the citizens who write. However, they do offer some information that might be of value in understanding how citizens perceive contacts with the police.

Many police departments are turning to formal citizen surveys to obtain information on a number of subjects, including citizen satisfaction. The Reno, Nev., Police Department conducts citizen surveys every six months in conjunction with a local university. In Newport News, Va., and Baltimore County, Md., officers regularly conduct neighborhood surveys on their problem-solving efforts. In St. Petersburg, Fla., the police department conducts surveys annually to measure progress on its community problem-solving policing efforts, as well as to gauge citizen satisfaction. Table 1 compares some of the results from a community survey conducted in 1991 and 1994 in St. Petersburg.

Table 1

St. Petersburg Community Survey

1991 n = 1,448   1994 n = 2,438

Change in Safety of Your Neighborhood in Past Year

	1991	1994
Became safer	7.7	10.7
Stayed the same	57.9	66.8
Became less safe	33.3	18.9
No answer	1.1	3.6

Most Serious Crime Problem in Your Neighborhood

	1991	1994
Assault/robbery	8.8	6.1
Burglary/theft	50.8	29.3
Domestic violence	1.2	0.7
Drugs	12.4	10.6
Noise/nuisance	10.2	1.0
Rape/sexual assault	1.2	0.2
Truancy	n/a	2.9
Vandalism	n/a	5.8
Vehicle theft	n/a	2.9
Other	0.0	3.1
None	11.9	23.2
No answer	0.9	10.1

Level of Concern for Neighborhood Problems

	% Very Concerned	
	1991	1994
Crime	65.3	41.7
Feeling safe/secure	50.8	37.5
Adequate police patrol	49.3	29.3
Juveniles	36.3	26.9
Homeless people	34.6	15.8
People in your area	31.4	15.4
Litter/trash	29.0	17.1
Traffic/parking	25.6	14.1
Noise	23.0	12.6

Level of Concern for Neighborhood Crime Problems

	% Saying Big Problem	
	1991	1994
Burglary	53.2	21.5
Vandalism	46.6	13.3
Drugs	46.2	19.1
Vehicle theft	36.0	12.0
Assault/robbery	32.4	11.1
Sexual assault	32.0	3.1
Gangs	27.1	7.3
Neighborhood decay	24.7	8.4
Noise/nuisances	16.2	7.3
Domestic violence	17.3	6.8
Drunk driving	n/a	9.5
Fraud/scams	n/a	6.1
Loitering	n/a	8.9
Prostitution	n/a	4.7
Speeding traffic	n/a	17.3
Truancy	n/a	10.6

Fear of Being out Alone in Neighborhood

	% Reporting Being Afraid	
	1991	1994
At night	46.4	41.1
During the day	7.6	6.7

*Rating of Police Service in Your Neighborhood

	% Rating as Good	
	1991	1994
Courtesy of officers	74.4	84.2
Courtesy of call-takers	n/a	84.0
Professionalism	70.0	85.8
Overall satisfaction	59.0	n/a
Emergency response	59.0	78.1
Sensitivity of officers	54.9	79.6
Help with nonemergencies	40.1	65.3
Availability of officers	n/a	59.7
Problem-solving skills	56.2	75.6
Officers' appearance	92.0	n/a
Officers' conduct	83.4	n/a
Officers' concern	71.2	73.2
Officers' helpfulness	72.4	80.2
Officer put you at ease	63.1	n/a
Communication skills	n/a	79.5

Listening skills	n/a	78.6
Judgment	n/a	76.4
Fair treatment	n/a	78.4
Treated with dignity	n/a	83.5
Language/behavior	n/a	86.5

	1991 % Yes
Treated you fairly	91.8
Used good judgment	85.6
Language offensive	4.0
Listened to you	91.3
Behavior offensive	9.7

*Question changed to good/fair/poor rating in 1994.

Who is most responsible for neighborhood quality of life?

	1991	1994
Residents and police	81.4	78.0
Residents	15.5	17.4
Police	2.4	1.4
No answer	0.7	3.2

Are you personally responsible for neighborhood quality of life?

	1991	1994
Yes	56.5	73.1
Somewhat	32.5	15.0
No	10.6	10.5
No answer	0.4	1.4

Are you aware of community policing/joint problem solving?

	1991	1994
Yes	44.5	54.3
No	55.1	43.6
No answer	0.4	2.1

Have you participated in a problem-solving activity?

	1994
Yes	24.1
No	75.5
No answer	0.4

Do you know your community policing officer?

	1991	1994
Yes	4.2	20.6
No	94.8	78.9
No answer	1.0	0.5

Can you name your community policing officer?

	1991	1994
Yes	2.8	7.6
No	96.0	92.2
No answer	1.2	0.2

Do you know your neighborhood patrol officers?

	1994
Yes	11.8
No	87.9
No answer	0.3

Can you name those patrol officers?

	1994
Yes	4.3
No	95.7
No answer	0.0

Have you been a crime victim in the past year?

	1991	1994
Yes	20.8	17.8
No	78.9	81.9
No answer	0.3	0.3

Did you report the crime of which you were a victim?

	% of Total Victims	
	1991	1994
Yes	83.7	82.7
No	16.3	17.1
No answer	0.0	0.2

How was the police report handled?

	1994
Officer/detective came	77.1
Taken over telephone	18.1
Form mailed	0.3
Went in person to HQ	2.8
Don't know/no answer	1.7

The St. Petersburg survey provides considerable information on how citizens feel about a number of issues of great importance to the police. Not only does it address issues of satisfaction, but it also deals with citizen perceptions of the extent of the problems in their neighborhoods and their level of concern about them. Of greatest importance as a measure of police performance is the amount of change from one survey to the next. On the first question, for example, 77 percent of the respondents felt that the level of safety had stayed the same or improved during the previous 12 months, as opposed to 65 percent who felt that way in 1991. Although one could argue the change had nothing to do with the police, a stronger case can be made that the police have contributed (at least in part) to this change. Surveys are not a measurement panacea, but they can be very useful gauges of citizen satisfaction when they are properly conducted.

Repeat Business

With the increased sophistication of information systems has come the confirmation of something the police have suspected for many years—much of their work is concentrated. In outlining their rationale for the importance of the police's moving from an almost exclusive focus on incidents to one that emphasized problems, Spelman and Eck (1989) pointed out the repeat nature of police work (see table 2).

Table 2

Repeat Business

10% of Locations	account for	60% of Calls for Service
10% of Offenders	account for	55% of Offenses
10% of Victims	account for	42% of Victimizations

In a two-year period, an Austin, Texas, convenience store was criminally victimized 385 times, with 90 percent of the victimizations being gasoline drive-offs. In Newport News, one convenience store accounted for over 500 calls for service during a 12-month period. In St. Petersburg, police responded to one 10-unit apartment complex over 150 times in a year. In Philadelphia, police responded to a neighborhood tavern over 600 times in a six-month period, after an anonymous caller complained about noise. Unquestionably, the repeat nature of police work offers an opportunity to identify problems and measure results. If police or community action can effect a reduction in the number of calls at a specific location, it not only can serve as an indication of effectiveness, but it can also free up time for officers to work on other problems.

Displacement

It is not unusual to hear it argued that displacement is an indication that police or community action has been ineffective in dealing with a problem. If one applies pressure on one side of a balloon, it will take a different shape—but it will still contain the same volume of air. The same argument is made about crime—pressure in one location causes it to move to another, and it returns when the action against it ceases. Displacement most often occurs in one or more of three forms.

The first, and the one the police most often think about, is when the crime problem simply moves from one geographic area to another, where the activity can take place with less interference. This often occurs when the police substantially increase their presence in an area where problems have surfaced.

Second, the problem is often displaced temporally. Offenders shift the time of their activity to one when the police or community residents are not present.

Third, displacement takes place when offenders shift from one crime to another. In the early 1990s, as auto thefts began to decline in some areas, "carjackings" became a major new crime in many urban areas across the nation. Some informed observers thought that alarms, new ignition systems and new locking mechanisms had increased the difficulty of stealing cars. Offenders responded by taking occupied vehicles by force, which is considered a more serious crime than stealing an unoccupied car. Others thought the carjacking problem was related more to the crack-cocaine epidemic, which brought with it an increase in all types of street violence. Whatever the cause, no one wants to make a problem worse through the response. Displacement is an important aspect of measuring the effect of a response to problems, and it should be given serious consideration.

In some cases, displacement may reduce the harm. For example, police elect to respond to a drug-dealing problem at a street intersection by maintaining high visibility. The dealers move to another location several blocks away, where they are observed setting up shop. Is there any value in moving the location of the enterprise? A case can be made that there might be some value if customers do not make connections with the dealers because they cannot find them or they are afraid to venture into a new area. Disrupting the market has the potential for reducing sales and, perhaps, consumption. Both are desirable ends. In fact, Kleiman (1987) offers some evidence from studies in Lawrence, Mass., and New York City that market interruption does reduce both sales and consumption. Kleiman argues that the more obstacles the buyer has to overcome to connect with the seller, the fewer sales will take place. For the casual user, the obstacles might be sufficient to substantially reduce use. For the heavy user, consumption is likely to be reduced if it takes longer to connect between uses.

Eck (1993) points out three general implications for planning and measuring anticrime efforts in a thoughtful paper on displacement. First, efforts aimed at a "unique" problem rather than a general problem will cause less displacement. Second, displacement can be minimized if the strategy includes steps to address likely displacement targets. Third, to identify methods to minimize displacement, a careful analysis must be done before choosing a response to the problem. Given a better understanding of displacement, the police might use it as an indication of success rather than failure.

Neighborhood Indicators

The police have been much more willing in recent years to acknowledge their limitations in dealing with crime. They have begun to talk about crime and violence in the context of neighborhood conditions, education, economic factors, and other demographic factors that are present or absent in areas with the greatest problems. Yet most police departments have not considered changes in these conditions as possible measures of their contributions.

Fortunately, some police departments are beginning to look at these factors to determine the effect of initiatives aimed at neighborhood problems. One example is the appearance of the neighborhood. Building on the theory of "Broken Windows," police departments, working with neighborhood associations, other arms of government and the private sector, have begun to consider change in the way a neighborhood looks as a positive impact of their collective efforts. An improvement in the way a neighborhood appears could possibly translate into less fear or higher property values. Both of these variables can be measured.

From the police perspective, what is the value of a new or expanded business in a neighborhood? Can the new job opportunities help divert individuals from criminal activities to legitimate forms of work? Can the foot and vehicular traffic associated with new business contribute to safer streets? Can police engage in programs or adopt policies that will enhance neighborhood improvement and investment? Is the reduction of truancy a valid measure of police performance? Does an increase in occupancy of an apartment complex where police have worked on problems reflect a positive contribution? Obviously, the answers to these questions depend in part on the interventions that police have initiated in cooperation with the community—but they may very well provide greater insight into police effectiveness than many of the measures that have traditionally been used.

Integration of Tradition and Community Problem-Solving Policing

> Meaningful, lasting change in policing cannot be achieved in isolation. Policing is like a large, intricate, complex apparatus with many parts. Change of any one part requires changes in many others and in the way the parts fit together (Herman Goldstein, Aug. 24, 1993).

When General Motors makes a major model change, they shut the assembly line down for several weeks. During this time, they make the necessary adjustments in the line to assemble the new model. They train the workers to produce the new model. They test the new line configuration and procedures, then make modifications to produce the car to quality specifications before returning to full production.

The most significant challenge facing the police is managing the colossal change associated with the introduction of community problem-oriented policing and performance measures. Unlike General Motors, the police cannot stop the assembly line for several weeks, retrain all employees, and then start with the new methods or procedures firmly in place and clearly understood by everyone whom the change might affect. The police must introduce change while the assembly line is running. The complexity of changing methods, procedures, policies, attitudes, and outcomes while the "assembly line" is moving is enormous. That is why many police departments never begin the process of change, and many of those that do, fail.

Ensuring the successful implementation of community problem-oriented policing requires the careful blending of the traditional approaches to policing developed over the years with the knowledge gained from research that points to practices that may have a greater long-term impact on crime. To do that, the police will have to think differently about the measurement of effectiveness, the way human resources are used, and the priority given prevention in relationship to arrest, prosecution and incarceration as the most important response to crime.

Measuring Effectiveness

The issue of measuring effectiveness is not entirely one of discarding the old and replacing it with new measures. It is one of putting the traditional measures in perspective (using them when appropriate) and placing greater emphasis on outcomes than process or "proxy measures." Some measures, traditional and new, may not be worth the investment required to collect and maintain information. For each measure, the police should ask some basic questions:

1. *What do we want to know?*   Are we interested in the resources invested (inputs) in solving this particular problem? Do we need to know if procedures (processes) were followed? Are we interested in the impacts (outcomes) of the effort? While these questions and their answers may appear to be obvious, depending on the problem or issue, it may not be necessary or feasible to address each of them.

2. *What information is required?*   What type of information is needed to learn what we want to know?   Where is that information? Is it currently collected? Will it be necessary to develop special methods to collect it? If available, is it in a form that is readily adaptable for the new use?

3. *What is the cost of collecting/storing the information?*   Is the answer to a question worth the cost of collecting the information?   The police invest considerable resources in collecting and storing information. Since much of the cost of collection is in human resources, creating a new report or changing an old one, the real cost is often not given much consideration.

4. *Who is interested in the answers to the questions?*   It is important to consider who is concerned about the answers to the questions.   Is the audience primarily organizational personnel, or is the audience the community?

Dealing with questions like these will help in making decisions about what will be measured, how and at what cost. As police departments make the transition from traditional policing methods to community problem solving, the measures used will gradually change in concert.

Shift in Resource Utilization

As one thinks about the future of policing, it is hard to imagine a time when the police will not be required to have the capability to respond immediately to citizens in need of help. It is equally difficult to imagine a time when the police will not have to have effective mechanisms in place to conduct retrospective criminal investigations.   These fundamental requirements of policing increase the complexity of making the changes proposed under a community problem-solving philosophy because a considerable portion of the available resources must be devoted to these activities. Many departments have responded by creating special units to do community policing or problem solving, while call response and criminal investigation remain the work of the majority of their personnel. And most of these departments eventually report that the special units face considerable animosity from their colleagues because the officers are no longer engaged in "real police work." Experience with the special-unit approach seems to indicate the immediate advantages quickly give way to the disadvantage of involving only a small portion of the department's resources in its philosophy of policing. While special units or split forces offer an expedient (and perhaps necessary) way of introducing the department and community to the new philosophy, the department must gradually move toward involving the entire workforce if the philosophy is to survive.

If one agrees that the police must maintain an immediate response and a retrospective criminal investigative capacity, then the issue becomes one of how to introduce a new *proactive* policing philosophy that must coexist with *reacting* to calls and crimes. One way to deal with this issue is to look at it in terms of how much time officers or investigators devote to reactive activities vs. how much time they devote to working with the community to solve problems. For the sake of discussion, if officers currently commit 65 percent of their time to handling calls and administrative activities, they can devote 35 percent of their time to problem solving. As officers and the community become more adept at solving problems, there should be a reduction in calls, which will allow for more time for problem solving. While obviously an oversimplification of a complex interaction, the point is the same: full and effective implementation of community problem-solving policing comes down to shifting the greatest proportion of an officer's (or detective's) time to working with the community to solve problems. Although it is difficult to say with any precision what the time mix should be, it seems clear that it should eventually be a *minimum* of an even split and, even better, broken down so that 65 percent of police time is spent on problem solving and 35 percent on call response and criminal investigation.[6]

That time mix can be achieved in several ways. One is by adding more police officers. Clearly, that is one of the most expedient approaches to implementing community policing. Financial constraints limit the value of that solution in many communities, so departments have to develop alternatives. Call management policies, use of civilian personnel in positions that have traditionally been staffed by police officers, telephone reporting, and the like are all effective approaches to creating more time for problem solving. And, over time, it can be achieved through more effective and lasting responses to the repeat business that consumes so much of police resources.

Focus on Prevention

Almost from the time that Sir Robert Peel set forth the principle that the effectiveness of the "preventive police" should be measured by the absence of crime and disorder—not by police efforts to deal with these problems—police have struggled with measurement problems. That struggle has essentially given way to doing exactly what Peel thought inappropriate: measuring inputs and process as a way of justifying their existence. Input and process measures have emerged as the proxies for gauging effectiveness and performance in part because of the great difficulties with establishing clear relationships between inputs and outcomes. They also emerged as proxy measures because the police alone could not be held accountable for the environmental conditions that produced crime. Peel was right, however, about the importance of prevention. Nevertheless, the police in America have effectively deemphasized the importance of prevention because of the emphasis on proxy measures like arrests, clearances and response times.

A critically important aspect of the transition from traditional to community problem-oriented policing is the emphasis placed on prevention. Prevention activities—other than the deterrent effects of arrest, prosecution and incarceration—must have equal emphasis. Just as wellness has become the medical profession's focus, creating safe communities through prevention must emerge as the police's primary goal.

Conclusion

> [I]f the police are serious about defining goals and measuring progress toward them, they will inevitably have to do so by identifying problems relevant to citizens' concerns at the neighborhood level, specifying possible solutions, and measuring the effect of those strategies. This is what is meant by problem-oriented policing (POP), which, in my view, is the heart of COP and what makes POP (and COP, properly defined) different from police-community relations (Wilson 1993).

The challenge of policing in America is enormous, and it seems to grow in complexity as the frequency and intensity of crime and violence increase. In many urban areas, the police are hard-pressed to answer the calls for help and seem overwhelmed by the cases that need follow-up investigation. Officers are frustrated by a criminal justice system that cannot keep the promise to isolate those who have been convicted of crimes from the rest of society. In Florida, the average prisoners serve about one-third of their sentence, and they generally are not sentenced to prison until they have committed several serious felonies. In this atmosphere, it almost seems like an empty academic exercise to talk about concepts like establishing a partnership with the community to solve problems and shifting from input and process measures to outcomes. Yet that is exactly what must be done.

The police—particularly executives and union leaders—must focus all the energy they can muster on the future. They must engage in the hard work required to develop true partnerships with citizens and other government agencies. They must acknowledge the limitations of the traditional approaches to policing and work to help others understand the importance of their responsibility for creating safe communities. The police must provide the leadership necessary to ensure that responses to crime, violence and disorder reflect our knowledge of these problems and our commitment to democratic values.

Notes

[1]I must acknowledge that I fall within the group of advocates. My experience and understanding of research on policing force me to conclude that we must change the way we approach our work and relate to the community. A focus on problems in a partnership with people affected by those problems makes a great deal of sense to me.

[2]The Consortium was created by the U.S. Department of Justice's Bureau of Justice Assistance (BJA). It consists of the Police Executive Research Forum (PERF), the International Association of Chiefs of Police (IACP), the National Sheriff's Association (NSA), and the Police Foundation. These organizations have come together with funding from BJA to further the development and implementation of community policing throughout America. Part of their role is to provide training and technical assistance. The passage quoted comes from an early draft of a document John Eck prepared in 1992.

[3]Although I place a great deal of emphasis on the research, these institutions contributed a great deal more than research. LEAA, for example, created the Law Enforcement Education Program, which helped officers attend college. They also provided travel and training opportunities that helped open the police up to new ideas by reducing their isolation.

[4]It is important to remember in this discussion that there is a vast difference in the development and thinking of police across America. Some police departments have attempted to expand the scope of what they considered for many years. They have tried to capture resource commitments

or inputs, process measures and, to a more limited extent, outcomes. Others (police, politicians and community members), even today, emphasize reported crime, arrests and response time as the key measures of police effectiveness. Obviously, measuring outcomes or impact on reported crime is a minefield for the police. Not only is it difficult to determine how much crime occurs, but it is also even more difficult to establish clear relationships between what the police do and how much crime occurs.

[5]Although citizens cannot *easily* take their services elsewhere, there is growing indication they are turning elsewhere to increase their sense of security. The security business is a growth industry. Alarm systems, private guards, personal safety devices, and gun ownership are all increasing. There are those in policing who see this as a loss of the public police "market share" and are concerned about the public's willingness to underwrite both public and private police.

[6]Community-oriented problem solving clearly involves much more than manipulating the amount of time officers spend on certain activities. Officers (and supervisors) must adopt a different attitude about the time they spend on calls and follow-up investigations. They must ask different questions on each call and crime report: Have we been here before? What is causing this situation to occur or reoccur? How can it be prevented? What should the police do? The callers? The victims? The community? The government? The time mix is my estimate of where a department should be to make a maximum contribution to safety within the range of affordability.

References

Bennett, T. 1994. "Community Policing on the Ground: Developments in Britain." *The Challenge of Community Policing: Testing the Promises.* Edited by D.P. Rosenbaum. Thousand Oaks, Calif.: Sage Publications.

Campbell, J.S., et al. 1970. *Law and Order Reconsidered: Report of the Task Force on Law and Law Enforcement to the National Commission on the Causes and Prevention of Violence.* New York: Bantam Books.

Cordner, G.W. 1985. *The Baltimore County Citizen-Oriented Police Enforcement (COPE) Project: Final Evaluation.* Baltimore: Criminal Justice Department, University of Baltimore.

Couper, D.C., and S.H. Lobitz. 1991. *Quality Policing: The Madison Experience.* Washington, D.C.: Police Executive Research Forum.

Eck, J. 1985. *Solving Crimes*. Washington, D.C.: Police Executive Research Forum.

_____. 1993. "The Threat of Crime Displacement." *Criminal Justice Abstracts* 25(3) (September):527-548.

Eck, J.E., and W. Spelman. 1987. *Problem Solving: Problem-Oriented Policing in Newport News*. Washington, D.C.: Police Executive Research Forum.

Goldstein, H. 1994. Foreword. *The Challenge of Community Policing: Testing the Promises*. Edited by D. Rosenbaum. Thousand Oaks, Calif.: Sage Publications.

_____. 1993. "The New Policing: Confronting Complexity." Speech presented at conference on community policing sponsored by National Institute of Justice. Washington, D.C.

_____. 1979. "Improving Policing: A Problem-Oriented Approach." *Crime and Delinquency* 25:236-258.

Greene, J.R., and S.D. Mastrofski, eds. 1988. *Community Policing: Rhetoric or Reality*. New York: Praeger.

Greenberg, B. 1972. *Analysis and Conclusions*. Vol. I of *Enhancement of the Investigations Function*. 4 vols. Menlo Park, Calif.: Stanford Research Institute.

Greenwood, P.W., and J. Petersilia. 1975. *Summary and Policy Implications*. Vol. I of *The Criminal Investigation Process*. 3 vols. Santa Monica, Calif.: The Rand Corp.

Kaminer, W. 1994. "Crime and Community." *Atlantic Monthly* (May).

Kelling, G.L., T. Pate, D. Dieckman, and C.E. Brown. 1974. *The Kansas City Preventive Patrol Experiment: A Technical Report*. Washington D.C.: Police Foundation.

Kleiman, M.A.R. 1987. "Crackdowns: The Effects of Intensive Enforcement on Retail Heroin Dealing." Working paper #87-01-11. Cambridge, Mass.: Program in Criminal Justice Policy and Management, JFK School of Government, Harvard University.

Klockars, C.B. 1988. "The Rhetoric of Community Policing." *Community Policing: Rhetoric or Reality.* Edited by J.R. Greene and S.D. Mastrofski. New York: Praeger.

Lurgio, A.J., and D.P. Rosenbaum. 1994. "The Impact of Community Policing on Police Personnel: A Review of the Literature." *The Challenge of Community Policing: Testing the Promises.* Edited by D.P. Rosenbaum. Thousand Oaks, Calif.: Sage Publications.

La Vigne, N.G. 1991. "Crimes of Convenience: Tackling Convenience Store Crime in Austin, Texas." Public affairs comment. Austin, Texas: Lyndon Johnson School of Public Affairs, The University of Texas at Austin.

Kansas City, Mo., Police Department. 1977. *Response Time Analysis.* Washington, D.C.: U.S. Department of Justice, National Institute of Law Enforcement and Criminal Justice.

Manning, P.K. 1988. "Community Policing as a Drama of Control." *Community Policing: Rhetoric or Reality.* Edited by J.R. Greene and S.D. Mastrofski. New York: Praeger.

National Advisory Commission on Standards and Goals. 1973. *Police.* Washington, D.C.: Government Printing Office.

Neuborne, E. 1994. "Fearful Shoppers Play it Safe." *USA Today* (June 3).

President's Commission on Law Enforcement and Administration of Justice. 1967. *Task Force Report: The Police.* Washington, D.C.: Government Printing Office.

Spelman, W., and D. Brown. 1981. *Calling the Police: Citizen Reporting of Serious Crime.* Washington, D.C.: Police Executive Research Forum.

Spelman, W., and J.E. Eck. 1989. "Sitting Ducks, Ravenous Wolves and Helping Hands: New Approaches to Urban Policing." Public affairs comment. Austin, Texas: Lyndon Johnson School of Public Affairs, The University of Texas at Austin.

Taft, P.B., Jr. 1986. *Fighting Fear: The Baltimore County C.O.P.E. Program.* Washington, D.C.: Police Executive Research Forum.

Trojanowicz, R.C.   1994.   *Community Policing: A Survey of Police Departments in the United States.* Washington, D.C.:   Federal Bureau of Investigation.

Trojanowicz, R.C., and B. Bucqueroux.   1989.   *Community Policing: A Contemporary Perspective.* Cincinnati: Anderson.

Wilson, J.Q.   1993.   "The Problem of Defining Agency Success." *Performance Measures for the Criminal Justice System.* Bureau of Justice Statistics/Princeton project, Washington, D.C.: Government Printing Office.

Chapter 7

The Effectiveness of Street-Level Drug Enforcement

Robert E. Worden

Introduction

The quality of street-level drug enforcement—police activities that are intended to directly affect retail drug transactions[1]—seems to defy quantification and systematic evaluation, at least inasmuch as it is seldom an element of police management. Quantification in the management of street-level drug enforcement normally reflects the more general concern in policing with *means*—e.g., numbers of arrests made and cases closed, amounts of drugs seized—and an inattention to *ends*, such as the size of the user or addict population, or the amount of nondrug crime perpetrated by (or against) users and sellers. This is in some ways understandable. The impacts of drug enforcement on social conditions are in practice difficult to detect, since a host of other more powerful social and economic forces also affect these outcomes. Furthermore, data on some of these outcomes usually are not readily obtainable. But if the quality of police services, including street-level drug enforcement, inheres in their impacts on social conditions, then information about these outcomes is essential to the assessment and management of quality.

The difficulties in quantifying quality notwithstanding, I believe that the quality of street-level drug enforcement could be improved if those who practice it and those who manage it were to give more attention to the ends, and accordingly, consider adjustments in means. The quantification of the ends and means will not suffice by itself to improve street-level drug enforcement, because the numbers cannot speak for themselves and, even if they could, they tell only part of the story. But quantified measures of police activities and of outcomes, i.e., the conditions that enforcement is intended to impact, can form the partial basis for better-informed managerial choices. In this chapter, I will try to explain why I believe this is true, and how quantifying quality might be accomplished.

I would hasten to add at the outset that the quantification of quality in street-level drug enforcement, or in policing more generally, cannot merely imitate private-sector efforts to better manage quality in the production of a good. Such efforts are, ideally, based on a well-developed understanding of the relationships between production activities and production outcomes. A television manufacturer, for example, can readily assess changes in production processes in terms of production outcomes. The products (or a sample thereof) can be subjected to direct quality checks. The consumers of televisions also can reliably assess the quality of the product, and through the number and dollar value of units they buy, the manufacturer can gauge customer response to changes in production processes and to resulting changes in the products' attributes. In drug enforcement, by contrast, production activities (e.g., investigations) bear uncertain and sometimes tenuous relationships even to the most proximate outcomes (arrests), and still more uncertain and tenuous relationships to less proximate outcomes (e.g., the supply of drugs or the incidence of drug-related crime). Moreover, and only partly as a consequence of the foregoing conditions, police managers cannot estimate the value that society attaches to an outcome—say, a reduction in crime of a given magnitude—in terms of the price that it willingly pays for it; through its taxes, the public buys services, not outcomes. Gauging customer response is especially problematic when, as in drug enforcement, the service is not provided directly to individual consumers (as it is when, say, a patrol officer takes a theft report); the "consumer" of local drug enforcement is not an individual but a community, and moreover, the consumer may be largely or wholly unaware of the provision of the service. Given that little is currently known about the effectiveness of street-level drug enforcement strategies, quantifying the quality of street-level drug enforcement should lay the foundation for a process whereby police can learn about the intermediate and ultimate outcomes of strategic and tactical choices. This process would make it incumbent on police managers, and perhaps the rank-and-file as well, to specify intended outcomes and to measure both the content of enforcement activities and the relevant outcome variables.

Such a process could yield important insights, and it could challenge police managers to contemplate alternative goals and strategies. To illustrate, let us consider "high-level" drug enforcement, which is directed toward (a) apprehending and (b) convicting those at high levels of drug distribution networks, and thereby (c) reducing the supply of drugs, (d) raising the price of drugs and (e) reducing the volume of drug consumption.

Quantifying the quality of high-level enforcement would involve the collection and analysis of information not only on the immediate outcomes of enforcement (a and b), but also on the intermediate (c and d) and ultimate (e) outcomes. The connections among these outcomes are usually taken as an article of faith (even though many police officers will simultaneously stress that enforcement alone cannot solve the drug problem), but as one analysis suggests, and as I discuss below, this faith may be partially misplaced. The complexity of the problem far outstrips the simplicity of such intuitive suppositions, as the apprehension and incapacitation of high-level drug distributors may not have the expected effects on either the supply or the price of drugs.

Street-level drug enforcement can be directed toward these same outcomes, serving as a preliminary step in higher-level enforcement, but street-level enforcement might be directed instead toward other goals. My impression is that police officers hold street-level enforcement in some contempt, as it requires much less of the investigative skill that must be brought to bear in higher-level investigations, and that many police managers regard street-level enforcement as a form of enforcement that they practice only when they lack the resources to practice higher-level enforcement, or when the community demands that the police "do something" about street drug markets. This view is unfortunate, because the other goals to which street-level enforcement might be directed—e.g., reducing the violence and disorder associated with street drug markets, and otherwise improving the civility of neighborhoods in which street drug markets operate—are valuable and perhaps more achievable (see Kleiman and Smith 1990), and the potential of street-level enforcement is unlikely to be fully realized unless it is organized and managed with these goals in mind.

My purpose here is not to specify how drug enforcement units should be organized and operated; answers to questions about these matters are contingent on the nature and scale of local drug problems and on the resources available for drug enforcement, including not only money, but also the number and especially the talent of enforcement personnel. Instead, I outline a general framework in terms of which strategic and tactical questions can be formulated and issues defined, whereupon the expertise of both police management and the rank-and-file can be applied to improve drug enforcement. More specifically, I specify some goals toward which street-level drug enforcement might be directed, and some corresponding outcomes in terms of which street-level drug enforcement might be assessed, and I briefly describe some sources of information that might be used to quantify these outcomes.

My discussion begins, however, with a description of the continuities and changes in street-level drug enforcement over the past two decades or so, in order that one might better understand how the quantification of quality must alter the conventional practices of investigators and managers. The inertial force of these conventional practices is arguably the greatest impediment to quality management, greater even than the technical difficulties of collecting and processing relevant information (see Manning 1992).

Continuity and Change in Street-Level Drug Enforcement

The 1970s[2]

Accounts of drug enforcement practices at the local level in the 1970s indicate that street-level drug enforcement was then predominantly seen as an adjunct to higher-level enforcement. Buying up the chain had to begin somewhere, and it was often at the retail level, as users/sellers were arrested and "flipped" or "turned" to serve as informants. Thus, the rationale for drug enforcement generally—namely, supply reduction and the presumably concomitant increase in price and decrease in use and the user population—was also the rationale for street-level drug enforcement.

There were some compelling reasons to emphasize higher-level enforcement. First, higher-level enforcement was presumed to be more effective. "They [investigators who focus on longer-term investigations] pointed out that one large dealer can supply fifty to a hundred users, and thus one such major arrest is equivalent to fifty street arrests" (Manning 1980: 243). Second, and relatedly, the federal Drug Enforcement Administration (DEA) had established a classification system that distinguished and targeted "major violators," i.e., those at high levels of the drug distribution pyramid (see Moore 1977:202-206; Manning 1980:136-138; Wilson 1978), and because the DEA was arguably the most prestigious agency that specialized in drug enforcement, its strategy was a model for local agencies to emulate. Third, higher-level enforcement presumably allowed for tighter controls on investigators' activities, and hence on corruption and abuses of authority (see Moore 1977:195).

I would add that high-level drug enforcement almost certainly achieved a degree of success, if only by making credible the statutory prohibition of drug distribution; in the absence of such enforcement activities, the supply of illicit substances probably would have been greater, the prices lower, and the consumption higher. But to illustrate the complexity of the strategic problem, one careful analysis suggests that a little high-level enforcement might go a long way, and that investments of enforcement resources in high-level investigations quickly reach a point of sharply diminished returns (Reuter and Kleiman 1986). Distributors are easily and quickly replaced, and the cost of replacing drugs confiscated at high levels is sufficiently low that, at the margin, successful investigations add little to the street prices of drugs. This implies that increases in the scale of high-level enforcement do not necessarily yield corresponding decreases in supply and consumption. Beyond what may be a rather low threshold, further investments of enforcement resources in high-level investigations might be less beneficial than other uses to which the resources could be put.

The day-to-day, operational objective of drug enforcement was to "make cases," that is, to assemble physical and/or testimonial evidence sufficient to establish the legal guilt of people suspected of violating drug laws (Manning 1980; Moore 1977:ch. 3), and especially of "major violators." It was difficult or impossible to anticipate where or to whom leads in a case might take an investigator, and investigators exercised considerable autonomy in selecting targets, in recruiting and working informants, and in determining when and how to close cases. Supervision revolved largely around investigators' use of search warrants and surveillance equipment, and their expenditures of money to either pay informants or buy drugs (the latter of which was often on a post-hoc basis) (Manning 1980:esp. 152-154). Furthermore, investigators' activities were subject to little or no *strategic* planning or evaluation, other than the stated emphasis on major violators; investigation was opportunistic.[3]   The exceptions to this rule included operations—usually of short duration—explicitly targeted at the retail level and directed toward the goal of reducing predatory crime committed by users, and efforts to target drug dealing organizations.

A particularly remarkable feature of drug enforcement in the 1970s is that the rationale and operational objective were often honored in the breach. Indeed, it appears that the commitment to high-level enforcement was more symbolic than it was real, and that the actual investment of enforcement resources in high-level enforcement was a good deal smaller than the major-violator focus would imply.[4]   Some agencies lacked the resources—especially money with which to pay informants and to purchase larger quantities of drugs—to buy up the chain and make cases against higher-level dealers (Williams et al. 1979). In some agencies, perceived pressure for documentable productivity in the form of arrests was incompatible with high-level and necessarily long-term investigations, and as a result, investigations were often truncated at a low level (Manning 1980). But in either case, supply reduction remained the *stated* goal, and investigators continued to work autonomously and opportunistically, subject to little or no strategic direction. Even when the goal was unachievable as a result of resource constraints, its acceptance served to legitimate drug enforcement activities, and it seemed to foreclose a consideration of other goals toward which enforcement might be directed and of other ways in which enforcement might be organized.

This disjuncture between stated goals and actual performance can perhaps be attributed to several factors. First, the police did not receive from policymakers or the public a sufficiently clear mandate to allocate scarce police resources among competing drug enforcement priorities. Second, the police could draw on only limited information about the nature of the problem and about drug markets, and on hardly any knowledge about the relationship of alternative enforcement strategies to the dynamics of drug use and distribution. Consequently, the police constructed a set of working assumptions and rules of thumb that made action possible (Williams et al. 1979).

These working assumptions were not—and for the most part, I suspect, have not been—reevaluated, as strategic planning and systematic evaluation of unit performance were generally discredited in drug enforcement. Manning explains:

> Police officers view paperwork as a kind of "dirty work." The police define their real work as clinical, tactical, face-to-face interaction with people in need of help or control. They see the work as being bounded by and limited to the street, concretely defined in terms of persons and events.... Paper, because it is viewed as negative and "unreal," cannot serve as a meaningful locus of planning. More specifically, long-range planning is systematically eschewed because it involves written ideas, intent, shared conceptions of actions and priorities, and a set of limitations on individual discretion that would be both anticlinical and tactical (1980:220-221).

> Officers deny the legitimacy of formal authority as a basis for evaluating their work, supervisors claim that they are aware of what each officer is doing and why and that they trust them. They subscribe to a personalistic, individualistic and context-bound view of the work and of the evaluation process itself.... They have confidence in sources they personally view as trustworthy and in informal means of gathering information on their colleagues. If a narcotics officer were to adopt fully the formal means of evaluation, he or she would be denying the centrality of trust (1980:224-225).

Furthermore, while one might expect that a prime indicator of the quality of high-level drug enforcement would be the location in the drug distribution network of the dealers in whose apprehension investigations result (and perhaps whether the dealer is convicted and of what charge), this was not generally true at the local level:

> Although general and rather abstract goals can be elicited in interviews, there is no consensus about what the overall aim is

and what relationships there are, if any, between these goals and the indices of success, such as seizures, arrests, charges, search warrants served, drugs bought, etc. (Manning 1980:225).

It appears, then, that the quantification of outcomes was inconsistent with and even undermined the stated goal of drug enforcement.

The 1980s

In 1977, Mark Moore planted a conceptual seed with the publication of his book, *Buy and Bust*. Moore argued that enforcement at the retail level could itself have beneficial effects on drug consumption and related social ills. Retail enforcement, he maintained, could affect the availability of drugs not only or primarily by increasing the monetary price, but also by increasing the other (nonmonetary) costs of acquiring drugs—the time, hassle and inconvenience of locating willing sellers, to which Moore summarily referred as "search time." Increases in search time, he argued, might have effects on consumption, especially by novice users who are not well-integrated into drug distribution networks, and by long-term, hard-core users who are fatigued by the lifestyle.

The ground for this seed became a bit more fertile in the 1980s with the introduction and proliferation of crack, and with it, the violence associated with retail drug trafficking. These developments seem not only to have prompted the commitment of greater resources for drug enforcement, but also to have prompted the commitment of a larger share of those resources to street-level enforcement (see Hayeslip 1989); it also seems to have generated more concern for reducing violence and other drug-related crime, and for improving the orderliness of neighborhoods in which drugs are sold (especially in open-air markets). For example, the New York City Police Department formed tactical narcotics teams (TNTs), whose object is to crack down on retail drug selling, usually through buy-and-bust operations, in selected target areas for delimited periods of time (Kleiman and Smith 1990:98; Sviridoff, Sadd, Curtis, and Grinc 1992). The Detroit Police Department committed most of its Narcotics Division, with over 200 officers, to street-level enforcement (Kleiman and Smith 1990:100-102), the scale of which is documented in quantifiable activity; in 1991, for example, the division conducted 3,859 raids, most of retail drug sales locations (Bynum and Worden 1994). In 1990 and 1991, the division implemented focused crackdowns in selected target areas. The Tampa, Fla., Police Department formed QUAD squads (later dubbed Quick Uniform Attack on Drugs), which adopted conventional and unconventional approaches including, but not limited to, intensive enforcement, to close retail "dope holes" (Kennedy 1993). While these specific forms of street-level enforcement differ somewhat from each other, they all involve intensified street-level enforcement applied to more or less specific locations (e.g., addresses or beats).

Despite this commitment of resources to street-level enforcement, Moore's seed may have yet to sprout, inasmuch as it is not at all clear that the basic practices and management of street-level drug enforcement have changed with the scale on which they are conducted. My impression is that, with some exceptions (such as Tampa's QUAD squads), the operational objective of street-level enforcement is still to make cases, albeit cases at low levels; the working assumptions and rules of thumb that guided drug enforcement in the 1970s are still widely shared today; arrests and drug seizures remain the outcomes of principal interest; and the organization of enforcement activity is not consciously directed toward other, less proximate outcomes. Enforcement is opportunistic, and thus more or less randomly distributed across drug markets and over time; as a result, enforcement poses a fairly low risk for drug dealers. The creation or expansion of units devoted to street-level enforcement has, I suspect, increased the level of enforcement activity without altering the largely nonstrategic nature of police efforts.

Police managers need to think carefully about the goals of such drug enforcement units, and about how the operation and management of those units should be structured to achieve those goals. It may be time to question the working assumptions and rules of thumb, to think carefully about how relevant outcomes can be measured, and to analyze that information to assess results and to thereby test the understanding of the problem and appropriate police action against data. In this way, police might learn more about the effects of alternative strategies and alternative operational structures.

Outcomes and Strategy

Outcomes

Drug enforcement programs in New York City (Sviridoff et al. 1992), Detroit (Bynum and Worden 1994), and elsewhere (Uchida, Forst and Annan 1992) have each been evaluated in terms of one or more of the following outcomes: (a) the level and form of street drug market activity; (b) drug-related crime (e.g., robbery, burglary, larceny, auto theft); and (c) residents' perceptions of the amount and visibility of street drug trafficking, their perceptions of other potentially drug-related problems in the neighborhood (disorder, prostitution, traffic), their fear of crime, and their assessments of quality of life. These evaluations illustrate the outcomes that might be measured and how they might be quantified. I first discuss how these conditions may be affected by street-level drug enforcement.

Insofar as intensified street-level enforcement increases the risk of arrest (and of other enforcement-related risks, such as the seizure of drugs) perceived by drug sellers, one might expect that it would prompt sellers to alter their practices to reduce their exposure and vulnerability (Kleiman 1988). This expectation has been confirmed. In both New York City (Sviridoff et al. 1992) and Detroit (Bynum and Worden 1994), sellers adapted to intensified enforcement: They became more circumspect about when and to whom they sold drugs. They were less likely to sell to people they did not know. They held smaller quantities of drugs at a time, and consequently, they were more likely at any given time to have run out. They altered the locations from which they sold from day to day. They complicated the transactions by involving more people on the sales end.

Such responses by dealers to the stimulus of intensified street-level enforcement might be taken to imply that street-level enforcement is futile— that for each move by police, dealers counter in a way that permits them to continue dealing—but these adaptations could represent social benefits, because the form and perhaps the scale of dealing change. Many such adaptations reduce the visibility of a drug market to residents. Furthermore, to the extent that such adaptations increase users' search time (increases that might be especially pronounced for users who do not have a regular source), the volume of sales and of consumption might be reduced. Some users would make fewer purchases; some would search for other "copping" areas; and others might desist altogether—novices giving up their experimentation, and hard-core users seeking treatment. In these respects, a drug market would shrink in size. Such results of intensified enforcement have been documented in New York City (Zimmer 1990) and in Lynn, Mass. (Kleiman 1988).

We might expect that these intermediate outcomes would, in turn, produce still other outcomes. In users and sellers, a street drug market attracts "motivated offenders" and "suitable targets" to the same area (Cohen and Felson 1979; Rengert and Wasilchick 1990), and if a shrunken drug market attracts fewer such people, one could expect to find less nondrug crime there. Insofar as users' consumption declines (even short of desistance), one might further expect to observe associated decreases in nondrug crime, based on the research that shows that users' consumption and rates of offending rise and fall together (e.g., Anglin and Speckart 1988; Nurco, Hanlon, Kinlock, and Duszynski 1988). These expectations have received mixed support from the results of evaluative research, as decreases in nondrug crime have been reported in some jurisdictions (Kleiman 1988, on Lynn; Zimmer 1990) but not in others (Bynum and Worden 1994; Kleiman 1988, on Lawrence; Sviridoff et al. 1992).

The shrinkage of a street drug market, and any associated decrease in nondrug crime, could also be expected to improve residents' quality of life. As a street drug market shrinks, the disorder and other "incivilities" associated with the market also diminish, and with these changes one would expect that residents would become less fearful of crime, more likely to use and enjoy neighborhood amenities, and more satisfied with their neighborhood as a place to live. Although drug enforcement units should not bear the onus of single-handedly restoring (or establishing) a high quality of life in urban neighborhoods (any more than they should bear the burden of single-handedly controlling drug abuse), it is reasonable to expect that drug enforcement can contribute to—and should strive for—improving residents' quality of life.

Strategy

One promising line of analysis suggests that street-level drug enforcement could achieve its greatest effects if it followed a "crackdown-backoff" strategy (Sherman 1990; also see Kleiman 1988; Kleiman and Smith 1990). Such a strategy would entail a series of geographically focused crackdowns, i.e., abrupt and dramatic increases in enforcement activity, each of brief duration and followed by a period of reduced enforcement activity—the backoff. Such a strategy capitalizes on the uncertainty that it creates in offenders' minds about the risk of arrest; if drug users and sellers adapt to the pressure of a crackdown, and if they remain, for at least some time, unaware of the backoff, then the targeted area reaps the benefits of enforcement pressure even after the police have begun a crackdown in another area.

The effectiveness and practicality of this strategy hinge largely on the intensity of the crackdown relative to the scale of the drug market, and on the timing of crackdowns and backoffs. The crackdowns must be of sufficient intensity and duration to affect sellers' and/or users' perceptions of the risks of apprehension. Furthermore, the period of the backoff should be not much longer than it takes for sellers and/or users to recognize and adjust to the reduced risks, whereupon another crackdown would commence. Moreover, the timing of the crackdowns and backoffs must be unpredictable. If sellers and users can anticipate the duration of crackdowns and the resumption of crackdowns after backoffs, the effectiveness of street-level enforcement is almost certain to be confined to the crackdown periods; this, it appears, was one of the shortcomings of TNT operations in New York City (Sviridoff et al. 1992).

I do not mean to imply that a crackdown-backoff strategy is the only strategy of street-level drug enforcement that is compatible with the goals identified above, or with efforts to quantify quality. It is one strategy that appears potentially effective with respect to the outcomes that I have discussed, and it illustrates how a consideration of outcomes can guide the development of a strategy. A crackdown-backoff strategy of street-level drug enforcement is directed not at accumulating arrests, but rather at affecting the practices of retail drug dealers, with the expectation that this impact would have effects on less proximate outcomes.

Be that as it may, this analysis leaves unresolved a number of issues on which quantified experience with such a strategy could be brought to bear. First, this analysis holds that the intensity of the crackdowns must be roughly commensurate with the scale of the markets to which they are applied, but trial and error will probably be necessary to determine the level of enforcement pressure needed to affect sellers' and/or users' perceptions of risk.[5] The analysis also holds that the crackdowns may be "brief," but it does not specify the practical meaning of "brief"—a few days, a couple of weeks or a few months? The crackdowns must be of sufficient duration to make a lasting impression on offenders' perceptions of risk. Again, trial and error will probably be necessary to ascertain the optimal duration under particular circumstances.   Finally, this analysis does not specify the geographic scope of crackdown target areas—a few blocks, a police beat or a precinct? If a drug enforcement unit were to implement a crackdown-backoff strategy, the quantification and analysis of both means and ends would be necessary to refine the strategy in the context of local conditions.

Data Sources and Indicators

It is one thing to say that the outcomes of street-level drug enforcement should be measured quantitatively, and another to specify how the outcomes can be quantified. Police managers are aware of the inaccuracies and omissions in departmental records, and the collection of data other than those that police agencies routinely compile calls for the expenditure of resources on what might appear to be luxury items (e.g., a survey of residents). But some of the data in police records are, as I shall explain, useful for *strategic* planning and evaluation, and more probably could be done to supplement readily available data for these purposes.

Police Records

Police tend to be rather skeptical of the accuracy of the records that they keep. Records that are based partly or entirely on information provided by citizens of unknown veracity are, of course, suspect. But so, too, are internally generated records. The contents of some records are shaped to serve or meet administrative needs or expectations; reports may be written to justify actions taken (and actions not taken), and forms on which officers record numerical activity totals are sometimes called "cheat sheets." In some instances, record-keeping serves no known or apparent purpose, which hardly inspires officers to be meticulous, and the maintenance of some records reflects officers' distaste for paperwork: records may not be filed, or records may be incomplete.

Nevertheless, police records are potentially a valuable source of quantified (or quantifiable) information on the means and ends of street-level drug enforcement. No measure of any phenomenon is completely accurate; in both the physical sciences and the behavioral sciences, every measure contains some error. Provided that the error is not too great and that adequate allowances are made for measurement biases in reaching conclusions, then the analyses of those measures can be informative.

Furthermore, the accuracy of the information in police records is probably affected by the purposes to which it is to be put. One can expect some distortion if the records are used to evaluate and assess the performance of individual investigators or squads. But if the records are intended only for internal consumption (rather than for public dissemination) and used to assess and, as necessary, redirect the performance of the unit as a whole, then one might expect less (but still some) distortion. If, moreover, the personnel responsible for creating the records understand their utility, then one might expect fewer omissions. In other words, if the analysis of police records has some recognizable utility for police and, at the same time, poses little or no threat to individuals, then the information the police collect and maintain may be enhanced.

Enforcement activity. Quantifying enforcement activity is useful less because these phenomena are intrinsically valuable than because any effort to adjust, modify or redirect enforcement strategies must rest on information about the nature, amount and location of actual enforcement activity. One cannot presume that an enforcement strategy is implemented precisely according to its design, and police managers must first ascertain the shape of actual enforcement patterns if they are to then formulate strategic alterations or refinements. Fortunately, many of these phenomena can be quantified in terms of police records that all or most agencies already keep on arrests, search warrants executed, drug seizures, and so on.

Such phenomena can be and, for many purposes, should be enumerated in a fashion that allows police managers to see some of the contours of enforcement. One can, for example, distinguish among felony, misdemeanor, and other arrests and citations, and among types of drugs. One can also break the totals down by precinct, neighborhood or other appropriate geographic units. (For example, the Jersey City, N.J., Police Department demarcated 107 street drug markets in Jersey City, on the basis of arrest data, citizen tips and a citizen survey [Weisburd and Green 1994]). Such spatial disaggregation is particularly important if the enforcement strategy is geographically focused. The measurement of enforcement activity and of other outcomes should coincide as closely as possible with the targeted areas' boundaries (see Worden, Bynum and Frank 1994).

However, not all of the activity in which drug enforcement units engage is captured in data on arrests and drug seizures, especially when the unit sometimes adopts more unconventional practices. Tampa's QUAD squads, for example, rely partly on traditional enforcement practices and partly on other tactics in closing "dope holes." As Kennedy (1993:7) describes it, "the QUAD team's job was to do anything it legally could to make dealers' and buyers' lives miserable.... The QUAD teams thought that the resulting displacement might even work in their favor, since dealers might not feel as safe or work as readily in new locations...." In addition to conventional enforcement tactics against dealers and reverse stings against buyers, the squads had "the city trim trees and shrubs that provided shade from the hot Florida sun," and they used civil abatement and code enforcement procedures to "close businesses...that were fronts for or catered to drug dealing" (Kennedy 1993:10). Any quantitative picture of enforcement should include these less traditional activities.

Market adaptations. Information on any illicit market is hard to come by, for obvious reasons, and it might seem hopelessly naive to suppose that the police would have and keep information on the basis of which one could quantify market adaptations to enforcement pressure. But police undercover operations put them in close touch with market dynamics; undercover purchases of illicit drugs, for example, provide information on the retail (and wholesale) prices of drugs, and this information is routinely kept to reconcile police accounts. However, since street-level drug enforcement may affect price, if at all, less than it affects availability, information other than that on prices should be systematically collected and analyzed.

One form of information that could be and sometimes is recorded (and rarely, I suspect, analyzed) concerns unsuccessful attempts by undercover officers (and informants) to buy drugs. If, as both our expectations and the results of evaluative research indicate, drug dealers respond to enforcement pressure by adopting more conservative practices, and users consequently encounter more difficulty in buying drugs, then one would expect that undercover officers and informants would also encounter more difficulty in buying drugs. Officers in Detroit reported precisely this experience in the wake of the crackdowns there: suspected dealers, approached by informants or undercover officers, were more likely to deny that they sell drugs, to refuse to sell to a stranger, or to report that they were temporarily out of the product (Bynum and Worden 1994). If police recorded these experiences with a modicum of detail, then they would form the basis for a quantified measure of market practices and adaptations therein. One needs only information on the date and the specific location (e.g., address or intersection) at which the attempted buy was made, and the apparent reason that it was unsuccessful (e.g., refusal to sell to unknown buyer, no drugs on hand, etc.). Even investigators with the stereotypic police aversion to paperwork might be induced to record such information.[6]

Police also have other contact with drug markets, as they interrogate arrestees and others who they suspect are involved in selling, buying and/or using drugs. The information gleaned from these interrogations is normally oriented toward and used for making cases, against either the subject of the interrogation or others (e.g., a source). But these interrogations could also be used to collect information on the market conditions and practices in which street-level enforcement might prompt changes, provided that interrogators ask the right questions and record and store the information in a form that lends itself to later analysis.

Visibility of street drug markets. Other police records, particularly records of the events about which citizens call, are a source of information about the frequency and visibility of retail drug sales, market-related problems (e.g., loitering, prostitution) and drug-related crime. Citizen complaints about retail drug dealing that are phoned in to 911, to a dedicated drug "tipline" or "hotline," and perhaps to other police numbers are a source of quantifiable information on drug activity, and especially on the kind of retail activity that most concerns citizens and on which the police may be best able to have an impact. Police are usually quite skeptical about the accuracy of citizens' reports of drug trafficking; some complaints are based on ignorance or misconceptions and are unfounded, and others are based on motives other than civic duty and may be quite misleading. Individually, many complaints may be indicative of nothing criminal, and investigations that follow up on these complaints may often prove fruitless. But *in the aggregate*, such complaints may be a useful indicator of the volume of retail activity in a street drug market, because the "noise" that unfounded complaints represent might well be a more or less constant proportion of the total;[7] thus, differences across neighborhoods and changes over time could with some caution be construed as differences or changes in the amount and/or visibility of retail drug trafficking.[8]

Drug-related problems. Calls for service are also a source of information about drug-related problems: reports of gunshots, disturbances, suspicious people, and the like. Even if some individual calls are unfounded (or misclassified by police call-takers), in the aggregate such calls could be taken as roughly indicative of the incidence and visibility of neighborhood problems. Even though it is probably not feasible to discriminate individual calls that are directly or indirectly drug-related from those that are not, neither is it necessary; but it is desirable and probably feasible to identify *categories* of calls of which one could reasonably suppose a significant proportion stem from street drug markets.

Drug-related crime. When police analyze outcomes of enforcement other than the immediate outcomes of arrests and drug seizures, they typically examine reported crimes. Such analyses usually focus on index crimes, or on violent crimes, and usually for an area (a precinct or the entire jurisdiction) that is much larger than the area in which drug dealing and enforcement are (or were) concentrated. As in the analysis of calls for service, analysis of crime levels should focus on categories of crime that bear the most substantial relationships to drug sales and use, and it should measure crime in the most appropriate geographic units (e.g., targeted neighborhoods).

It may be necessary to take unprecedented steps to make these data accessible for the purpose of strategically planning and evaluating street-level drug enforcement, but several police departments recently proved that it could be done. Under the Drug Market Analysis Program (D-MAP) sponsored by the National Institute of Justice, five police departments developed information systems that integrate relevant police (and other agencies') databases, to which computer mapping technology and other analytic techniques can be applied (Hebert 1993). It remains to be seen how, if at all, drug enforcement practices have changed or will change in these departments, but much of the needed infrastructure for measuring outcomes is in place.

Resident Surveys

Resident surveys are a complementary source of data on some outcomes, and the only source of systematic data on others. Survey data complement police data on the visibility of street drug markets to residents, and on the existence and severity of drug-related problems; survey data on these outcomes are arguably superior to police data, since they tap the perceptions of residents who do not call the police as well as the perceptions of residents who do. Survey data are uniquely well-suited for measuring residents' fear of crime and their subjective quality of life. Since general information on the application of surveys in policing (including instrument construction, sampling procedures and the like) is available elsewhere (Bureau of Justice Assistance 1993), I dwell on the particulars of using survey data to measure the outcomes of street-level drug enforcement: what should be asked, and of whom.

Visibility of street drug markets. Several survey items can be and have been used to measure the visibility of street drug markets to residents (see, e.g., Uchida et al. 1992; Bynum and Worden 1994). Survey respondents can, for example, be asked how easy they think it is for people who want to buy drugs to do so on their block (or the area immediately around their block, or in their neighborhood), with response categories of "very easy," "fairly easy" or "not very easy." Respondents can be asked whether they think that street drug selling is a "big problem" in their neighborhood, "some problem" or "no problem at all." Respondents can be asked whether they know of a place on their block from which drugs have been sold (in, say, the preceding six months) or are being sold. The use of multiple items like these, of a similar but not identical nature, allows one to combine the items to form a composite measure that better calibrates residents' perceptions than does any one item by itself.

Drug-related problems. A battery of items could also be used to measure residents' perceptions of neighborhood problems. With respect to each of a list of conditions, respondents can be asked whether the condition is a "big problem," "some problem" or "no problem at all." The conditions about which the survey might inquire include, for example, (1) people drinking on the street or in other public places, (2) groups of people hanging around on the street or in parks or vacant lots, (3) prostitution, and (4) vacant or abandoned houses in the neighborhood. One analysis of survey data of this kind found that responses tend to reflect perceptions of either social disorder (including numbers 1 and 2, above) or physical disorder (including number 4) (Skogan 1990:190-191; also see Sviridoff et al. 1992; Bynum and Worden 1994). Some conditions about which a survey might ask bear, on their face, a stronger or more direct relationship to the existence and size of street drug markets, but many of these conditions (Skogan analyzed 14 such items) bear at least an indirect relationship. Once again, items that are related to one another, such as items concerning social disorder, can be combined to form a composite measure.

Fear of crime. Surveys are uniquely useful in quantifying residents' fear of crime. Such measures have been constructed to evaluate not only street-level drug enforcement, but also preventive patrol (Kelling, Pate, Dieckman, and Brown 1974) and, more recently, community policing (e.g., Cordner 1986; Pate 1989; Pate, Wycoff, Skogan, and Sherman 1986; Police Foundation 1981). Fear of crime may be measured by asking respondents how worried they are that (for example) someone will try to break into your home while no one is there (very worried, somewhat worried or not worried?); that someone will try to rob you or steal something from you while you are out in the neighborhood; or that people involved with drugs around your home will harass or bother you on the street. Fear of crime can also be measured by asking respondents the following: (a) How safe would you feel being alone outside around this neighborhood at night (very safe, somewhat safe, somewhat unsafe, or very unsafe)? (b) How safe do you think young children are when they go out by themselves at night in this neighborhood? (c) Is there any particular place in this neighborhood where you would be afraid to go alone either during the day or after dark? and (d) How often does worry about crime prevent you from doing things you would like to do in your neighborhood?

Quality of life. Residents' subjective quality of life has also been measured for many previous evaluations of police strategies and programs. Respondents have been asked, for example, (a) On the whole, how do you feel about this neighborhood as a place to live? Would you say you are very satisfied, somewhat satisfied, somewhat dissatisfied, or very dissatisfied? (b) In some neighborhoods, people do things together and help each other. In other neighborhoods, people mostly go their own way. I'd like to know which kind of neighborhood you think this is. In general, is it mostly one where people help each other, or one where people go their own way? (c) Do you really feel like this is a neighborhood, or do you think of it more as just a place to live? and (d) How familiar are you with the neighbors on your block? Do you know no one, know some by sight or name, know most by sight or name, or know everyone by sight or name?

Survey population. The last issue concerns the population to be surveyed. Police can survey the general public, i.e., the entire service population, or specific subpopulations such as those who have contact with the police (see, e.g., Couper and Lobitz 1991). To quantify the outcomes of street-level drug enforcement, it is probably unnecessary (in most jurisdictions) to survey the entire service population; a more efficient use of survey resources would entail surveying those who reside (and/or work) in the immediate vicinity of street drug markets, where the problems and, presumably, enforcement are concentrated, and where impacts are most likely to be felt and detected. Within these areas, the population as a whole—and not subpopulations thereof—should be sampled for the survey, because respondents should be as representative as possible.[9]

Analysis

Analyses of police and/or survey data should be as rigorous as possible, but it would be ill-advised, in my view, to hold analyses for management purposes to the standards applied to social science. There is, to be sure, some danger in relaxing these standards, which are intended to guard against reaching erroneous and potentially misleading conclusions. But if police managers must choose to rely either on analyses that can withstand scientific scrutiny or on no analysis at all, they will ineluctably choose the latter in most instances, because the former is seldom feasible. Police departments can conduct useful analysis themselves, even if it does not conform to models of scientific experimentation.[10] It is a source of information on which strategic decisions can be based, in part; the purpose of such analysis is not merely or at all to demonstrate success or failure, but rather, to inform adjustments in enforcement strategy and tactics to enhance effectiveness. Analysis might also serve a heuristic purpose, stimulating thought about the forms that street-level drug enforcement might take and the outcomes toward which it might be (re)directed.

Most such analysis will probably take the form of before-and-after comparisons of outcomes in the areas to which strategic interventions are applied. The principal danger in drawing inferences about enforcement impacts from such comparisons is that short- and long-term changes might not be attributable to enforcement. A change, e.g., a decrease in calls to a drug hotline, could be part of a longer trend for which the police are not responsible. It could be a manifestation of the instability and randomness of events that produces short-term increases and decreases around an average or typical level. It could be a result of some other factor—changes in the physical, social or economic environment that effect changes in drug use and related phenomena. Police managers should be careful not to leap to the conclusion that any beneficial changes are due to enforcement activities; they should consider the plausibility of alternative explanations before concluding that enforcement impacts are the most plausible explanation for observed changes.

Conclusion

Street-level drug enforcement is a form of enforcement that could play a uniquely valuable role in addressing the drug problem, which by many accounts includes not only drug abuse by individuals, but also the community problems that stem from the illicit drug trade. It may be, as some argue, that prevention is the key to drug abuse control, but until that key is turned, countless neighborhoods will suffer the spillover effects of street drug markets. Street-level drug enforcement might better serve to contain and reduce these effects if it were strategically directed toward these outcomes. Quantifying the quality of street-level drug enforcement could, I believe, facilitate the formulation and refinement of effective strategies.

Notes

[1]This definition of street-level drug enforcement thus excludes preventive education efforts by the police (such as the DARE program), and it also excludes general efforts to mobilize community residents and other resources against neighborhood problems. I exclude these activities, even

though they may play important roles in drug control, because their quality is better measured in terms of other outcome variables in addition to or instead of those discussed here.

[2]Much of this section is based on studies by Moore (1977), Williams, Redlinger and Manning (1979), and Manning (1980), which are certainly the principal empirical studies of drug enforcement at the local level in the 1970s. I caution the reader that these and other studies, of which there are few, form a basis for only very tentative generalizations about drug enforcement.

[3]This is not to say that investigators did no *tactical* planning (e.g., on search warrant raids and the like), although by some accounts even the tactical planning was rather loose (Manning 1980).

[4]As Manning (1980:125, 132-136) points out, the category of major violators was sufficiently ambiguous that it allowed for several different operational definitions, and this ambiguity itself compromised the stated goal.

[5]The intensity of the initial crackdown in an area might need to be greater than the intensity of subsequent crackdowns in the same area; this, too, would be the subject of trial and error.

[6]I have perused activity reports from which such information could be easily retrieved (and which, I am convinced, were not mere fiction), as well as activity reports—prepared by different squads in the same unit—that contained no usable information of this kind. That some reports contained such information even though it was not, to my knowledge, put to any purpose, suggests that with some incentive to do so, investigators would willingly keep such records.

[7]One could examine, say, monthly totals of such calls, or monthly totals of the locations about which calls are received. The latter may differ from the former by a substantial margin, as numerous calls may be received about a specific location, especially if nearby residents adopt an organized response to the operation of street drug markets that includes calling the police.

[8]Changes over time would have other interpretations as well; see Cook and Campbell (1979), and below.

[9]It would be a mistake, for example, to collect survey responses only from citizens who participate in neighborhood watch or other community

groups, because citizens who participate in such organizations are not representative of their neighborhoods (see, e.g., Skogan 1990).

[10]Some police departments have also formed short-term or even long-term collaborative relationships with university-based social scientists. Such relationships can be beneficial to both parties, particularly if they are sustained long enough for each of the parties to appreciate the other's needs.

References

Anglin, M.D., and G. Speckart.   1988.   "Narcotics Use and Crime: A Multisample, Multimethod Analysis." *Criminology* 26:197-233.

Bureau of Justice Assistance. 1993. *A Police Guide to Surveying Citizens and Their Environment.* Washington, D.C.: Author.

Bynum, T.S., and R.E. Worden. 1994. *The Impacts of Police Drug Crackdowns.* Unpublished report to the National Institute of Justice. East Lansing, Mich.: Michigan State University.

Cohen, L.E., and M. Felson. 1979. "Social Change and Crime Rate Trends: A Routine Activity Approach." *American Sociological Review* 44:588-608.

Cook, T.D., and D.T. Campbell. 1979. *Quasi-Experimentation: Design and Analysis Issues for Field Settings.* Chicago: Rand McNally.

Cordner, G.W. 1986. "Fear of Crime and the Police: An Evaluation of a Fear-Reduction Strategy." *Journal of Police Science and Administration* 14:223-233.

Couper, D.C., and S.H. Lobitz. 1991. *Quality Policing: The Madison Experience.* Washington, D.C.: Police Executive Research Forum.

Hayeslip, D.W., Jr. 1989. "Local-Level Drug Enforcement: New Strategies." *NIJ Reports* 213:2-6.

Hebert, E.E.   1993.   "NIJ's Drug Market Analysis Program." *National Institute of Justice Journal* 226 (April):2-7.

Kelling, G.L., T. Pate, D. Dieckman, and C.E. Brown. 1974. *The Kansas City Preventive Patrol Experiment: Technical Report.* Washington, D.C.: Police Foundation.

Kennedy, D.M.   1993.   *Closing the Market: Controlling the Drug Trade in Tampa, Florida.*   Program Focus.   Washington, D.C.:   National Institute of Justice.

Kleiman, M.A.R.   1988.   "Crackdowns: The Effects of Intensive Enforcement on Retail Heroin Dealing."   *Street-Level Drug Enforcement: Examining the Issues.*   Edited by Marcia R. Chaiken.   Washington, D.C.:   National Institute of Justice.

Kleiman, M.A.R., and K.D. Smith.   1990.   "State and Local Drug Enforcement: In Search of a Strategy."   *Drugs and Crime.*   Vol. 13 of *Crime and Justice: A Review of Research.*   Edited by Michael Tonry and James Q. Wilson.   Chicago: University of Chicago Press.

Manning, P.K.   1980.   *The Narcs' Game: Organizational and Informational Limits on Drug Law Enforcement.*   Cambridge, Mass.:   MIT Press.

_____.   1992.   "Information Technologies and the Police."   *Modern Policing.*   Vol. 15 of *Crime and Justice: A Review of Research.*   Edited by Michael Tonry and James Q. Wilson.   Chicago: University of Chicago Press.

Moore, M.H.   1977.   *Buy and Bust: The Effective Regulation of an Illicit Heroin Market.*   Lexington, Mass.:   D.C. Heath.

Nurco, D.N., T.E. Hanlon, T.W. Kinlock, and K.R. Duszynski.   1988.   "Differential Criminal Patterns of Narcotic Addicts Over an Addiction Career."   *Criminology* 26:407-423.

Pate, A.M.   1989.   "Community-Oriented Policing in Baltimore."   *Police & Policing: Contemporary Issues.*   Edited by Dennis Jay Kenney.   New York: Praeger.

Pate, A.M. , M.A. Wycoff, W.G. Skogan, and L.W. Sherman.   1986.   *Reducing Fear of Crime in Houston and Newark: A Summary Report.*   Washington, D.C.:   Police Foundation.

Police Foundation.   1981.   *The Newark Foot Patrol Experiment.*   Washington, D.C.:   Author.

Rengert, G., and J. Wasilchick.   1990.   *Space, Time and Crime: Ethnographic Insights into Residential Burglary.*   Unpublished report to the National Institute of Justice.   Philadelphia: Temple University.

Reuter, P., and M.A.R. Kleiman. 1986. "Risks and Prices." *Crime and Justice: A Review of Research.* Vol. 7. Edited by Michael Tonry and Norval Morris. Chicago: University of Chicago Press.

Sherman, L.W. 1990. "Police Crackdowns: Initial and Residual Deterrence." *Crime and Justice: A Review of Research.* Vol. 12. Edited by Michael Tonry and Norval Morris. Chicago: University of Chicago Press.

Skogan, W.G. 1990. *Disorder and Decline: Crime and the Spiral of Decay in American Neighborhoods.* Berkeley, Calif.: University of California Press.

Sviridoff, M., S. Sadd, R. Curtis, and R. Grinc. 1992. *Neighborhood Effects of Street-Level Drug Enforcement: An Evaluation of TNT.* New York: Vera Institute of Justice.

Uchida, C.D., B. Forst, and S.O. Annan. 1992. *Modern Policing and the Control of Illegal Drugs: Testing New Strategies in Two American Cities.* Washington, D.C.: National Institute of Justice.

Weisburd, D., and L. Green. 1994. "Defining the Street-Level Drug Market." *Drugs and Crime: Evaluating Public Policy Initiatives.* Edited by Doris Layton MacKenzie and Craig D. Uchida. Thousand Oaks, Calif.: Sage.

Williams, J.R., L.J. Redlinger, and P.K. Manning. 1979. *Police Narcotics Control: Patterns and Strategies.* Washington, D.C.: U.S. Government Printing Office.

Wilson, J.Q. 1978. *The Investigators.* New York: Basic.

Worden, R.E., T.S. Bynum, and J. Frank. 1994. "Police Crackdowns on Drug Abuse and Trafficking." *Drugs and Crime: Evaluating Public Policy Initiatives.* Edited by Doris Layton MacKenzie and Craig D. Uchida. Thousand Oaks, Calif.: Sage.

Zimmer, L. 1990. "Proactive Policing Against Street-Level Drug Trafficking." *American Journal of Police* 9:43-74.

Chapter 8

Assessing Alternative Responses to Calls for Service

Dorothy H. Bracey

Introduction

The traditional response to a call for police service has been the immediate dispatch of a sworn officer. In the mid-1970s, a number of police departments began to question whether that expensive reaction was always necessary. The 1977 Kansas City Response Time Study indicated that, in many instances, the rapidity of the response had no effect on the outcome of the incident prompting the call. At the same time, a spate of municipal fiscal emergencies forced police administrators to consider budgetary matters with a new urgency. As a result, the 1970s and early 1980s saw a series of attempts to respond to citizen calls in innovative and more cost-effective ways. These alternatives became known collectively as *differential police response* (DPR) and included delaying patrol officers' response, having civilians rather than sworn officers respond, directly referring calls to specialized police units, taking reports by telephone, asking callers to go to a police station, sending report forms to be returned by mail, and referring calls to other agencies.

Effect on Arrest and Detection

In spite of the results from Kansas City, there was still fear that responding to calls for service in nontraditional ways might lower arrest and detection rates. Several pieces of research addressed that concern. William

Spelman and Dale Brown (1981) examined over 3,300 serious crimes in Jacksonville, Fla.; Peoria, Ill.; Rochester, N.Y.; and San Diego. They found that only 25 percent of these crimes were reported while they were being committed, that these were the only cases in which rapid response might make a difference, and that an arrest could be attributed to the speedy arrival of the police for only 2.9 percent of reported serious crimes. A 1980 reexamination of the Kansas City data (Caron) indicated that rapid response led to an arrest in under 3 percent of the cases sampled; a later study (Eck and Spelman 1987) showed that there was a chance of an immediate arrest for only 5 percent of the calls studied. Sumrall et al. (1981), in a survey of 175 police agencies, found that rapid response had no effect on gathering evidence. This conclusion was strengthened by a 1983 study showing that in the absence of eyewitnesses or other leads, many departments did not assign investigators to a case; this indicated that the crime report could just as effectively be taken over the phone (Eck).

In fact, analysis of the data from several of these studies suggested that uniform rapid response could actually reduce police effectiveness, since dispatchers might send cars from adjoining districts or interrupt officers who were performing other duties. The implication of the sum of all this research was that if it were possible to identify that small number of calls that would benefit from a uniformed officer's rapid response, the others could receive alternative responses with no diminution in effectiveness.

Citizen Reaction

How did citizens respond to these untraditional responses? Are efficiency and savings worthwhile if they produce a population convinced that the police perceive their problems to be a low priority? Actually, a number of studies have come to the same conclusion—citizen satisfaction is more closely related to expectations and honesty than to rapid response.

The first of these studies involved four surveys from the Kansas City Preventive Patrol Experiment (Pate et al. 1976). In the surveys, citizen satisfaction with response time ranged from 54 to 71 percent. The most striking finding, however, was that satisfaction was directly related to the difference between expected and observed response time. If the dispatcher told the caller that the police would arrive at a certain time, and the police did indeed arrive at that time, the caller was satisfied. If the dispatcher led the caller to believe that the police would arrive earlier than they actually did, the caller was dissatisfied.

This observation was strengthened by Percy's 1980 study of Rochester, N.Y.; Tampa, Fla.; and St. Louis. A survey of 12,000 people who had had recent contact with the police indicated that 62 percent were satisfied with the police's actions. The *best* predictor of citizen satisfaction, however, was the closeness of expected and reported response times. Both Percy and Pate suggested that a promise of rapid response might actually produce dissatisfaction if the patrol car were to arrive later than the caller expected; an accurate prediction, even one that indicated a delayed response, would actually *increase* citizen satisfaction with the police. The evaluation of the Wilmington, Del., Split Force Experiment (Tien 1977) also noted that citizen satisfaction was more a function of expectation than of any other single factor.

Early Experimentation

In fact, it was satisfaction with the split-force concept—in which the patrol force was split into a basic patrol section that responded to calls for service, and a structured patrol section that carried out preventive patrol— that motivated the Wilmington Police Department to continue experimenting with ways to increase efficiency and effectiveness. Since this early program addressed so many of the issues fundamental to any discussion of alternative responses to calls for service, it is worth describing it in some detail.

Wilmington adopted a management of demand (MOD) or demand-side management approach; this is a strategy pioneered by utility companies that consists of making supply match demand by reducing demand, mainly through greater efficiency (Wald 1994:C6). In law enforcement, MOD is based on the premise that the pattern of demand for police services can be managed or changed so that the police can better supply that demand. In doing so, the Wilmington Police Department tackled the widely held belief "that the public demand for police services, particularly for 911 rapid-response services, is largely out of police control" (Kennedy). In brief, Wilmington decided to upgrade the existing complaint-taking function to one of complaint-screening, "so that calls for service could be prioritized and, if applicable, designated for an alternative response" (Cahn and Tien 1981:vi).

Screeners had five options: they could dispatch a patrol unit, formally advise the caller of a 30-minute delay in police response, adjust the complaint on the phone, ask the complainant to come to police headquarters to make the complaint, or refer the complaint to a call-back officer. The call-back officer would contact the complainant and, based on further information obtained during this call, exercise one of five additional options: ask communications to send a basic patrol unit, adjust the complaint over the phone, take a report over the phone, ask the complainant to make the complaint at police headquarters, or schedule a meeting with a specialist unit.

During the experimental period, 18.9 percent of calls for service were diverted away from the basic patrol force (p. viii). Phone adjustment accounted for 3.5 percent, walk-in for 1.6 percent, phone report for 11.2

percent, and appointment with a specialist unit for 2.6 percent. In addition, formal delay of response accounted for 3.6 percent. The evaluators of the project felt that, given the positive responses of the Wilmington citizens, the percentage of calls diverted or officially delayed could have been doubled.

Since it was the desire for increased effectiveness *and* efficiency that inspired the MOD program, the program could only be considered successful if it saved resources. For this reason, the basic patrol unit was reduced in size in proportion to the number of calls diverted; this amounted to approximately 20 percent. Efficiency, measured by calls for service, per effective eight-hour officer increased by 15.8 percent.

Wilmington citizens appeared at least as satisfied with police services after the introduction of MOD as they were before; in fact, "a slightly higher percentage felt that their recent police contact during the MOD program had raised their opinion of the WPD...and that the quality of police services was good or excellent" (p. 179).

Police officers were satisfied with the alternative responses, but they were deeply dissatisfied with the reduction in the size of the basic patrol force. They believed this reduction resulted in greater danger to police officers and citizens. Although there was absolutely no evidence during the experimental period that danger did increase, the police officers remained concerned.

Early Evaluation

Although the Kansas City and Wilmington experiences motivated a considerable number of police departments to divert nonemergency calls from an immediate mobile response, many of them confined their reactions to refusing to respond to nuisance calls, while others declined to provide services such as escorts and house checks. Only a few implemented a "comprehensive system to handle all calls for service—a system [that] included call classification, intake processing and alternative service delivery" (McEwen et al. 1986:1). To test the effectiveness of such a comprehensive plan, the National Institute of Justice designed the Differential Police Response Field Test Program in October 1980; the test was eventually carried out in three cities—Garden Grove, Calif.; Greensboro, N.C.; and Toledo, Ohio.

The NIJ test design called for the participating departments to implement a number of response alternatives; these included (1) a telephone response unit to take reports over the telephone; (2) procedures for delaying mobile response for 30 to 60 minutes; (3) procedures for referring calls to other agencies; and (4) at least one other response, such as a scheduled appointment, walk-in or mail-in (p. 8). In addition, all three departments agreed to randomize incoming nonemergency calls. This enabled them to compare control and experimental groups during the same period, as well as compare "before/during" measures of citizen satisfaction (p. 9).

Although the results varied somewhat from one department to another, the evaluators found the test to be successful in all three of them. More than 90 percent of the callers who received alternative responses in the three cities were satisfied with the response the police offered; the only exception was the return-by-mail option, which was rarely used and not very popular when it was (p. 17). Although the experiment's design limited the number of alternative responses actually used, nearly half of all calls for service received during the experimental period could be handled with one of the alternatives (p. 16). And even with the limitations the experiment imposed, patrol workload in the three cities was reduced by as much as 20 percent (p. 101). Other research supports these findings; some departments can handle as many as 45 percent of their reports over the phone (Sweeney 1982). The meaning of these numbers in terms of resources saved is not hard to calculate. In Toledo, the evaluators estimated that four report-takers in the headquarters telephone unit were worth 10 officers in the field. The Garland, Texas, Police Department estimates that eliminating or modifying the response to certain calls can save the time of approximately five-and-one-half officers a year. In larger departments, the savings can result in staggering numbers. The very modest set of alternatives the New York City Police Department practices frees up the time of 750 patrol officers in a year.

Although police officials initially approached the MOD program with some caution, fearing adverse citizen reaction or situations jeopardizing officer safety (Cahn and Tien 1981:190), by the end of the experimental period, they were pleased with the results. This was not unexpected. One of DPR's implicit promises is that it increases the chief's control over police resources and policy. When a force immediately dispatches a patrol car in response to every call for service, the chief surrenders control and resource allocation to any citizen with a telephone. Crime prevention, peace-keeping and other programs calling for long-term investment of police time take second place to keeping up with what appears to be a constantly increasing, citizen-generated workload. Dispatchers take on the role of first-line supervisors since they, rather than sergeants, actually control the patrol force's activities. Implementing DPR implies a policy that directs dispatchers to respond to calls for service in standardized ways, removing discretion and control from complaint-takers and dispatchers and placing them, instead, in the hands of those who make the policy.

An important implication, therefore, is that the officer-hours saved by DPR are a resource that those in policy-making and administrative positions can utilize. If DPR is not accompanied by changes in the patrol force's organization, the officer-hours saved may simply be dissipated. Plans to "harvest" these resources must be an integral part of any DPR program. A parallel fear is that the economies of DPR will be used against the department at budget time; the resources saved can be a rationale for not providing additional resources.

Waddington (1993) notes that these observations are consistent with others that have pointed out that the amount of discretion necessarily vested in the police organization's lower ranks makes it difficult for the upper ranks to exercise "command and control." In this case, the discretion belongs not only to patrol officers, but also to complaint-takers and dispatchers—who are often civilian employees.

Underutilization of Alternatives

With this in mind, it is worth noting that one factor that appears in the Wilmington study and in every subsequent one is that alternative responses are consistently underutilized. This is not necessarily a result of complaint-takers' deliberately trying to undermine the program; rather, it is the consequence of institutional constraints. If an operator or dispatcher immediately sends a sworn officer to a call for which such a response turns out to be unnecessary, the worst that can happen is that a superior reprimands him or her. On the other hand, if an alternative response is used for a call that would actually have benefited from a swiftly dispatched police officer—especially if the alternative results in harm to the caller—the consequences, in terms of both career and personal anguish, can be substantial. There can also be negative consequences for the department, in terms of bad publicity and legal liability. There is every reason, therefore, for the complaint-taker to be ultra-conservative in using alternatives: the rewards for using alternatives are small, and the consequences of mistakes can be disastrous.

> Alarms activated at the start of the working day are almost invariably set off by the staff opening the premises. But the operative words here are "*almost* invariably." On one occasion, recalled by some of the control room staff, a local gunshop's alarm was activated as the owner arrived to start the working day. However, the reason for this was not the owner's carelessness, but because he was attacked and robbed as he opened the door. One of the guns stolen on that occasion was used to hold up a building society office in south London and was the weapon that killed a young clerk (Waddington, p. 165).

One of the earlier English studies (Ekblum and Heal 1982) called attention to this "just in case" rule. It emphasizes the complaint room personnel's perceived need to "cover their backs" against possible criticism. Rather than try to obtain as much information as possible from the caller, complaint-takers often responded to the imprecision surrounding a call by dispatching a car, often with a backup. The assumption was that sending a car could always be justified, doing anything else could be risky, and patrol officers on the scene could always get a clearer picture of the circumstances than could an operator relying on a telephone connection (p. 24). The "just in case" rule is, therefore, not just an instance of self-protection against those who might criticize with the benefit of hindsight. It is also a decision to err on the side of safety—the safety of responding police officers and the safety of victims, actual and potential.

Responses to Underutilization

Evaluators of DPR have tended to respond to the underutilization of alternative responses by calling for better training and reduced discretion for communications personnel.

> Some police departments have developed detailed protocols for call-takers to follow in gathering information to select the best response. The call-taker makes an *initial* decision as to which of several classifications best characterizes the call. Then a predetermined set of questions is asked that [is] pertinent to calls falling into the selected category....[T]here are several common items that facilitate the selection of a response: time of occurrence...whether a suspect is at or near the scene, whether there are weapons present, and whether the situation is life threatening. The nature of the "correct" response is specified by departmental rules, which indicate a particular priority code for each combination of possible responses in each call classification category. Department policy also specifies which priority levels require an immediate response.... Policy also stipulates which can be delayed, and which can or must be diverted to alternate methods of response. Although some systems allow the communications personnel to use their own judgment to "override" the predetermined response priority for a given call, others do not. Given recent advances in computer-aided dispatch (CAD) systems, it is now possible for the call-taker to serve *only* as an information gatherer, while the computer itself carries out the priority selection and unit assignment tasks [emphases added] (Worden and Mastrofski, p. 18).

Worden and Mastrofski describe several call classifications. Houston, for example, is reviewing a system with the following categories: accidents, property crimes, auto thefts, patrol calls, crimes against persons, police transport calls, noncriminal service calls, assist the officer, and hospital checks.

This underscores the fact that a department that wishes to make more than perfunctory use of alternative responses must devise a call classification system that bears little resemblance to the legally oriented "10-code" ones most commonly used. These systems only provide information on the criminal code designation of the call, information that is sufficient when most calls are routinely answered with rapid mobile response (McEwen et al.:47). But when a decision from among a number of alternative responses is being made, more information is required. The NIJ evaluation of DPR suggested that in addition to categories such as those listed above, "descriptors" such as type of injury, likelihood of apprehension, availability of witnesses, and existence of non-crime hazards should also be part of the system. Of all the categories, the most important is "time of occurrence," which is most often described as (1) in progress, (2) proximate/just occurred or (3) cold (McEwen et al.:48-49).

Decision-Making

Such classifications ignore the fact that these categories are not embedded in the outside world, but are actually conclusions, conclusions operators make on the basis of information that callers give them—and calls are often surrounded by confusion and ambiguity. As Shapland and Vagg (1988) point out, there are times when callers are indeed clear in their own minds as to "exactly what they are reporting and whether they see it as 'crime' or not," and once the police have investigated, they, too, make up their minds about the nature of the incident. "During the brief period of conversation on the telephone between the two, confusion is rife" (pp. 37-39).

The fact is that callers rarely present uninterpreted information. First, they may have a vested interest in their version of the incident. This is particularly true if the caller is assuming the role of the victim or aggrieved party. The call-taker has no way of knowing whether the caller is actually the aggressor or is lodging a complaint motivated by irritation or malice. Second, the caller's perspective is limited and may be only one inference based on facts that would support others. Waddington gives as an example a report of an automobile accident; the caller saw from his bedroom window that a car had left the road and had crashed through a fence. The caller believed that people were trapped inside the car and called the police within seconds (p. 112). However, from the information given, it would also be possible to assume that the people inside the car were simply gathering their wits, were drunk or were planning their escape (p. 164).

We can begin to see the problems in the common suggestion (e.g., Ekblum and Heal 1982) that if call-takers collected more information, they would be better able to match the response to the call and thereby reduce the underutilization of alternative responses. One problem with this assumption lies in the very concept of information, information that is needed to classify a call and assign the correct response. Manning (1977, 1988) argues that calls for police services are typically imprecise; it is the complaint-taker who must interpret the content of the call. This is done by mentally reconstructing the circumstances prompting the call, and in doing this, Manning suggests, the complaint-taker relies not only on policy and classification systems, but also on a body of beliefs and assumptions about calls and callers, beliefs and assumptions that reflect not only the complaint-taker's own personal history, but also the police culture's beliefs and assumptions. Before the call classification system can take effect, someone must interpret the words of the caller—words that are themselves interpretations—so that they match one of the system's categories. The fact that the call-taker elicited the words through a standard set of questions and feeds them into a computer does not change the situation at all.

> Whether a call relates to, in the words of the official policy, a "life-threatening condition," "an offense in progress," or indicates the "presence of a suspect at the scene" or "important physical evidence that will be lost if not retrieved," or has "a potential for further violence," very largely (though not entirely) depends [on] the interpretation of what the caller says and [his or her] credibility in the eyes of the listener (Waddington, p. 156).

A second objection to the demand for more information from callers relates to the fact that callers can give only *their* version of events; if that version is untrue, mistaken or exaggerated (p. 164), further questioning will not give the caller a better understanding or the call-taker a more accurate interpretation. It can only provide more information about the caller's version—or interpretation—of the incident being reported.

Following this line of thought, referring to the call-taker as *only* an information gatherer underestimates immeasurably the effects of information gathering. The really important classification judgments are made by the person who gathers information from the caller and translates it into categories the computer accepts. The discretionary work is already done *before* the detailed protocols, predetermined questions and computer-driven priority selections ever come into play.

It is a fact of police life that most of the incidents that prompt a call for service did not occur, dissipate before the police can get there, or are beyond the ability of the police to handle. DPR enthusiasts work on the assumption that it is both possible and desirable to identify those calls that require rapid police response and that to use a rapid response for any other call is a failure of the system.

> Nobody doubts that for that crucial 5 percent, the response should be immediate and authoritative. But in the other 95 percent, the scene is cold and the officer can do little more than take a report and soothe the victim (Kennedy).

The implication is that the call-taker can, given the proper training and equipment, unerringly select from all the calls received the 5 percent that involve the possibility of an immediate arrest or of a rescue from immediate danger. Any doubts about a person's ability to make such a selection can be allayed by delegating the selection to a computer. If the doubts are really great, the computer can be programmed to reject a human override.

But consideration of the type of information that call-takers receive and of the ways they process and interpret that information should lead to doubts as to whether unerring selection is really possible. Even under optimum conditions—conditions that are rare in a police control room—we would be forced to predict a significant number of mistakes. In this context, underutilization of alternative responses is not a failure of the program, but rather is a realistic way of handling a situation fraught with dangers.

The Symbolic Function of Policing

In the last analysis, DPR is another of those ideas that appear to be solely about efficiency and economy but that quickly force a reexamination of the police's role in the social order. Waddington (p. 168) suggests that it is all too easy to overlook the police's *symbolic* role. He approvingly quotes Ericson (1982, pp. 198-199) to the effect that citizens often call the police because they "have defined a situation as 'out of order,' and they want the authority of the police officer as one powerful resource to assist them in putting things back in order." He also notes that Maguire's 1982 survey indicates that when burglary victims call the police, they do not necessarily expect that the police will catch the burglar; calling the police is a way of "reestablishing the order of things," of receiving "what they [regard] as the *appropriate response to the incident*" (p. 137).

These considerations provide a context for Kennedy's remark, quoted above, that in many cases, all the police officer can do is "take a report and soothe the victim." These seem to be the very acts that do "reestablish the order of things," that begin to restore the level of social order that existed before the incident that prompted the call. Hoover (1992, p. 23) agrees that a patrol officer can do little when summoned to the scene of an auto theft other than note, "By golly, you're right. Your car isn't there anymore."

> On the other hand, a citizen victimized by a $10,000 to $30,000 theft perhaps "deserves" to talk to a real live representative of her or his local *law enforcement* agency. Such a citizen might legitimately respond, when queried by her or his neighborhood community-oriented officer about what the police can do to improve the quality of life in the area, by saying, "Come when I call you" [emphasis in the original].

A final question, one that arises in other studies, is whether use of alternative responses affects crime reporting. Do alternatives such as requiring citizens to go to the police station or mail in forms make it more difficult for citizens to report crime, and thus lower reported crime figures? Or does requiring the extra effort reduce false reporting? It is suspected that the results are quite crime-specific, calling again for a careful and knowledgeable matching between crime and response.

Evaluation

Total quality management teaches the importance of ongoing evaluation, evaluation consisting of as many measures as are found to be relevant to the program's goals. Differential response programs are deceptively easy to evaluate quantitatively. Such programs produce a number of easily counted outcomes—calls diverted, calls eligible for alternative responses, officer-hours saved, effects on reported crime rates, types of alternatives available, and satisfaction rates of citizens, officers and administrators. Even such apparently simple measures may produce results that are easy to misread. For example, citizens who never believed in their police department's promise of rapid response may be more pleased with alternatives than citizens with more confidence in their department.

Wordon and Mastrofski give excellent advice on collecting data on variables such as these. They also point out, however, that a careful examination of a police department's goals may indicate other factors that are not so easily measured. Problem-oriented policing, for example, calls for analysis of situations that produce repeated calls for service from one location; police collect information as well as deal with the incident that prompted the call. If call-takers immediately refer some calls to other agencies, or even to a number of different police units, less information may be gathered for analysis. If this is true, the goals of problem-oriented policing are being subverted, as problem-solving is sacrificed for short-term effectiveness and economy (pp. 26-27).

A second example involves the distribution of alternative responses. Calls for police service are not distributed equally throughout the community; they vary with the ethnic, racial and income levels of neighborhoods. It is important to know whether alternative responses are being allocated solely on the basis of the information given during the call, or whether they reflect the callers' personal or demographic characteristics (p. 29)

A third example involves policing's symbolic function. A rapid police response conveys respect for the caller's interpretation of events, concern for whatever it is that has disturbed the caller, and a willingness to restore order to a situation that has been defined as being out of order. Is it possible to convey these attitudes in other ways? And how do we measure the results?

Clearly, a meaningful use of alternatives raises issues relating to training, supervision, career development, reward systems, civilianization, officer safety, citizen satisfaction, data collection, and relationships between police and community. The question is not necessarily whether a department should use DPR; DPR offers extremely attractive opportunities for increases in economy and effectiveness. Rather, it is a question of developing a differential police response program that furthers *all* of a department's goals.

References

Cahn, M., and J. Tien. 1981. *An Alternative Approach in Police Response: Wilmington Management of Demand Program.* Washington, D.C.: National Institute of Justice.

Caron, N. 1980. *Response Time Analysis, Vol. III: Part II Crime Analysis.* Kansas City, Mo.: Kansas City Police Department.

Eck, J. 1983. *Solving Crimes: The Investigation of Burglary and Robbery.* Washington, D.C.: Police Executive Research Forum.

Eck, J., and W. Spelman. 1987. *Problem-Solving: Problem-Oriented Policing in Newport News.* Washington, D.C.: Police Executive Research Forum.

Ekblum, P., and K. Heal. 1982. *The Police Response to Calls From the Public, RPU No. 9.* London: Home Office.

Ericson, R. 1982. *Reproducing Order.* Toronto: University of Toronto Press.

Hoover, L. 1992. "Police Mission: An Era of Debate." *Police Management: Issues and Perspectives.* Edited by L. Hoover. Washington, D.C.: Police Executive Research Forum.

Kennedy, D. N.d. *The Strategic Management of Police Resources.* Available on the Internet: NIJ documents.

Kansas City Police Department. 1977. *Response Time Analysis: Executive Summary.* Kansas City, Mo.: Kansas City Police Department.

_____. 1977. *Response Time Analysis: Vol. II-Analysis.* Kansas City, Mo.: Kansas City Police Department.

Maguire, M. 1982. *Burglary in a Dwelling.* London: Heinemann.

Manning, P. 1977. *Police Work.* Cambridge, Mass.: MIT Press.

_____. 1988. *Symbolic Communication: Signifying Calls and the Police Response.* Cambridge, Mass.: MIT Press.

McEwen, J., E. Conners, and M. Cohen. 1986. *Evaluation of the Differential Police Response Field Test.* Washington, D.C.: National Institute of Justice.

Pate, T. 1976. *Police Response Time: Its Determinants and Effects.* Washington, D.C.: Police Foundation.

Percy, S. 1980. "Response Time and Citizen Evaluation of Police." *Journal of Police Science and Administration* 8:75-86.

Shapland, J., and J. Vagg. 1987. *Policing by the Public.* London: Routledge.

Spelman, W., and D. Brown. 1981. *Calling the Police: Citizen Reporting of Serious Crime.* Washington, D.C.: Police Executive Research Forum.

Sumrall, R., J. Roberts, and M. Farmer. 1981. *Differential Police Response Strategies.* Washington, D.C.: Police Executive Research Forum.

Sweeney, T. Jan. 11, 1982. "Managing Time—the Scarce Resource." *Law Enforcement News.*

Tien, J., J. Simon, and R. Larson. 1979. *An Alternative Approach to Police Patrol: The Wilmington Split-Force Experiment.* Cambridge, Mass.: Public System Evaluation.

Waddington, P. 1993. *Calling the Police.* Aldershot, U.K.: Avebury.

Wald, M. May 19, 1994. "A New Mantra From Utility Companies: Use *More* Electricity." *New York Times,* p. C6.

Worden, R., and S. Mastrofski.   N.d.   *Differential Police Response: A Program Evaluation Package.* Huntsville, Texas: Bill Blackwood Law Enforcement Management Institute of Texas (unpublished).

Chapter 9

Rethinking Detective Management
or, Why Investigative Reforms Are Seldom Permanent or Effective

John E. Eck

The Detective Cycle

Plainclothes detectives may be the oldest form of public police. The Bow Street Runners, created by Henry Fielding in London during the late 18th century, spent considerable time pursuing highwaymen (Fitzgerald 1888). A uniformed London Metropolitan Police did not appear until 1829. Yet the English parliamentary debates leading up to the creation of the London Metropolitan Police depict the conflict between uniformed and plainclothes policing that persists to this day, and that is likely to continue far into the future. That is, plainclothes officers can blend with the public and, presumably, get closer to the criminals they are pursuing. But the fact that they are not obviously police officers creates public suspicion that these agents may be engaged in dubious behaviors. These suspicions, often held by police administrators and sometimes exaggerated, are not misplaced.

Detectives' abuse of authority has a long history, as long as the history of the profession (Kuykendall 1986). A colorful example is Jonathan Wild. Wild was a private "thief taker" before the creation of any public police in England. To understand how Wild operated, one has to understand the nature of property theft in 18th century England. The well-to-do owned many things, but most of their possessions were too bulky to be stolen easily. However, they did purchase from skilled artisans small objects made of precious metals and jewels, such as snuff boxes, jewelry and other personal items.   Because these items were not mass-manufactured, each was distinctive. And each was valuable enough to attract the attention of thieves. In the absence of a public police, a gentleman whose wife's jewels were stolen would hire a thief taker like Jonathan Wild. The thief taker's primary job was to recover the stolen artifact for a reward. If possible, he would also capture the thief. Wild was particularly good at recovering stolen property *and* apprehending offenders. Because of his prowess, Wild was known as the "Thief Taker General" (Howson 1970).

The penalty for theft was death, and this was the secret of Wild's success. For as it turned out, Wild did not only recover property and send a few errant individuals to the gallows, but he also organized the thieves and planned thefts from the start. Those thieves who did not cooperate with him were threatened with apprehension and death. A number of individuals were executed because they resisted Wild's attempts to organize the underworld. When Wild was discovered, he was sent to the gallows himself (Howson 1970).

Wild's familiarity with the thieves and his ability to use his intimate knowledge for corrupt purposes were lessons that were not lost on early police reformers. Also not lost were the lessons from using undercover officers in Napoleonic France to ferret out threats to the government (Forssell 1970; Critchley 1979). Concerns over corruption and political influence resulted in the London Metropolitan Police's focusing almost entirely on uniformed officers. But the advantages of having a few specialists out of uniform who could mix with offenders could not be ignored (Cobb 1957). Consequently, a small number of constables were assigned to plainclothes work. The number of these detectives increased as they were able to demonstrate some successes, and declined when they became involved in political or corruption scandals (Cobb 1957; Critchley 1979). After one particularly major scandal, a special inquiry was established to determine what should be done. Howard Vincent was asked to head the inquiry. Vincent had studied the French and other continental European police systems, and he recommended the establishment of a special detective bureau to investigate crime and to help combat Fenians (Irish rebels) who were terrorizing England. Thus, the outside threat overcame the inside threat and resulted in the creation of the detective force commonly referred to as Scotland Yard. It also resulted in the formation of the antiterrorism section then called the Irish Special Branch (Critchley 1979; Porter 1987).

We see in this sketch of the early history of detectives a cycle that continues to this day. First, plainclothes work is criticized for corruption, ineffectiveness, political interference, or any number of possible scandals associated with detectives. This leads to the marginalization of detective work and the reduction of its capacity to operate. After some period of time, the police agency confronts a serious problem that refocuses attention on the need for increased detective capacity. (In late 19th century England, it was

Irish terrorism.   In late 20th century Washington, D.C., it was the historically high homicide rate.) This leads to the expansion of detective operations. This expansion eventually, if not initially, begins to conflict with the demands of other parts of the police agency, in particular, uniformed patrol. Then, when the next scandal occurs—as it always does—a group interested in curtailing plainclothes operations surfaces within the police agency.

Detectives are particularly vulnerable to cycles of scandal and reform (Sherman 1978) for a number of reasons. First, as a distinct minority with relatively advantageous working conditions (out of uniform and with more discretion than patrol officers), they incur the jealousy of the majority of the police force. Second, detective work appears to be secretive, even when it is not. Detectives are not known to share information routinely or often, and they have the same aura that surrounds spies, even when they are not conducting undercover work. Third, it is never clear what they are accomplishing. This puts detectives in a difficult position. Knowing that they are judged in part by their productivity, detectives often seek opportunities to enhance their records, even at the expense of others in the police service. Finally, detectives are invisible to their supervisors. Thus, there is uncertainty as to what they are really up to. And when a few detectives exploit this invisibility for personal gain, the discovery of malfeasance reinforces the suspicions. For all these reasons, specialized investigation sections are seldom popular, except with their members and the entertainment media.

At the beginning of the 1970s, the United States was entering the first step of this cycle. Corruption scandals, civil rights violations and other problems put the police under a great deal of scrutiny at a time when fear of crime was rising. Thus, when research began to question detectives' effectiveness, many police administrators were mentally prepared to cut back the number of plainclothes detectives.

Investigations Research

Over the last 25 years, the results of investigative research have been pessimistic for supporters of specialized plainclothes detective sections. For police officials who are skeptical of such units, it has been a breath of fresh air. Let's look briefly at this line of research.

Though observational studies of investigations had been published before 1970 (Skolnick 1967), and the President's Commission on Law Enforcement had used quantitative data to examine detectives' effectiveness (Isaacs 1967), much of this went unnoticed by policing. But in 1970, the New York City RAND Corp. issued a damning report on follow-up investigations of burglaries and assaults in New York City. Though it found some evidence that investigations of assaults increased arrests, the report's authors claimed that the solution of burglary cases had virtually nothing to do with detective effort. Instead, the report stated, the solution of these cases was due solely to the evidence available to the patrol officers who first arrived at the scene. If patrol officers did not gather the relevant information, detectives were unlikely to collect it later. Further, the availability of information necessary to solve cases is random (Greenwood 1970). In short, there is little follow-up investigators can do to solve burglaries except to process reports.

This conclusion was important for several reasons. First, it gave a coherent and empirically supported explanation for detective work that conflicted with the explanations detectives gave. By highlighting the important role of patrol officers, the study drew attention to a neglected aspect of investigations, an aspect that was hard to deny once attention was drawn to it. Though people could claim that patrol officers were not as thorough as detectives, they could not deny their importance. But the report went further. It claimed that on average, detective work contributes little additional value to the case once it leaves the hands of a patrol officer. Second, the New York City RAND Corp. had the ear of decisionmakers at the highest level of the police department, and these people were not great fans of detectives (Daley 1971; Murphy and Plate 1977; Seedman and Hellman 1974). Finally, the researchers went on to conduct a study of investigations nationally that came to similar conclusions.

Five years later, another study, by some of the same researchers, examined solved cases from the Kansas City, Mo., Police Department and came to the same conclusion. In particular, they found that the activities detectives engaged in to solve those crimes were common, everyday police work; they took no special actions. They also surveyed police agencies across the United States and found no relationships between various ways of organizing detective operations and clearance and arrest rates. This was the now-famous RAND report on detectives (Greenwood, Petersilia and Chaiken 1977). This study nationalized the New York City conclusions and forced police officials across the United States to confront the possibility that their detectives might not be as useful as once thought.

Finally, from the early to late 1970s, a series of studies in California (Greenberg, Yu and Lang 1973), Minnesota (Johnson and Healy 1978) and nationally (Eck 1979) examined solved and unsolved burglary cases. These studies came to similar conclusions: detectives solved few burglary cases; the information that led to arrests was collected by the first patrol officer at the scene, not by the follow-up investigator; this patrol information came from victims and witnesses, for the most part; and absent this information, there was little that could be done to solve the case. These studies recommended that police managers use statistical tools to predict case outcomes and screen out cases that could not be solved. Thus, detectives should get only those cases that had the information needed to make an arrest. In short, the detective was viewed as a report processor, not a case solver.

The findings from all of these studies, although never implemented to the extent that the researchers recommended, fell on fertile ground. Corruption scandals in New York and other places had tarnished the public image of detectives and reinforced the position of uniformed branch supporters. Civil libertarians had become more vocal about police abuses, and some of their concerns centered on the activities of plainclothes police. Finally, police managers trying to reform law enforcement operations found that the detective branches were often quasi-independent power sources that resisted reform efforts. In academic circles, criticism of the police had greater support than support for the police. Thus, police practitioners, policy makers outside of police agencies, and academics gave the research findings far more credence than an objective view of the evidence would suggest.

These studies had several problems. First, none of them directly measured the level of detective effort that went into cases and compared this with case outcomes. Therefore, statements about the absence of a relationship between detective effort and case solution had no direct empirical support. Second, the RAND analysis of the Kansas City data only looked at solved cases. Consequently, it could not find differences between solved and unsolved cases that could be due to detective work, if such differences existed. Third, though studies showed that information patrol officers collected was critical to solutions, no study examined what information detectives collected. Thus, though these studies created a very plausible theory of how cases were solved, there were sufficient problems with the study designs that their conclusions and recommendations should not have been taken as "facts." But for many police officials and researchers, these findings were interpreted as having settled the question of detective effectiveness (Kuykendall 1986).

In 1980, the Police Executive Research Forum (PERF) began a study to overcome some of the limitations of the earlier work (Eck 1983). Unfortunately, this was the last major study of detective work, and consequently, research still cannot answer many questions.

The study was designed to overcome the main problems with earlier research. First, patrol and detective efforts were measured directly by having the police officials complete detailed logs of their activities, the time spent on each activity, and the information the activity produced. Second, solved and unsolved cases were examined so that comparisons between these types of cases could be made. Third, the logs allowed examination of the additional information detectives collected beyond that available to patrol officers. Finally, burglary and robbery investigations were examined at three sites: St. Petersburg, Fla.; DeKalb County, Ga.; and Wichita, Kan. (Eck 1983).

Two theories of detective work were developed for comparison. The first theory, called the Effort-Result Hypothesis, claimed that cases were solved because of detectives' work. In short, the more effort by detectives, the better the results. The second theory, called the Circumstance-Result Hypothesis, was based on the RAND researchers' ideas. That is, the availability of information to the patrol officer depended on circumstances beyond the control of the police, and additional work by the detective did not help solve the case. In short, cases were solved through random factors.

In comparing the two hypotheses, it was found that both are right and both are wrong. Some cases were solved through circumstances beyond the police's control. Some cases could not be solved within the resource constraints the police agencies faced. And some cases were solved because of the additional efforts of detectives.

In other words, detectives are neither heros nor demons. Follow-up investigations of property crime will have low solution rates because offenders avoid being seen. Nevertheless, absent detective work, some of these offenders will not be arrested. Both hypotheses make exaggerated claims, but both contain more than a little truth.

Why Investigate?

Up to this point, we have assumed that there is a need for investigators, without clearly stating exactly what this need is. Addressing this question is of fundamental importance if police agencies are to manage investigations effectively. There are only three goals. The first two are often confused, and the third is seldom discussed. We will examine each.

Crime control through law enforcement is the first goal. It is achieved by apprehending offenders. Detective units attempt to achieve this goal by arresting offenders. But once offenders have been caught, at least one of three objectives must be met: deter other offenders by making them believe that if they commit the same offense, they, too, will be caught; incapacitate the apprehended offender so that he or she cannot commit another crime for some specified period of time; or rehabilitate the offender so that, when released, he or she does not continue to offend. The research about the criminal justice system's ability to accomplish any of these three objectives will not be reviewed here. It is sufficient to state that research does not suggest that any of them are remotely close to being the silver bullet for crime (Blumstein, Cohen and Nagin 1978; Blumstein et. al. 1986; Sechrest, White and Brown 1979). Nevertheless, some people are rehabilitated; recidivism is not 100 percent. Clearly, a serial murderer in prison is not killing women on the street. And some people do stay away from crime because they are afraid of getting caught. Still, if detectives solved more crimes and arrested more offenders, would this translate into noticeable reductions in crime? Though there is no direct evidence that can answer this question, it does seem dubious, especially given the problems of courts and corrections.

There is a possibility of an alternative answer. The Washington, D.C., Metropolitan Police faced an increasing homicide rate, with no increase in the number of homicide investigators. Recently, the number of homicide investigators was increased and supplemented with investigators from the FBI and other federal agencies. Furthermore, there has been a decline in the number of homicides. Whether the increase in staffing caused the decline or whether it just happened to coincide with the decline is impossible to tell from the anecdotal evidence available.

The second goal, often confused with the first, is justice. From a pure justice perspective, it does not matter whether crime declines as a result of apprehending offenders. One tries to catch offenders because they have done something bad and they should be punished. Because humans are fallible, the court system stands between the arrest and the punishment. From a justice perspective, what matters is that the public, through the courts, can examine the case and the offender and then determine the penalty, if appropriate. Detectives contribute to justice if they catch the right offenders and provide prosecutors with the relevant information. If this also happens to result in fewer crimes in the future, so much the better.

There is a third goal that is seldom discussed. This is crime prevention. Though one can call crime control crime prevention, we will make a distinction between the two goals, principally because crime prevention does not depend exclusively on apprehension of offenders. Crime prevention will be discussed more extensively when we examine problem-oriented policing and problem solving. Though neglected, this is an area that detectives should be more involved in and where they have special expertise that can be applied to this goal.

Reactive Investigation Management

Investigations are usually divided into two categories: reactive and proactive. The research described earlier examined reactive investigations, that is, investigations of crime events after they occur because a citizen initiates the investigation through a request. Proactive investigations are police-initiated, sometimes before any crime has been committed.

The research on reactive investigations has been relatively pessimistic, in large part because these investigations begin after the crime has taken place. Nevertheless, research into the productivity of criminal investigations led to a national program to change the way investigations were managed. Throughout the latter half of the 1970s, the Managing Criminal Investigations (MCI) program produced seminars, sponsored training sessions and published manuals for police officials (Cawley et al. 1977; Greenberg and Wasserman 1979). Among many elements, the MCI program emphasized four points.

1.   Police officers need to collect as much information as possible during the first stages of an investigation. The difference between solvable and unsolvable cases is in large part, but not entirely, determined by the quality of patrol officers' work.
2.   Investigative managers need to sort those cases that cannot be solved from those that may be solved. Putting time into unsolvable cases wastes resources and diverts attention from cases that may be solved if more effort is put into them.
3.   Of those cases that may be solved, some will, in essence, solve themselves, while others will require more effort. It is this last group that should receive the greatest attention.
4.   Investigators should examine patterns of crime to link bits of information from several offenses. This point seems particularly obvious, but as we will see later, it has some implications beyond crime control.

The first point emphasizes one of the main conclusions from the research. It assumes that there is substantially more information to be gained at the earliest stage of the investigative process. Though there is evidence that this is the case for physical evidence (Peterson 1974), there is no scientific data that more witnesses can be found or that victims will recall more information if patrol officers make a more detailed initial investigation.

Case screening (point 2) makes the best out of a bad thing. Though it diverts attention from unsolvable cases, by itself it does nothing to put resources to productive use. Often, case screening is just a mechanism for dealing with cutbacks in staffing or increases in caseload. In this sense, it prevents things from getting worse. To make improvements, attention must be shifted toward productive activities. Points 3 and 4 suggest ways of doing this. Another approach is to use the resources to target offenders proactively.

Reform and Three Laws of Investigations

Though little research has been conducted on reactive investigations in the last decade, virtually no comparable work has been done on proactive investigations. The studies that have been conducted have focused on career criminals and narcotics investigations. These studies have found that targeting offenders is highly productive in generating arrests, but the costs of such efforts can be very high and there are many concerns about how offenders are selected for targeting (Martin and Sherman 1986; Sherman 1983).

Proactive investigations are very expensive because a great deal of investigative time must be spent watching people and places, waiting for something to happen (Pate, Bowers and Parks 1976). Undercover work also requires a substantial resource investment. Adding to the expense are the extra personnel needed to ensure the safety of the undercover officers and to ensure that informant funds are not misallocated. Reactive investigations are relatively cheap because the victim or witness brings forth information, and the investigation can be curtailed if no useful information is found. Proactive investigations are expensive because one starts with the least information, and detectives need to spend a great deal of time looking for it. Thus, there is a fundamental dilemma, which will be called the *First Law of Investigations:* relying on cheaply obtained information results in few solutions, but to get many solutions, one must gather expensive information. Technology can help make the First Law of Investigations less onerous, but it cannot eliminate it.

Targeting offenders proactively presents a different problem. Investigators like to select targets, and they often do so based on the information at hand. If the investigation is proactive, then the information will have to come from people with direct contact with offenders, often criminal informants. So proactive investigations are likely to be informant-driven. If the investigation is reactive, then the information will come from victims and witnesses. But in neither case are detectives in direct control over the direction of the investigation. In both circumstances, persistent and dedicated management practices can reduce the negative aspects of this—by case screening in reactive investigations and by careful informant control procedures for proactive investigations—but it cannot eliminate the problem. Thus, the *Second Law of Investigations* is that the direction of all investigations is largely out of the investigators' control, and the more control that is desired, the more expensive the investigation will become.

Ideally, one would have some objective form of targeting based on explicit goals. One might want to target the most violent offenders for proactive investigations, for example. Then information, much of it from police records of prior offenses, would be used to rank-order potential targets. One could target the most active offenders, regardless of their propensity for violence. Or one could target offenders who prey on special victims (children, for example). One could target offenders active in a specific neighborhood. Once a rank-order target list was prepared, additional information could be collected. This approach would target the worst offenders, not just the easiest-to-get offenders. The first and second laws of investigations assert, however, that this approach will be labor-intensive and expensive.

Another standard reform is to rotate personnel through investigations sections. This may improve communications throughout the agency and decrease the isolation of investigative units. However, because it does little to address the difficulty of gathering information, and does nothing to focus outcomes, it does not get to the heart of the problem of detective work.

The third type of investigative reform includes decentralization and despecialization. These reforms have received considerable attention in the context of community policing (Skolnick and Bayley 1986), just as they did during the late 1960s, when community policing was being examined (Bloch and Bell 1976; Schwartz and Clarren 1977; Sherman, Milton and Kelly 1973). Decentralization moves investigations from a central command location to area commands, from headquarters to precincts. It often involves disbanding or shrinking the separate investigations bureau and putting the decentralized detectives under the direct control of the area commander. Whatever centralized independent investigative bureau that remains focuses on the most serious and rarest crime—homicide, for example.

Despecialization reduces the number of special units within investigations. For example, the separate burglary, larceny and auto theft squads are combined to form a single property-crime unit. An extreme form of despecialization involves moving investigative functions into patrol and shrinking the investigative section. Decentralization almost always requires some form of despecialization. This is because when detectives are moved to area offices, each detective must take on a more heterogeneous caseload, since there are seldom enough cases of each particular type to keep a specialist detective busy. Despecialization does not require decentralization, however. One could keep all of the detectives at headquarters, while combining the specialty units.

Despecialization and decentralization are useful under some circumstances. To the extent that the investigation of each crime type requires distinctive skills and knowledge, specialization is defensible. If distinctive skills and knowledge are not required, then specialization is not justifiable. When the jurisdiction is very large and the areas within the jurisdiction are very different, decentralization makes a great deal of sense. In medium-sized and smaller cities, it is not clear how much difference decentralization will make. But in jurisdictions with relatively few crimes, either because the jurisdiction is small or because it is relatively safe, despecialization may be very useful. Under such circumstances, there are too few crimes to justify having specialists. In large cities and other cities with large numbers of crimes, despecialization may not be warranted.

This leads us to the *Third Law of Investigations:* the circumstances that call for specialization also call for decentralization, and the circumstances that require centralization require despecialization. Small cities and towns have few problems with this law: everyone works out of the same building, patrol officers conduct the investigations, and if there are any detectives, they handle all crimes. But in large cities, the third law explains why investigative units are constantly being reorganized; there is no formula that simultaneously satisfies the needs of (de)specialization and (de)centralization. When a large department decentralizes its investigations, it also despecializes. Decentralization brings the detectives closer to the peculiarities of the areas, but the despecialization makes it more difficult to develop and mobilize expertise in particular crimes. Later, under different leadership, the department recentralizes and respecializes. This solves the problem of expertise but reduces the detectives' interaction with the areas. Bayley (1992) has noted that debates about centralization vs. decentralization seem to have little impact on agency performance.

The three laws of investigations limit the effectiveness of the standard reforms police managers have attempted over the last 15 years. Each attempt to manage investigations is a little useful. That is, each of these types of reforms can help under some circumstances, but each brings with it difficulties of its own. One should not throw out these approaches, but one should not expect too much from them, either. And none of these approaches provides permanent fixes. In fact, one could argue that there are no permanent fixes to the problems that the standard reforms are meant to address.

But whether one accepts or rejects these laws and their implications, there is a deeper criticism of the standard reforms. None of them does much to change the nature of investigations. One can shift from reactive to proactive investigations, thereby increasing the amount of information, but at greater expense. Or one can invest considerable resources to exercise greater control over the direction of investigations. Or one can decentralize and despecialize. Still, none of these efforts will substantially increase the ability of investigations to achieve the goals of crime control and justice.

Thus, we need to rethink not only how we manage criminal investigations, but also the goals that we are trying to achieve. One cannot and should not abandon justice as a goal. The public has a right to demand that the police pursue the ends of justice, at least within the bounds of the resources available. We should downplay the goal of crime control through law enforcement, however, and substitute for it the goal of crime prevention. Simply put, investigators (and all others in police agencies) should work to keep crimes from occurring. When, despite these efforts, crimes do occur, the detective's job (shared with others in the agency) is to bring the offender to the prosecutor. More elaborately, we can suggest four guiding principles.

1. Abandon crime control through apprehension as a principle goal of investigations. There is little evidence that increased apprehensions by detectives make much of a difference in crime levels, except under special circumstances (see below).
2. Detectives should focus on justice. Offenders should be arrested because they violated the law. Detectives should find out who the offenders are and bring their evidence forward.

3. The special circumstances mentioned in item 1 are clear crime patterns. Obviously, arresting a repeat rapist or killer prevents crimes. And as we will see in point 4, focusing on patterns allows detectives to combine enforcement powers with many other techniques.

4. Crime prevention through problem solving should be emphasized. Detectives should look for patterns of crimes, determine why the patterns exist and implement programs that stop the patterns. Criminal apprehension is one technique that may be useful, but there are many other techniques (some illustrated next) that can be used in conjunction or as substitutes.

The Problem-Solving Detective

Problem-oriented policing is a style of policing that is designed to make the police more effective. Many see problem-oriented policing as an aspect of community policing (Moore 1992), while others do not (Goldstein 1990). Community policing is such an ambiguous term that debating this point is not particularly productive. Though problem solving has been most often discussed with regard to patrol officers, there are many cases in which detectives have applied a problem-oriented approach. The principles of problem solving have been explained in other books and reports (Goldstein 1979; Goldstein 1990; Eck and Spelman 1987), and the basic approach can be easily adapted to detectives. In fact, because detectives are not tied to a radio and have more control over how they use their time, it is possible that they would find it easier to address problems than would patrol officers. Rather than go over the details of problem-oriented policing, we will examine three examples of how detectives have addressed problems.

Domestic Homicides

One of the very first examples of how detectives used a problem-oriented approach occurred in Newport News, Va., during the first effort to use problem solving throughout an agency. One of the homicide detectives felt that as satisfying as it was to solve murders, it would be more satisfying to prevent them from occurring. He noted that half of the homicides the department had investigated in the previous year were related to domestic violence. Moreover, in half of these cases, the police had been to the address in the past. This led him to consider the possibility of early intervention with the couples involved.

He brought together representatives from many public and private organizations—the prosecutor's office, the women's advocates, the hospitals, the local newspaper, the military, and many others. Together, they developed a program that forced the couples into mandatory counseling. Under very specific circumstances (e.g., serious injury, presence of a gun or knife, and so forth), arrests of the assaulter were mandatory. The prosecutor agreed to refuse to drop charges unless the abuser and the victim entered counseling. If they completed the counseling and if the victim allowed, the charges could be dropped. The goal was to reduce repeat domestic violence and domestic homicides, while keeping families intact. No formal evaluation has been conducted, so it is impossible to be certain of the results. Nevertheless, the police department reports that domestic homicides and repeat domestic violence declined in the first years after implementation.

Gas Station Robberies

The Edmonton (Alberta, Canada) Police Service, as part of its community policing reforms, has undertaken a variety of changes throughout the agency, including decentralization and despecialization of detectives. Additionally, detectives are encouraged, like patrol constables, to address problems. Patrol constables and decentralized detectives are focused on geographically based communities, i.e., neighborhoods. The headquarters detectives are encouraged to look for nongeographic communities. For example, two detectives are members of the bankers association and attend its meetings.

One robbery detective noted that one chain of gas stations had a very high robbery rate. Because of the high cigarette tax in Canada, there is a thriving black market for cigarettes, and cigarette theft can be lucrative. The detective reviewed the crime reports and found that many of the robberies involved the theft of cigarettes and nothing else. He visited those stations and noted that the single attendant was in a small booth stocked with candy, cigarettes and other small items. The detective worked with the managers of the gas station chain. Together, they identified a number of simple changes that could be made to the booth, cigarette displays and attendant procedures. The gas station chain made the changes. The police service reports a major decline in the robberies of these gas stations.

Drug Houses

Cities throughout the United States have seen an increase in street drug sales over the last decade. More recently, some cities have seen a decline in open street sales. Trends in sales from indoor locations are more difficult to determine because these places are harder to detect. The San Diego Police Department's narcotics section noted that their investigators were repeatedly called back to the same apartment buildings and rental houses. They asked the question, Is there something that can be done about repeat drug places? One approach was to go directly to property owners. Owners were told about the use of their rental property for drug dealing, and their cooperation was sought in evicting the dealers. Though landlords were rarely uncooperative, the police used civil law—nuisance abatement—in conjunction with criminal law to close down drug houses. If, after the police warned a landlord about the drug dealing, the dealing continued, and it was determined that the landlord had done nothing to curb the problem, the police asked the city attorney to file a civil suit in state court to seize the house as a public nuisance. This approach has not solved the drug problem in the city, but it has resulted in the elimination of a number of persistent drug locations. In combination with the abatement approach, San Diego detectives (like police officials in other cities) put on training courses for landlords to help them manage their property better and keep out drug offenders.

Problem-Solving Typology

These examples were selected because they demonstrate the diverse nature of problems and solutions detectives have addressed. They also illustrate that problem solving can be an effective method of preventing crime. And they show how strict enforcement can be used as part of a comprehensive prevention strategy. If detectives increase their overall arrest rate, chances of a reduction in crime are small. But if they target their efforts and use their powers of arrest along with other tactics, it is possible to have an impact on crime.

Problem solving requires the examination of crime patterns, a management reform consistently recommended by advocates of managing criminal investigations. Three basic types of patterns can be examined. First, one can look for common offenders. This is the most common approach to applying crime analysis to investigations. Another approach is to look for common victims or targets. The Edmonton detective who noted that one chain of gas stations was suffering a high number of robberies illustrates this example. By determining what is similar about the victims and targets and how they differ from nonvictims and nontargets, one can make some headway toward solutions. A third approach, illustrated by the San Diego example, is to focus on repeat places and ask the question, Why are crimes occurring here instead of at other, similar places?

Conclusions

In this chapter, we have examined some of the developments in investigative reform. We have seen how plainclothes investigations have gone through cycles of popularity and decline. We have seen how, in the last 25 years, research has attempted to examine the productivity of detectives. We asked, What are the goals of investigations? Then we examined the changes police officials have made in investigative operations, changes that have often been lumped together under the title of "managing criminal investigation." We noted how the reforms have severe limitations and summarized these limitations with three laws of investigations. Finally, we reviewed the proposal that detectives focus more on justice and crime prevention and focus less on crime control through law enforcement.

A recurring theme of this chapter is that managing criminal investigations involves conflicting difficulties. Addressing one almost necessarily ensures that the other will get worse, thus forcing change in another direction. We see cycles of expansion and contraction of specialized investigative units; movements from centralization to decentralization, and back; enthusiasm with proactive tactics, followed by focusing on reactive investigations; and so on. One of the reasons for this seeming lack of permanent, unassailable management principles is that we try to force investigative units to do too much with too little.

Instead of recognizing that justice is an important goal in and of itself, some have emphasized the crime-control efficacy of investigations. Though there are some important exceptions, follow-up investigations are unlikely to have much influence on overall crime rates. If detectives focused on justice and crime prevention, then there would be some possibility that more progress could be made. If detective work were more than tracking down and arresting offenders, detectives would have to interact with communities. They would also have to work more with other sections of the police force and other public and private groups to achieve their objectives. Since most of this work would be open, there would be less likelihood of corruption and abuse of authority, perceived or otherwise. One must be careful about making greater claims for police reforms than can be delivered. Nevertheless, even modest improvements would be welcome.

References

Bayley, D.H. 1992. "Comparative Organization of the Police in English-Speaking Countries." *Modern Policing.* Edited by Michael Tonry and Norval Morris. Crime and Justice Vol. 15. Chicago: The University of Chicago Press.

Bloch, P.B., and J. Bell. 1976. *Managing Investigations: The Rochester System.* Washington, D.C.: Police Foundation.

Blumstein, A., J. Cohen, and D. Nagin (eds). 1978. *Deterrence and Incapacitation: Estimating the Effects of Criminal Sanctions on Crime Rates*. Washington, D.C.: National Academy of Sciences.

Blumstein, A., J. Cohen, J.A. Roth, and C. Visher (eds). 1986. *Criminal Careers and "Career Criminals,"* Vol. 1. Washington, D.C.: National Academy of Sciences.

Cawley, D.F., H.J. Miron, W.J. Araujo, R. Wasserman, T.A. Mannello, and Y. Huffman. 1977. *Managing Criminal Investigations: Manual*. Washington, D.C.: U.S. Department of Justice, Law Enforcement Assistance Administration.

Cobb, B. 1957. *The First Detectives*. London: Faber and Faber.

Critchley, T.A. 1979. *A History of Police in England and Wales*. London: Constable.

Daley, R. 1971. *Target Blue: An Insider's View of the NYPD*. New York: Delacorte Press.

Eck, J.E. 1979. *Managing Case Assignments: The Burglary Investigation Decision Model Replication*. Washington, D.C.: Police Executive Research Forum.

_____. 1983. *Solving Crimes: The Investigation of Burglary and Robbery*. Washington, D.C.: Police Executive Research Forum.

Eck, J.E., and W. Spelman. 1987. *Problem Solving: Problem-Oriented Policing in Newport News*. Washington, D.C.: Police Executive Research Forum.

Fitzgerald, P. 1888. *Chronicles of Bow Street Police Office With an Account of the Magistrates, "Runner" and Police; and a Selection of the Most Interesting Cases*, Vol. 1. London: Chapman and Hall.

Forssell, N. 1970. *Fouche: The Man Napoleon Feared*. New York: AMS Press.

Goldstein, H. 1979. "Improving Policing: A Problem-Oriented Approach." *Crime and Delinquency* 25:2.

_____. 1990. *Problem-Oriented Policing*. New York: McGraw Hill.

Greenberg, B., O.S. Yu, and K. Lang. 1973. *Enhancement of the Investigative Function—Volume 1: Analysis and Conclusions.* Springfield, Va.: National Technical Information Service.

Greenberg, I., and R. Wasserman. 1979. *Managing Criminal Investigations.* Washington, D.C.: U.S. Department of Justice, Law Enforcement Assistance Administration.

Greenwood, P. 1970. *An Analysis of the Apprehension Activities of the New York City Police Department.* New York: Rand Institute.

Greenwood, P., J. Petersilia, and J. Chaiken. 1977. *The Criminal Investigation Process.* Lexington, Mass.: D.C. Heath.

Howson, G. 1970. *Thief-Taker General: Jonathan Wild and the Emergence of Crime and Corruption as a Way of Life in Eighteenth-Century England.* New Brunswick, N.J.: Transaction.

Isaacs, H.H. 1967. "A Study of Communications, Crimes and Arrests in a Metropolitan Police Department." Appendix B in the President's Commission on Law Enforcement and Administration of Justice, *Task Force Report: Science and Technology.* Washington, D.C.: U.S. Government Printing Office.

Johnson, N., and D. Healy. 1978. *Felony Investigation Decision Models.* St. Paul, Minn.: Minnesota Statistical Analysis Center.

Kuykendall, J. 1986. "The Municipal Police Detective: An Historical Analysis." *Criminology* 24:1(175-201).

Martin, S., and L.W. Sherman. 1986. "Selective Apprehension: A Police Strategy for Repeat Offenders." *Criminology* 24:155-73.

Moore, M.H. 1992. "Problem-Solving and Community Policing." *Modern Policing.* Edited by Michael Tonry and Norval Morris. Crime and Justice Vol. 15. Chicago: The University of Chicago Press.

Murphy, P.V., and T. Plate. 1977. *Commissioner: A View From the Top of American Law Enforcement.* New York: Simon and Schuster.

Pate, T., R.A. Bowers, and R. Parks. 1976. *Three Approaches to Criminal Apprehension in Kansas City: An Evaluation Report.* Washington, D.C.: Police Foundation.

Peterson, J.L. 1974. *The Utilization of Criminalistics Services by the Police: An Analysis of the Physical Evidence Recovery Process.* Washington, D.C.: U.S. Department of Justice, Law Enforcement Assistance Administration.

Porter, B. 1987. *The Origins of the Vigilant State: The London Metropolitan Police Special Branch Before the First World War.*   London: Weidenfeld and Nicolson.

Schwartz, A.I., and S.N. Clarren. 1977. *The Cincinnati Team Policing Experiment: A Summary Report.* Washington, D.C.: Police Foundation.

Sechrest, L.B., S.O. White, and E.D. Brown (eds). 1979. *The Rehabilitation of Criminal Offenders: Problems and Prospects.* Washington, D.C.: National Academy of Sciences.

Seedman, A.A., and P. Hellman. 1974. *Chief!* New York: Arthur Fields Books.

Sherman, L. 1978. *Scandal and Reform: Controlling Police Corruption.* Berkeley: University of California Press.

_____. 1983. "From Whodunit to Who Does It: Fairness and Target Selection in Deceptive Investigations." *ABSCAM Ethics: Moral Issues and Deception in Law Enforcement.* Edited by Gerald M. Caplan. Washington, D.C.: Police Foundation.

Sherman, L., C. Milton, and T. Kelly. 1973. *Team Policing: Seven Case Studies.* Washington, D.C.: Police Foundation.

Skolnick, J.H. 1966. *Justice Without Trial: Law Enforcement in Democratic Society.* New York: John Wiley and Sons.

Skolnick, J.H., and D.H. Bayley. 1986. *The New Blue Line: Police Innovation in Six American Cities.* New York: Free Press.

Chapter 10

Evaluating Tactical Patrol

Gary W. Cordner

Introduction

This chapter (1) describes a variety of forms of tactical patrol, including evidence on effectiveness; (2) discusses a number of practical and methodological problems that interfere with any attempt to quantify the success or failure of tactical police patrol operations; and (3) suggests techniques that police can use to overcome or alleviate these problems as much as possible, providing several concrete examples. While it can be extremely difficult, and sometimes impossible, to *prove* that a particular police program or strategy *caused* crime to decrease or something else beneficial to happen,[1] it is usually quite feasible to measure what the police did and what happened. This kind of simple, straightforward quantification may not be sufficient to authoritatively prove or disprove a research hypothesis (Sherman 1992a), but it can certainly help police executives decide whether to continue, revise or replace a tactical patrol practice (Goldstein 1990).

Tactical patrol has been out of the programmatic and research limelight over the last 10 to 15 years. More attention has been focused, instead, on community and problem-oriented policing, and on such specific policy issues as domestic violence, use of force and pursuit driving. An exception has been in the area of drug enforcement—new police patrol tactics have been introduced to target drug users, drug sellers, drug markets, and drug-related crime and disorder (see Hayeslip 1989), and the impact of crackdowns and other drug-focused patrol tactics has been studied (see Sherman 1990).

It falls to other chapters in this book to discuss quality measurement related to community policing, problem-oriented policing and drug enforcement, the major concerns of the past decade. Tactical patrol remains important, however, even if it has been out of the limelight lately. Almost all police departments still devote more resources to patrolling than to any other single strategy or tactic. Moreover, since the mid-1970s, police patrol has become less diffuse and more targeted. Today, many police agencies (1) expect their regular patrol officers to engage in directed, aggressive or other types of tactical patrol; and/or (2) assign specialized patrol officers to full-time tactical positions. Any police departments that employ tactical patrol and are serious about continuous improvement and customer satisfaction should want to know how effective their tactical patrol practices are and, therefore, should be concerned about quantifying quality.

Tactical Patrol

Doubts about the efficacy of routine preventive patrol began to increase in the 1970s among both police practitioners and researchers.[2] Following the landmark Kansas City, Mo., Preventive Patrol Experiment (Kelling, Pate, Dieckman, and Brown 1974), which suggested that neither eliminating nor doubling patrol coverage had any significant effects on reported crime, actual victimization, fear of crime, or citizen satisfaction with the police, many administrators began seeking alternatives to their traditional reliance on random visibility and reactive handling of calls for service. Methods that were more directed and more aggressive, employing tactics targeted to address specific problems, became increasingly popular, as did more substantive and prevention-oriented methods (see figure 1). Subsequent research and innovation have advanced our understanding of what works in policing (see Cordner and Hale 1992). We are still a long way, though, from having authoritative knowledge about which specific tactics work best against which types of problems in which kinds of settings.

The Evolution of Tactical Patrol

The evolution of tactical patrol out of the ashes of routine preventive patrol was aided immensely by research studies and accumulated police experience. For example, during a study of field interrogations (FIs) in San Diego in the 1970s, perhaps the first major test of tactical patrol, researchers found that suppressible crime increased significantly (by 39%) in areas where field interrogations were discontinued. Once the FIs were resumed, these same crimes returned to approximately their previous levels (Boydstun 1975). Quite importantly, this apparent FI effect was not simply a mask for an arrest effect, since arrests in the no-FI area actually increased by about 25

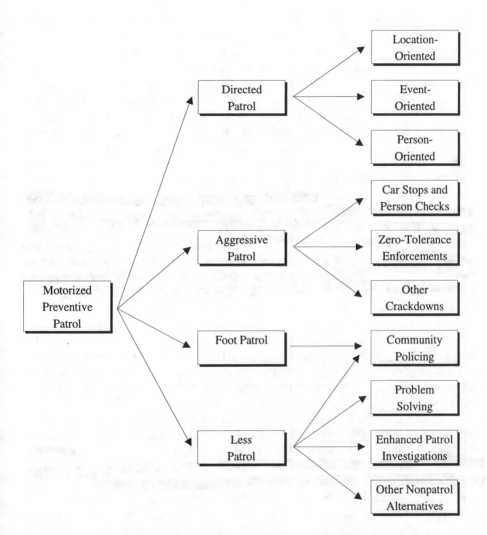

Fig. 1. Recent evolution of police patrol strategies and tactics

percent during the experimental period. In other words, the level of suppressible crime appeared to have been affected by the use or avoidance of field interrogations, independent of the number of arrests made in the area.

During the same time period, the Police Foundation tested the ability of crime analysis to support directed patrol and traditional patrol approaches to criminal apprehension in Kansas City (Pate, Bowers and Parks 1976). Two directed patrol programs were tested: Location-Oriented Patrol (LOP) and Perpetrator-Oriented Patrol (POP). As the names imply, the LOP

188 Evaluating Tactical Patrol

strategy directed patrol officers to pay close attention to *areas* with particularly high crime rates, while the POP strategy was to engage in surveillance of a selected group of suspected *offenders*. Both strategies were intended to increase arrests of suspects in the act of committing crimes, especially robberies and burglaries. To support these efforts, a special Criminal Information Center (CIC) was created within the police department to develop and disseminate suspect information intended to guide the efforts of both special units and a selected group of regular patrol officers.

When evaluators compared the three groups (LOP, POP and regular patrol), they concluded that the specialized units had outperformed the regular patrol officers for almost all comparisons. Results varied between LOP and POP, however. LOP officers were more efficient in terms of hours expended per arrest, they had a greater number of robbery arrests as a percentage of their arrest total, and they had more charges filed for prosecution per arrest. POP officers had a greater percentage of arrests resulting from officer-initiated activities, they arrested suspects with more extensive felony records, and they produced more information for CIC use and dissemination. POP officers also received fewer citizen complaints than their LOP counterparts. Considering all comparisons collectively, the Kansas City staff concluded that, from the standpoint of apprehending suspects, the location-oriented strategy was slightly superior to the perpetrator-oriented strategy, and substantially better than traditional patrol. Providing CIC information to the comparison group of regular officers, though, was found to have significantly increased their arrest rates as well.

In the late 1970s, Pontiac, Mich., experimented with directed patrol as part of the federally funded Integrated Criminal Apprehension Program (Cordner 1981). Over a period of nearly one-and-one-half years, directed patrol responsibilities were shifted from all patrol personnel to a special directed patrol unit, and then back to a divisionwide approach. The study concluded that target crimes could be decreased through the use of directed patrol based on crime analysis. Interestingly, in Pontiac, the most significant impact was achieved during the initial time period, when directed patrol assignments were widely distributed among all patrol officers. Overly large investments of time in limited areas, however, appeared to offer no additional effects—perhaps because of the relatively limited number of "opportunities" in any particular target area for aggressive patrol efforts.

Calling them "crackdowns," Sherman (1990) recently noted that efforts to direct patrol resources to specific problems became quite widespread during the 1980s. Drunk driving, public drug markets, street-walking prostitutes, and even illegal parking have each become targets for various directed patrol responses in programs throughout the country. Still, he notes, some observers remain skeptical about whether these tactical applications of patrol have any real effects; they argue that lasting impacts, especially deterrence, have not yet been demonstrated.

Extending the discussion, Sherman goes on to point out that the debates about tactical patrol fail to make an important distinction among the different kinds of deterrent effects possible. Specifically, most planners fail to separate the *initial* deterrence that might be achieved once a tactical operation is undertaken from the possible *residual* deterrence that may remain following its completion. Additionally, the extent to which such impacts *decay* during or after the effort is seldom considered (Sherman 1990:2). Determining these differential effects, he argues, might suggest new ways of utilizing tactical patrol to maximize effectiveness. An example might help to explain these varying forms of deterrence.

In the 1987 Minneapolis Repeat Call Address Policing (RECAP) Experiment, patrol officers were given directed assignments that called for problem solving at locations that had been identified as requiring frequent police services. The idea was to solve the problems generating the repeat calls, thereby reducing the volume of activity at those addresses. The officers involved in the project were formed into special teams. Each team participated in the repeat call analysis for its location, in the design of tactics for reducing the volume of calls, and in the implementation of the chosen tactics.

After six months, the RECAP officers had considerable successes to show—calls for service at their experimental addresses were reduced significantly. However, during the second six months, officers increasingly found their targets resistant to further improvement. In fact, by the fourth quarter of the project, all of the earlier results had disappeared.

To Sherman, the obvious conclusion was that an operational policy of short-term targeting might offer the best investment of police resources. Instead of attempting to maintain a tactical response over a long period of time, as many departments do, police might

> use their resources more effectively if crackdowns are seen as short-term efforts frequently shifted from area to area or problem to problem. By constantly changing crackdown targets, police may reduce crime more through residual deterrence than through initial deterrence. And by limiting the time period devoted to each target, police might also avoid wasting scarce resources on a decaying initial deterrent effect (Sherman 1990:3).

Varieties of Tactical Patrol

Obviously, any number of variations of tactical patrol are possible. Strategies focused on crime prevention might include directed assignments requiring officers to conduct security surveys, recommend housing repairs and self-protection steps, and encourage and work with citizen groups. Other programs focus more on crime deterrence. As suggested above, short-term tactics intended to raise the perception of risk might be most effective (and efficient). Included might be saturation patrolling, field interrogations, increased traffic enforcement, and other "aggressive" patrol procedures causing increased or high visibility. Still other strategies might concentrate on criminal apprehensions by employing covert and stakeout activities designed not only to deter but also to catch violators while they are committing crimes. Regardless, in each instance, virtually all tactical/directed patrol projects share four common characteristics (Warren, Forst and Estrella 1979):

1. They are proactive and aggressive.
2. Officers use noncommitted time to engage in purposeful activity.
3. Officers have specific instructions directing their activities.
4. These instructions ("directions") are based on thorough analyses of crime data.

Aside from the support it receives from recent research, tactical patrol is attractive to police managers for at least two additional reasons. One is its directed nature—seemingly the very opposite of random patrol, the approach so often criticized for not working. The other is that the strategy is neither officer- nor community-directed, but rather is information- and management-directed. Traditionally, calls for service have dictated the use of a substantial portion of patrol resources, and the use of the remainder of patrol officer time has been left to individual discretion. Tactical patrol strategies are a means for police managers to regain some control over their most significant resource, the time and activities of patrol officers. Careful implementation and evaluation are essential, though, if tactical patrol's goals are to be reached and its potential benefits realized.

As each agency designs its own directed patrol system, police managers have three basic models that they can follow. First, and probably most common, is a *location-focused* approach that attempts to increase the dosage of police presence within a specific geographic area. As with the LOP strategy in Kansas City described earlier, agencies using this approach should first identify, through analysis, those geographic areas that are experiencing problems of particular police interest. Of course, these may include crime or accident problems, frequent demands for police services, order maintenance problems, or areas where fear is especially high. The areas chosen could be as small as a single address or as large as a park, a section of road or highway, an area of several square blocks, or even a patrol beat or sector. Once assigned, the officers responsible for these areas—either routinely or as part of some special unit—then implement tactics selected to match the concerns identified.

One of the most recent studies of this location-based approach to tactical patrol was the Minneapolis Hot Spots Patrol Experiment (Sherman 1992b). In this study, extra police patrol presence (about three hours per day) was applied to 55 call-for-service "hot spots," while 55 other hot spots served as the control group (they received no special attention). The actions patrol officers took at the experimental group hot spots were left to their discretion, and mostly amounted to little more than "sitting on the spot." The results indicated that, among serious crimes, only robberies were reduced at the hot spots that received the extra patrol attention. Overall calls, though, including minor crimes and disorder, decreased 13 percent at the experimental hot spots, as compared with the control group hot spots.

With an *offense-* or *event-specific* approach, the agency seeks to change how it responds to some specific type of crime or incident, either in a target area or throughout the jurisdiction. Examples might include domestic abuse, traffic violations or parking problems. Regular patrol officers or officers in specialized units are provided with pattern and trend data and instructions to make arrests, issue tickets or take other appropriate actions wherever they encounter the problem.

A recent study by Sherman (1994) illustrates a combined location-based and offense-specific directed patrol operation that relied heavily on aggressive patrol tactics. A group of Kansas City patrol officers received special training and were deployed in a target area to focus on gun-related crime. They were encouraged to utilize pedestrian checks and vehicle checks whenever they had sufficient legal justification for such intrusions. The study indicated (1) that these officers conducted many more field interrogations and car stops than the patrol norm, (2) that they located and seized more firearms than other patrol officers and special units, and (3) that incidents of shots fired and gun-involved crimes decreased in the target area but not in a selected comparison area or citywide.

The third basic model of directed patrol is *person-oriented*. As in the Kansas City LOP/POP study, patrol officers may focus their attention on known or suspected offenders, for example, or on other categories of people, such as parolees, probationers or gang members. However, such attention need not necessarily be limited to people who have committed crimes or who create disorder problems—patrol officers could also focus on chronic or likely victims, for example (such as taxi drivers, tourists and pensioners), or on crime "facilitators" such as gun dealers and pool hall hustlers (the distinction between person facilitators and such location facilitators as taverns and all-night convenience stores gets hazy).

Most concentrated person-oriented policing efforts in recent years, or at least those practices that have been carefully evaluated, seem to have been predominantly specialized and investigative rather than genuine patrol functions. Repeat-offender programs, for example, in which the police concentrate attention on high-rate offenders, are typically staffed with plainclothes investigators and located within detective divisions or special operations divisions rather than patrol divisions. Since this variety of individual person-oriented tactical patrol almost always entails considerable surveillance activity and requires officers to follow suspects wherever they go, it is not usually well-suited for uniformed officers, especially those confined to patrol beats.

Distinctions probably need to be made among three types of person-oriented tactics: (1) those that involve constant surveillance of specific individuals, (2) those that involve periodic or episodic observations of specific individuals, and (3) those that encourage officers to pay attention to categories of people. The latter two would seem to be generally more appropriate tactics for patrol officers; the first, for plainclothes personnel. Several studies have examined the efficacy of investigator-based repeat-offender programs, with mixed but promising results (Martin and Sherman 1986; Spelman 1990). The LOP/POP study in Kansas City in the mid-1970s focused on type 2; no systematic evaluations since then have looked at the effectiveness of that type of person-oriented patrol, and none has tested the impact of type 3. Thus, we really do not have much credible evidence at this point, either positive or negative, on the impact of person-oriented *patrol*.

An important implementation question confronting the police manager concerns whether tactical assignments should be given to routine or to specialized patrol units. In general, if the assigned tactic requires only short periods of dedicated time, it may be preferable to use regular patrol units. Field interrogations, vehicle checks, security surveys, and saturation patrols can usually be conducted by regular officers without serious disruptions to their ability to handle other calls for service. As the amount of time needed to complete the directed activity increases, however, so does the desirability of developing specialized patrol or investigative capabilities. This would be a virtual necessity whenever the tactical assignment required an officer's full-time commitment, such as for covert surveillance, decoy operations and stakeouts. Fearing conflicts in communication and grumbling about elite units, some departments have created this capacity by relieving regular patrol officers for single tours of duty for special assignment. Others, however, have established specialized units with their own structure, training and deployment (Gay, Schell and Schack 1977).

Quality Issues

It seems fairly evident that defining and measuring quality in the public sector involves some additional complexities beyond those faced in the private sector. The policing situation is particularly complicated for a host of reasons, including the following:

1. The police have a multifaceted rather than a simple mission.
2. In a diverse and free society, the police must try to satisfy often conflicting interests.
3. The police share responsibility for much of their mission with other government agencies and cultural institutions.
4. The police are significantly restricted in the means that they are allowed to employ in trying to accomplish their complex, conflict-laden mission.
5. The very nature of policing makes "satisfying the customer" often unlikely and sometimes an irrelevant or even improper criterion (Wilson 1968; Goldstein 1977; Manning 1992).

No attempt will be made to fully discuss these important issues in this chapter, but a brief overview of several complications that specifically affect quality measurement related to tactical patrol is offered below.[3]

The Bottom-Line Problem

The easiest situations are those in which a single criterion suffices as the "bottom line" measure of quality and success. It is almost never the case in policing, however, even in the most narrow and compelling situations, that "only one thing matters." A specific police action will usually be judged according to several criteria (Was the officer courteous? Did he or she follow the law? Did he or she handle the matter efficiently? Did he or she actually solve the problem?). A police program, strategy or organizational unit, not to mention the entire department, will be judged by an even wider array of criteria. There is no universally accepted listing of the goals, objectives, performance measures, or criteria by which to evaluate police practices, but the set of objectives and important values for policing presented below illustrates the complexity of the situation.[4]

Objectives of Policing

1. Prevent and control crime and other seriously harmful conduct.
2. Resolve conflicts and maintain reasonable levels of order.
3. Create and maintain a feeling of safety in the community.
4. Aid and assist people who are crime victims, who need protection or who have nowhere else to turn.

5. Facilitate the safe and orderly movement of vehicles and pedestrians.
6. Protect constitutional guarantees and the democratic process of government.
7. Create and maintain public trust and confidence in the police.

Basic Values for Policing

1. Efficiency
2. Legality
3. Accountability
4. Equity
5. Integrity

When our task is to measure and assess the quality of a police tactic, a police tactical unit or the performance of a tactical patrol officer, some of these objectives and values are more likely to be applicable than others. When tactical patrol is directed at crime-related problems, as it most often is, its *effectiveness* will obviously be judged primarily by the accomplishment of the first objective, prevention and control of crime. If the tactic is principally focused on fear of crime, disorder or traffic-related problems, however, the corresponding objective would serve as the primary criterion of success. Some tactics might be focused on more than one kind of problem (e.g., crime and disorder) or might logically be expected to have an impact on more than one of these objectives (e.g., reducing disorder and enhancing feelings of safety), in which case they would be judged by two or more of these criteria.

The last objective listed above, which pertains to police-community relations, is frequently an important consideration when judging the overall quality of tactical patrol. Whenever the police utilize tactics that incorporate frequent intrusions and/or severe levels of enforcement, they run the risk of angering and alienating the citizens who get watched, stopped, ticketed, and/or arrested, as well as other citizens who do not approve of such practices. Of course, there may also be citizens who benefit from and support these kinds of tactics. The net effect on the public's sense of trust and confidence in the police can be positive or negative. The point is that some impact is likely and should therefore be measured.

Three of the basic police values are most likely to be pertinent to judging the quality of tactical patrol: efficiency, legality and equity. Tactical patrol will frequently provide a more efficient use of police resources than its most likely alternative, unfocused preventive patrol, but it may also arouse efficiency concerns, such as when the hours devoted to surveillance of a person become excessive or when a tactical assignment to a geographic area is left in place longer than necessary to achieve the maximum deterrent effect. Legality often becomes a concern with tactical patrol because of privacy, stop-and-frisk and search-and-seizure issues that are unavoidably intertwined with directed and aggressive patrol tactics. Equity is sometimes a key consideration when judging tactical patrol, because of the possibilities of discrimination on the basis of race, ethnicity, age, income, or other characteristics whenever police target people or areas for close attention and enforcement.

The key point is that we invariably have to consider *bottom lines* when judging the quality of a tactical patrol operation. Any particular tactical patrol officer, strategy or unit might have an impact on the police department's accomplishment of two or three objectives and its adherence to two or three basic police values. Often, the impacts are mixed—pros and cons. An aggressive patrol operation in a target area might decrease crime but impair community relations and create some inequitable uses of police authority. Or a directed patrol operation targeted toward risky driving behavior might have modest effects on serious accidents but be very time-consuming and costly, thus raising efficiency concerns. Because of such trade-offs, deciding whether such tactics should be continued, whether their effects represent improvements or declines over previous conditions, and whether they are preferable to other alternatives becomes a complex rather than a simple endeavor.

Effort vs. Outcome

In quantifying the quality of tactical patrol, it is the outcome that we are most interested in—did crime go down, was disorder reduced, were citizens satisfied? It is often important, however, to also quantify the effort applied toward accomplishing such objectives, for several reasons. One is that, in policing, the quality of the effort itself actually matters—whether it was legal and equitable, for example. Another reason is that we need to know what effort was undertaken if we are to learn what works and what does not. Simply knowing that an objective was achieved, without any reliable information about exactly what tactic deserves the credit, fails to help us very much the next time around. Finally, it is not always reasonable to hold the police accountable for accomplishing their objectives, because society's crime and disorder problems are rather intractable and because other agencies and institutions have as much impact on these problems as the police, if not more. Consequently, it is often important to know whether the police are doing the best they can, working as intelligently and as hard as possible, independent of the degree to which they are accomplishing objectives.

Beyond Bean Counting

Although it is important to measure tactical patrol effort as well as outcome, attention should be concentrated on quality as much as possible. If a directed patrol operation is targeted at reckless and risky driving, for example, the number of tickets issued would be a better measure of effort than simply the number of hours devoted to patrol, the number of moving-violation tickets would be better yet, and the number of hazardous-moving-violation tickets even better. A person-oriented tactical operation could be judged by the number or percentage of targeted people arrested, but seriousness of charges placed, length of prior records, prosecutions, and convictions would be even better measures of the quality of the effort applied.

Routine vs. Special Measures

It is always easier and cheaper to measure quality using information routinely collected than to undertake additional data gathering. Unfortunately, some of the most useful kinds of information for judging the quality of tactical patrol are not routinely collected by many police departments. Few police agencies routinely and systematically measure levels of fear of crime, disorder or citizen satisfaction, for example, either jurisdiction-wide or by separate neighborhoods. Nor do they measure the actual level of crime—police departments rely instead on reported crime measures, which are known to underrepresent the total amount of crime and which are unstable, since citizens' propensities to report crime can vary and can be affected by police tactics themselves. A very common and aggravating chain of events occurs when the police implement a new program and then crime seems to increase. What has probably happened is that the new program has encouraged citizens to increase their *reporting* of crime.

Of course, the business of policing is policing, not data gathering for quality measurement. Because increased data collection and special measurements cost money, they are not always feasible. Police departments need to (1) take maximum advantage of the data they routinely collect anyway, (2) look for cost-effective ways to enhance their routine data collection in support of quality measurement, and (3) undertake special measurements when the cost is not prohibitive and the need is substantial enough to warrant the extra effort. An example of the first point would be to use crime, arrest and traffic-ticket data in ways that go beyond mere bean counting, as described above. An example of the second approach would be to use senior-citizen volunteers or college students enrolled in research methods classes to conduct telephone surveys focused on citizens' fear of crime and satisfaction with the police, as several police departments have done.[5] An example of the third method would be to make systematic "compliance" observations of, say, seat belt usage, driving speeds or adherence to stop signs to determine whether tactical patrols are accomplishing their traffic-safety objectives.

Quantifying the Quality of Tactical Patrol

This final section of the chapter offers three specific suggestions for quantifying the quality of tactical patrol: (1) use *specific* measures of effort and outcome, (2) use *multiple* measures, and (3) use *creative* measures. Several examples of each of these suggestions are presented.

Specific Measures

Judgments about the quality of a tactical patrol operation (whether an individual officer, a special program or an organizational unit) should be based on carefully selected, specific measures of effort and outcome. If diffuse, general measures are mistakenly used, the chances are great that real accomplishments will be blurred or even totally obscured. If a person-oriented tactical effort is judged simply on the number of arrests made, for example, it might appear deficient, even if the quality of the arrests (based on convictability, seriousness of offense and/or length of prior record) is extremely high. Similarly, if a tactical patrol focused specifically on robberies is judged by the overall crime rate, it might seem ineffective, even if the rate of robberies declines considerably.

The field interrogation experiment conducted in San Diego (Boydstun 1975) provides a good illustration of the use of a specific outcome measure. In that study, reported Part I "suppressible" crimes were measured, using routine police records. These crimes included robberies, burglaries, auto thefts, thefts from autos, and other Part I crimes reasonably visible from the street, but not assaults or thefts occurring inside homes or businesses. As shown in table 1, such crimes increased substantially in the no-FI beat during the period that field interrogations were halted, and then decreased to "normal" levels once FIs were resumed. Neither a control beat with regular levels of FIs nor a special FI beat with increased levels of field interrogations experienced any significant fluctuations in suppressible crimes throughout the study periods. Quite possibly, this clear-cut demonstration of the impact of field interrogations might have failed had a less specific measure of outcome been utilized.

Table 1

The Impact of Field Interrogations in San Diego

	Part I Suppressible Crimes Monthly Averages		
	Before	During	After
Control	40.9	42.9	38.6
Special FI	57.7	60.2	56.6
No FI	63.1	83.2	63.2

Adapted from Boydstun (1975).

Another illustration can be drawn from the first major study of problem-oriented policing, conducted in Newport News, Va. (Eck and Spelman 1987). One of the POP projects undertaken in Newport News focused on thefts from autos in parking lots, especially shipyard parking lots. The primary response to this problem was directed preventive patrol and directed apprehension-oriented patrol based on careful crime analysis. As shown in figure 2, the results were rather dramatic. Thefts from autos in the downtown area were reduced by more than 50 percent over an extended period of time. Had this tactical effort been judged by the total amount of crime rather than just thefts from autos, however, or if it had been judged on the basis of citywide data rather than target-area data, its impact might have been missed.

One final example of the application of specific measures is provided by the evaluation of tactically-oriented overtime foot patrol in public housing in Lexington, Ky. (Cordner 1994). Because the police instituted these foot patrols largely in response to increased levels of disorder in the public housing sites, one of the measures used was the number of disorderly conduct and drunkenness calls the police department received from the sites. This measure was further refined by calculating the *rate* of such calls per 100 occupied residences. This was particularly important because the number of public housing units "in service" fluctuated substantially during the study period, due to efforts to reduce housing density and renovations of remaining housing units.

As can be seen in figure 3, the trends in the rate of disorderly conduct and drunkenness calls in the three target public housing sites (Bluegrass-

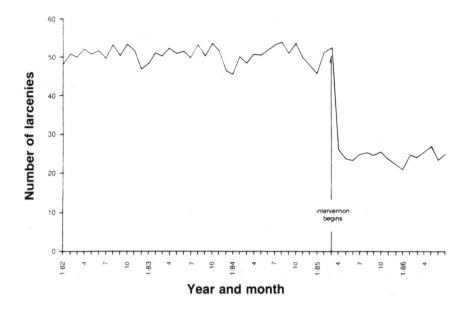

Note: This time-series has been exponentially
        smoothed to account for short-term fluctuations,
        long-term trends and seasonal variations. The
        estimated crime reduction due to police action is
        statistically significant at the .01 level or
        lower. Adapted from Spelman and Eck (1987).

Fig. 2. Larcenies from autos in the downtown area of Newport News, Va.

Aspendale, Charlotte Court and Pimlico Apartments) have been favorable
since 1991, when the overtime foot patrols began. This stands in contrast to
the trend for all calls for service—the overall demand for police services has
increased substantially in two of the three sites.   This once again
demonstrates the importance of specific measures for determining the quality
of tactical patrol operations.

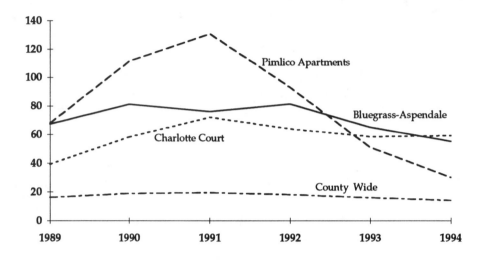

Fig. 3. The impact of overtime foot patrol in Lexington
Disorderly conduct and drunkenness calls per 100 residences: 1989-1994

Multiple Measures

Using multiple measures is critical for judging the quality of tactical patrol, for reasons outlined earlier in this chapter. The police have multiple objectives, they are expected to adhere to multiple values, and their efforts have multiple effects. The bottom line is that policing must be judged by *bottom lines*.

The San Diego field interrogation study, described above, utilized multiple measures as well as specific measures. Besides measuring Part I suppressible crimes, this study used community surveys to detect any effects of the FIs on general attitudes toward the police (there were none), and it measured the number of FI-related citizen complaints to detect any specific effects on police-community relations or police adherence to legality and equity values (again, no effects). These "no impact" findings on community relations and basic police values lent further credence to the conclusion that the effects of field interrogations on crime made an overall beneficial contribution to the quality of policing in San Diego.

An evaluation of directed patrol in Pontiac, Mich. (Cordner 1981), also used multiple measures of effort and outcome. As indicated in table 2, the amount of time devoted to directed patrol; the numbers of car stops, FIs and arrests made; and the changes in *target crimes* in *target areas* were all measured throughout three consecutive study periods. These multiple and specific measures, together with changing conditions during the three study periods, allowed two useful conclusions to be drawn: (1) the beneficial effects of directed patrol on target crimes resulted more from the level of activity undertaken (arrests, stops, etc.) than from the amount of time devoted to the patrols; and (2) the law of diminishing returns seemed to apply to the effects of directed patrol presence and activity—efforts in target areas beyond a certain level did not seem to have much, if any, additional impact on target crimes.

Table 2

The Impact of Directed Patrol in Pontiac

	Period 1	Period 2	Period 3
DP Minutes per Week	3,467	17,045	2,895
Car Stops and FIs per Week	13.4	60.6	3.8
Arrests per Week	1.8	4.4	0.4
Weekly Change in Target Crimes in Target Areas	-9.2	-9.1	-3.5

Adapted from Cordner (1981).

As another example, ongoing evaluations of tactically-oriented overtime foot patrols in public housing in Lexington, Ky., have utilized a variety of measures of crime, fear of crime, disorder, and police-community relations (Cordner 1993, 1994). Since the beginning of the project, in 1991, overall calls for service have gone up, while disorder-related calls have declined; crime victimization and fear of crime have gone down; both positive and negative contacts with the police have increased; and general satisfaction with the police has improved, but more residents also believe that "the police hassle people too much around here." Inevitably, the net result is a mixed bag of pros, cons and unknowns; this mixed picture provides a better reading of the quality of police efforts and outcomes than any one measure could, however.

Creative Measures

It is often possible to devise innovative measures of tactical patrol effort and outcome that are both superior to conventional measures and reasonably efficient to employ. To date, we have probably seen greater use of such creative measures in assessments of crime prevention, community policing and problem solving than in studies of more traditional patrol strategies,[6] but there is no reason not to apply some imagination when trying to quantify the quality of tactical patrol.

As an example, suppose a tactical operation was focused on graffiti and disorder in a target area. It would be relatively easy to "measure" the amount of graffiti in the area before the tactical operation began and at regular intervals thereafter. Similarly, it would not be difficult to systematically count, in specified locations, the number of panhandlers, homeless people, people hanging out on the sidewalk, people sitting in cars, or cars slowly cruising by. The best practice to follow would be, first, to precisely identify the nature of the "disorder" that is considered problematic in the target area, and second, to devise a scheme for measuring it systematically and periodically.

Similarly, if street robberies or panhandling is blamed for scaring shoppers away from a business area, the impact of a tactical operation could be measured not only in terms of the reduced incidence of robbery or the reduced presence of panhandlers, but also in terms of increased numbers of shoppers and increased revenue for businesses. Each of these conditions could be measured without much difficulty, if only a little imagination and initiative were employed.

So-called "compliance rates" provide another creative measure of the impact of tactical patrol operations. As mentioned earlier in this chapter, they apply nicely to many traffic safety situations—such matters as average speeds, adherence to traffic control devices and seat belt usage can be observed unobtrusively and used to monitor the impact of traffic-related efforts. Other compliance rates can be monitored as well: adherence to parking regulations, trash container regulations, subway fare turnstiles, house-numbering laws, drinking-in-public laws, loitering laws, and so forth. Such compliance rates, if monitored regularly, can be used both to measure the effects of tactical operations and to reveal deteriorating conditions in need of attention.

Conclusion

By its very nature, police tactical patrol tends to be more targeted than much of the rest of policing, and therefore more amenable to effort and outcome measurement. Still, such operations are likely to have multiple objectives, to have various intended and unintended effects, and to be held accountable for adherence to several important police values. To "quantify the quality" of tactical patrols, therefore, it is necessary to use multiple measures that are specific and creative. If such measures are employed regularly and systematically, police agencies should be able to refine their tactical patrols, increase customer satisfaction and generally engage in continuous improvement. It would be naive and unrealistic, though, to expect that police tactical patrol in our diverse society could ever please everyone or cease being a source of conflict and controversy.

Notes

[1]For a more extended discussion of methods for evaluating police tactical patrol, see Cordner and Kenney (1991). Also see Eck (1984) concerning police research generally.

[2]This section on tactical patrol is revised and updated from Cordner and Kenney (1991:1-9).

[3]Further discussion of measurement and evaluation issues affecting policing can be found in Cordner and Hale (1992:vii-xii), Sheehan and Cordner (1995:351-383) and Spelman (1988).

[4]These objectives and values are adapted from Goldstein (1977) and Sheehan and Cordner (1995).

[5]Police departments in Rapid City, S.D.; Reno, Nev.; and Tempe, Ariz., are known to have used creative methods such as these to conduct citizen surveys. To meet accreditation requirements and/or to gather data considered important for community policing, many other police agencies have undertaken citizen surveys of one kind or another over the last 10 to 15 years. See Eck (1994).

[6]For examples of creative measures used to evaluate crime prevention, community policing and problem solving, see Clarke (1992) and Rosenbaum (1994).

References

Boydstun, J.E.   1975. *San Diego Field Interrogation: Final Report.* Washington, D.C.: Police Foundation.

Clarke, R.V., ed.   1992. *Situational Crime Prevention: Successful Case Studies.* New York: Harrow and Heston.

Cordner, G.W.   1981. "The Effects of Directed Patrol: A Natural Quasi-Experiment in Pontiac." *Contemporary Issues in Law Enforcement.* Edited by J.J. Fyfe. Beverly Hills, Calif.: Sage.

_____. 1993. "Public Housing Drug Elimination Program II in Lexington, Kentucky: Final Evaluation Report." Richmond, Ky.: Eastern Kentucky University. Mimeo.

_____. 1994. "Public Housing Drug Elimination Program III in Lexington, Kentucky: Final Evaluation Report." Richmond, Ky.: Eastern Kentucky University. Mimeo.

Cordner, G.W., and D.C. Hale, eds. 1992.   *What Works in Policing?: Operations and Administration Examined.* Cincinnati: Anderson.

Cordner, G.W., and D.J. Kenney. N.d.   *Patrol Evaluation Package: Tactical Patrol Evaluation.* Huntsville, Texas: Law Enforcement Management Institute, Sam Houston State University (unpublished).

Eck, J.E. 1984.   *Using Research: A Primer for Law Enforcement Managers.* Washington, D.C.: Police Executive Research Forum.

_____. 1994.   *A Police Guide to Surveying Citizens and Their Environment.* Washington, D.C.: Bureau of Justice Assistance.

Eck, J.E., and W. Spelman.   1987.   *Problem-Solving: Problem-Oriented Policing in Newport News.* Washington, D.C.: Police Executive Research Forum.

Gay, W.G., T.H. Schell, and S. Schack. 1977.   *Improving Patrol Productivity: Volume I—Routine Patrol.* Washington, D.C.: Government Printing Office.

Goldstein, H.   1977.   *Policing a Free Society.* Cambridge, Mass.: Ballinger.

_____. 1990.   *Problem-Oriented Policing.* New York: McGraw-Hill.

Hayeslip, D.W.   1989. "Local-Level Drug Enforcement: New Strategies." *NIJ Reports* 213 (March/April):2-6.

Kelling, G.L., T. Pate, D. Dieckman, and C.E. Brown. 1974. *The Kansas City Preventive Patrol Experiment: A Summary Report.* Washington, D.C.: Police Foundation.

Manning, P.K. 1992. "Economic Rhetoric and Policing Reform." *Criminal Justice Research Bulletin* 7,4. Huntsville, Texas: Sam Houston State University. Reprinted in *Police Forum* 4, 3 (1994):1-8.

Martin, S.E., and L.W. Sherman. 1986. "Selective Apprehension: A Police Strategy for Repeat Offenders." *Criminology* 24, 1 (February):155-173.

Pate, T., R.A. Bowers, and R. Parks. 1976. *Three Approaches to Criminal Apprehension in Kansas City: An Evaluation Report*. Washington, D.C.: Police Foundation.

Rosenbaum, D., ed. 1994. *The Challenge of Community Policing: Testing the Promises*. Thousand Oaks, Calif.: Sage.

Sheehan, R., and G.W. Cordner. 1995. *Police Administration*. 3rd ed. Cincinnati: Anderson.

Sherman, L.W. 1990. "Police Crackdowns: Initial and Residual Deterrence." *Crime and Justice: A Review of Research*. Edited by M. Tonry and N. Morris. Chicago: University of Chicago Press.

_____. 1992a. "Book Review: Problem-Oriented Policing." *Journal of Criminal Law & Criminology* 82, 3:690-707.

_____. 1992b. "Attacking Crime: Policing and Crime Control." *Modern Policing*. Edited by M. Tonry and N. Morris. Chicago: University of Chicago Press.

_____. 1994. "The Kansas City Gun Experiment." *Update* (October). Washington, D.C.: National Institute of Justice.

Spelman, W. 1988. *Beyond Bean Counting: New Approaches for Managing Crime Data*. Washington, D.C.: Police Executive Research Forum.

_____. 1990. *Repeat Offender Programs for Law Enforcement*. Washington, D.C.: Police Executive Research Forum.

Spelman, W., and J.E. Eck. 1987. "Problem-Oriented Policing." *Research in Brief* (January). Washington, D.C.: National Institute of Justice.

Warren, J., M. Forst, and M. Estrella. 1979. "Directed Patrol: An Experiment That Worked." *The Police Chief* (July):48, 49, 78.

Wilson, J.Q.   1968.   "Dilemmas of Police Administration." *Public Administration Review* (September-October):407-417.

Chapter 11

Measuring Police Performance in Public Encounters

Stephen D. Mastrofski

Introduction

Calls for better police performance measures are as regular as the eruptions of the Yellowstone geyser, Old Faithful, but over the years neither researchers nor police seem to have produced results that give enduring satisfaction. The measures once thought to serve so well have been largely discredited. Ratios of officers to population, arrest rates, crime clearances, response times, and crime rates are now thought to be either irrelevant to desired outcomes (such as community peace and safety) or unreliable indicators of those states of affairs. The shift in the progressive movement that surfaced in the 1970s produced a new set of measures by which police might be evaluated: criminal victimizations, fear of crime, citizen confidence in and satisfaction with police. And as this movement crystallized under the rubric of community policing, other measures were added to the wishlists of the reform-minded: number of community "problems" solved, reductions in social disorder and physical decay, reductions in calls for service, amount of citizen "coproductive" and self-help activity (Bayley 1993:15). Despite this ferment, police continue to rely heavily on the traditional indicators of agency and program performance: those things that reflect inputs and activities (what Bayley terms indirect measures) or those outcomes for which data remain readily available (arrests, clearances, response times, and crime rates).

In this essay, I will argue that what is currently fashionable among reformers, as well as what once was, ignores some of the most fundamental aspects of police performance in a democratic society: how police use their authority when they encounter the public. What constitutes "good" and "bad" performance in the exercise of police power is sometimes obvious, but often not, and is consequently the object of contention. That there could be serious debate among lawyers and police experts about whether the Rodney King episode constituted good police work shows how complicated and controversial the matter is. Yet it is absolutely essential to conduct such debates and attempt to formulate criteria for how the police deal with the public in their day-to-day encounters, which constitute perhaps the most frequent, widespread and literally compelling form of human service delivery that local governments provide.

This essay will not resolve these issues, but it will present a framework that may prove useful for future efforts to develop measures of police performance in public encounters. It draws heavily on the work of Egon Bittner and David Bayley, who have argued consistently and persuasively for appraisals of police work focused on how police choose to exercise their powers with the public. I will first comment on the limitations of police performance measures previously and currently in vogue. I will then turn to a discussion of the need for measures that illuminate the core function of our most numerous police (the uniformed street officer): to investigate things that might be awry and to set them aright inasmuch as time and resources permit. Egon Bittner called this peace-keeping service the authoritative intervention in circumstances where "something-ought-not-to-be-happening-about-which-something-ought-to-be-done-NOW!" (Bittner 1974:30). I will then suggest several dimensions of police performance in these situations and some criteria for assessing performance. I will offer some methods for obtaining data on these indicators. I will propose an approach that gives skilled officers the central role in identifying performance criteria, that provides for support from social scientists and other experts, and input from interested citizen groups. It is an approach that will test the capacity of police and police researchers to advance professionalism and increase accountability.

Performance Measurement Then and Now: A Critique

The contemporary police department's system of performance measurement remains substantively rooted in the perspective of the reform wave that was gathering force in the 1930s under the leadership of August Vollmer, J. Edgar Hoover, the Wickersham Commission, and others. More effort is put into recording UCR data (arrests, clearances, reported crime) than any other indicators, and these data also tend to take up more space in annual reports and program evaluations than any other. The value of contraband seized and stolen property recovered is also frequently reported. Even the much-cited average response time, which may reflect on a broader range of services, is often presented as an indication of the department's capacity to apprehend offenders. Although innovations in police performance measurement since the 1970s have gone beyond crime control, this mission is still strongly articulated in crime victimization data and fear-of-crime surveys. Indeed, even though federal community policing initiatives such as "Weed and Seed" are couched in broader terms of improving the general quality of life in neighborhoods by meliorating a wide range of social and physical problems, the success stories are reported in terms of arrests made, drugs and arms seized, and crime rates reduced (U.S. Department of Justice 1992).

The above measures have a number of well-documented technical weaknesses (Whitaker et al. 1982), but they have a more compelling limitation at the policy level. We do not know what contribution the police make to crime control. Although most experts agree that police make an important contribution to the control of crime and disorder, researchers have not provided rigorous studies that indicate that police "control" or heavily influence crime.[1] Many other forces at work in a community or the larger society are believed to account for much of the variance in crime rate (demography, economy, unemployment, social inequality, fashion in family and child-rearing styles, and a variety of social and political forces), and the effects of police, though significant, may be quite marginal by comparison.[2] It makes about as much sense to hold the police accountable for fluctuations in the UCR as it does to hold weathermen accountable for fluctuations in the weather. Of course, Americans care very much about crime, and evaluators should continue to study the contributions police can make to its control, but until the police role in the technology of crime control is better understood, communities would be well-advised to pursue a broader agenda of performance indicators.

Police are expected to perform many other functions besides crime control, and there is growing interest among progressive chiefs today in using performance measures that reflect the broader range of services they provide. These include indicators of order maintenance and control, quality of life in neighborhoods, mobilization of the public to work with the police, and citizen satisfaction with the police. New data collection methods continue to emerge to accommodate the progressives' demand for a broader definition of the police role: fear-of-crime surveys (Pate and Skogan 1985), repeat-calls-for-service analysis (Sherman, Gartin and Buerger 1989), and surveys of physical and social disorder in public spaces (Skogan 1990). Although this ferment in performance indicators is encouraging, these new non-crime measures suffer drawbacks as well. Some are not yet well-established as accurate indicators of that which they are held to represent; calls for service may not be a reliable manifestation of the existence of a problem, and fluctuations in calls for service may bear an unexpected unpredictable relationship to the quality of service delivered. An effective or responsive police activity may produce more, not less, business for the department. Other measures may reflect outcomes of unknown or questionable value. Reducing fear of crime is not an unmitigated good if it results in subjective perceptions of the risk of crime that are considerably divergent from the *objective* risk of victimization (Mastrofski 1988); it could lull some people into a false sense of security. Measures of social and physical disorder are highly subjective; one person's noisy disturbance is another's music. A citizen complainant's assessment of police performance may be more influenced by his or her expectations and preconceptions of police than by the nature of the particular experience (Brandl et al. 1994).

There are, then, many challenges to overcome in developing and interpreting performance measures for the more eclectic vision of the police mission that is emerging under the movement toward community and problem-oriented policing. But the principal limitation of the new measures, as with the crime and enforcement-focused measures that they supplement, is that they ignore aspects of performance that have long been a central concern of Americans: how the police treat them. Crime rates, fear levels and citizen satisfaction—although keenly felt at the personal level—are hard to observe directly. But citizens have little difficulty observing and forming judgments about what officers *do* when they encounter them. It is not at all clear that the public holds the police accountable for the crime rate, but they do hold them accountable for their actions (Mastrofski 1994:401). Police officers, too, give a lot more credence to assessing how officers handle these situations and their immediate, observable consequences. The following section discusses why police-public encounters are key to understanding how police use their authority.

The Importance of Police-Public Encounters

One of the most enduring influences on the shape of policing in Britain and America has been a profound concern for how police exercise their authority with members of the public (Klockars 1985; Miller 1977). The use of uniforms, concentration of resources on the policing of public space in a highly visible manner (preventive patrol), and hierarchical control within the organization have all been enduring features of police organizations that originated as efforts to control police powers. Indeed, Muir has defined the quality of police work (1977:4) precisely in terms of how officers think and behave, not whether crime went down:

A policeman becomes a good policeman to the extent that he develops two virtues. Intellectually, he has to grasp the nature of human suffering. Morally, he has to resolve the contradiction of achieving just ends with coercive means. A patrolman who develops this tragic sense and moral equanimity tends to grow in the job, increasing in confidence, skill, sensitivity, and awareness....Achieving a tragic sense and a moral calm under the threatening circumstances of patrol work depends in part upon developing and enjoyment of talk....[I]n the paradoxical circumstances in which the policeman is forever working, of being powerful but not absolutely powerful, the absence of either the inclination or the opportunity to talk is likely to isolate him from both the public and his fellow officers. This isolation impedes developing a tragic outlook in combination with a moral equanimity about coercion. As a result, he tends increasingly to habits of avoidance, brutality or favoritism.

To place in perspective American society's sensitivity to police performance in the exercise of their authority, consider the impetus for some of the most powerful police reform trends in the United States in the 20th century. The Wickersham Commission was formed in reaction to well-publicized cases of police abuse of their coercive powers, and concern about police treatment of the public was also a driving force behind several blue-ribbon commissions investigating police since the 1960s (Walker 1985). Although these commissions also concerned themselves with enhancing the police's crime control capacity, the push for their creation was occasioned by troubled police-community relations, an outgrowth of apprehensions about the extent to which police treated the public with fairness, civility, attentiveness, and only that level of force necessary to restore the peace.

Although the pronouncements of blue-ribbon commissions are instructive as to the ostensible intentions of top policy makers, they are less valuable for identifying performance goals at the operational level, where the work gets done. At that level, from the perspective of police officers, their goals regarding their encounters with the public are several, they sometimes conflict, and the priority given to each may vary, depending on the officer and the circumstances. Bayley and Bittner (1984) suggest that officers have several such operational goals:

(a) meeting departmental norms,
(b) containing violence and controlling disorder,
(c) preventing crime,
(d) avoiding physical injury to themselves, and
(e) avoiding provoking the public into angry retaliation that threatens their careers.

The list is not exhaustive; other goals might well be added. Although there would be debate about the particulars, it is hard to imagine that a high degree of consensus could not be achieved among police constituencies that these are worthy, appropriate to guide performance measurement.

A significant feature of this list is that all but one of the goals involve outcomes that are observable in the here-and-now of the police-public encounter, not at some future time (Bayley and Bittner 1984). With the exception of preventing crime, the achievement of all these goals can be determined simply by knowing what transpired during the course of the encounter. This knowledge is not quite so easily obtained as one might imagine, but because the impacts are defined in terms of either police actions or consequences that are closely linked in time and space to those actions, encounter-level impacts offer an intriguing opportunity to develop meaningful performance measures. They are meaningful in two ways: (1) the police and public care about them, and (2) the police can be presumed to have the major influence on them, contrary to the case with broader social impact measures.

Unfortunately, police departments do little systematic performance evaluation of how police use their authority when they engage members of the public. Most departments attempt to tally the frequency of police-public encounters (number of "incidents" handled), but they do little to learn what happened during those encounters and to judge the quality of the police work done. They sometimes provide counts of certain actions taken during these encounters, such as arrests, citations and use of force. Virtually all departments mandate reporting arrests and lethal force, but policies about reporting other forms of police coercion are far more variable among American police agencies. A recent nationwide survey of police departments indicated that only 60 percent of municipal agencies required reports of dog attacks, only 36 percent required reports of wrist locks, and 29 percent required reports of handcuffing (Pate and Fridell 1993:68). It is even rarer for departments to make routine determinations of whether various forms of police authority were appropriately exercised. And it is even rarer still to make the results of such reviews available to the public. The same survey of police agencies reported that only 47 percent of municipal departments with over 500 officers published summary information on investigations of citizen complaints of officer misconduct; the number dropped to 21 percent for smaller departments (Pate and Fridell 1993:145). These reports tend to represent the most dramatic forms of police authority; departments rarely monitor and assess the use of other forms, such as searches and interrogations, threats and warnings, counseling, referrals, and other types of assistance. What follows is an attempt to illuminate a more *comprehensive* view of what is involved in assessing police performance in encounters.

Dimensions of Police Performance in Encounters With the Public

What constitutes police "performance" on those occasions when officers encounter the public? Because the nature of those situations varies greatly, it is difficult to provide more than some general performance dimensions applicable to all. The following, drawing heavily on Bayley and Bittner (1984), is a list of general criteria or "dimensions" that are applicable to virtually all police-public encounters:

- violence containment and disorder control,
- problem diagnosis,
- problem resolution,
- citizen response to police,
- people's safety,
- lawfulness of police response, and
- economy in police response.

Not included in the above list and subsequent discussion are measures of the long-term impacts of police action, events that might occur at some time after the encounter has concluded (e.g., offense violations, citizen self-help efforts, participation in community crime prevention programs). Knowing the long-term impact of patrol officer decisions in encounters is an important part of learning what works under what circumstances, but this chapter will focus on only those aspects of performance that can be observed within the context of the police-public encounter.

Violence Containment and Disorder Control

From the police officer's perspective, perhaps the strongest performance imperative in dealing with the public is maintaining order in the situation at hand, something that is necessary for the accomplishment of all other objectives (Bayley and Bittner 1984). Police "take charge" to reduce chaos, obtain information, resolve a problem, and establish citizen respect for police authority, and they can do so in different ways (Sykes and Brent 1980). In the vast majority of situations patrol officers handle, disorder is reduced by the officer's making his or her presence known. But disorder, rebellion or violence occur with sufficient frequency that officers are highly sensitive to threats and potential threats to their control of situations, even seemingly routine ones, such as cold property-crime calls. While it seems reasonable to consider as most challenging those cases where chaos, violence or rebellion are manifest at the outset, it is not entirely clear that these situations are necessarily the most challenging to the officer. Dealing with the uncertainty of the *possible* eruption of disorder, violence or rebellion requires keen observation and astute judgment (Muir 1977:164-168). Thus, different circumstances carry different risks of violence and disorder, and measures of officer performance should take into account not only the extent to which officers deescalate situations from chaos to order, but also the extent to which they prevent the escalation of events to greater levels of disorder and violence during the encounter.

Problem Diagnosis

If keeping the peace is the foremost consideration for police officers, diagnosing the nature of the problem at hand is certainly the most common element of any police intervention into citizens' lives.[3] This is an essential step in the process of resolving the problem, whether it occurs in an instant or takes hours. Police communications personnel screen many calls, but dispatched officers are the principal means by which the department and local government generally decide whether there is a "problem" that needs attention, and if so, whose (Prottas 1978). New police officers quickly learn that the dispatcher's description of the nature of a problem is highly provisional and subject to redefinition at the scene (Gilsinan 1989; Manning 1988). Indeed, officers understand that outward appearances are deceiving, which is the reason that their inquiries must go beyond accepting the obvious without validation. There are bureaucratic routines for many types of inquiries, and these are institutionalized in procedural manuals and various official forms that structure the information provided to the department. But these forms fail to capture much of what constitutes performance in conducting such inquiries—at least from the perspective of policing as a craft and as experienced by the public.

From the police perspective, good investigative performance means producing a diagnosis that accurately characterizes the situation at hand.[4] For some situations, the most relevant criteria are legal, evidentiary concerns: Is this a burglary, larceny or insurance fraud? Is this a minor spat between spouses, or the prelude to violence? Often, however, the law is not the issue. Is this a group of boisterous but harmless juveniles, or is this a significant disturbance of public order on the street corner?

The citizens present may also be interested in obtaining the most accurate police diagnosis of the problem, although often the dominant criterion for accuracy is agreement with their *own* reading of the situation. Indeed, citizens often jockey with each other and the police to establish their own interpretation as the one that ultimately prevails with police. Even when citizens are willing to defer to the officer's "professional" judgment about the nature of the problem, they are often concerned about the thoroughness of the officer's inquiry, particularly if they cast themselves in the role of victim, complainant or service recipient. The more thorough the inquiry seems to be, the greater the officer's concern for the citizen's problem, and therefore, the better the service.

From the police perspective, however, thoroughness carries a price (the officer's time), and so the degree of investigative effort appropriate depends upon such things as the importance of the matter and the degree to which the police may be able to do anything about it. It is therefore a misallocation of resources when an officer spends too much time investigating a minor problem, just as it is when an officer spends too little time on a serious matter. Any tension between the citizen's personal expectations and the officer's professional judgment can be resolved in a number of ways. One is simply to do things that impress the citizen with the degree of effort without actually expending much (e.g., cursorily searching an area, dusting for a few fingerprints, asking questions or taking notes when the citizen offers information). The other is to attempt to adjust the citizen's expectations (describing routine department procedure, describing more pressing matters that require the officer's attention, explaining the law).

Despite the critical diagnostic, gatekeeping role that patrol officers play, police departments do very little to assess the quality of performance. The accuracy of the officer's diagnosis has the greatest chance of being double-checked if he or she decides to give the situation an official crime designation, so that some police specialist may conduct a follow-up investigation. Often, however, such follow-ups are cursory and are themselves heavily determined by the information the patrol officer provides. Further, the follow-up investigator's assessment of the officer's diagnosis is often not communicated to anyone, much less systematically recorded and analyzed. Another occasion for validating the officer's diagnostic performance—occurring much less frequently—is when a citizen files a complaint about the officer's performance, which may occasion at least a cursory follow-up by the officer's sergeant, or internal affairs if the matter is deemed serious. When thoroughness is the issue, the department hierarchy generally discounts most complaints as unrealistic, although situations that appear truly egregious may be accorded a thorough investigation of their own. What is most remarkable about the agency's inattention to police performance of the diagnostic function is that it shapes so many other aspects of police work. It affects the official rate of crime, the workload of specialist units and the allocation of patrol resources—not to mention the prospects for a satisfactory resolution of the situation at hand.

Problem Resolution

Police are expected to provide a definitive resolution in nearly every encounter they have with the public.[5] In many instances, this is no more than establishing that there is no problem worthy of further attention.[6] Probably the most commonly recorded resolution of a problem is merely to make an official record that places it in one of the department's recognized problem categories (appearing on an incident report). Other official dispositions that are usually reported are making an arrest, using lethal force and releasing individuals to the custody of other government agencies (e.g., mental health, detoxification facility, homeless shelter). For the vast majority of police-public encounters, there is either no official record whatsoever, or only the vaguest indication of police action ("advised," "referred," "warned"). This is remarkable, because the dispositional choices available to officers are many, and those often regarded as "informal" and unworthy of detailed documentation are the most numerous (Bayley 1986; Bayley and Bittner 1984). Further, they offer very favorable prospects for more effective problem solving from the perspective of progressive reformers (Goldstein 1990:135). Determining the long-term effects of selecting one disposition or tactical choice over another is essential for validating craft knowledge about what works and under what circumstances (Bayley and Bittner 1984), yet departments are data-blind as to how police actually resolve most situations.

Short of a scientifically rigorous evaluation of the impact of various tactics, police have other criteria available to judge the suitability of a disposition, most of which are seldom applied systematically to police-public encounters. One set of criteria emanates from department "norms" (Bayley and Bittner 1984). Written policies may tell officers what dispositions are appropriate, inappropriate, preferred, or mandated under given conditions. Or the pronouncements of supervisors may similarly communicate such information. In a more general sense, the attention paid by the hierarchy to productivity statistics and the actions listed on report forms also structures the exercise of discretion in resolving problems. The law, of course, may also provide some indication as to the choice of disposition in cases where criminality or certain civil status (e.g., mental health, code violations) is in question—usually in terms of whether and how to stop, arrest, search and seize, and use force. Finally, certain informal craft norms about what constitutes good "workmanship" may be relevant regarding how to handle certain kinds of situations (Bittner 1983). The extent to which there is consensus about these norms may well have been overstated in early police ethnographies (Rubinstein 1973; Skolnick 1966; Westley 1970), and competing decision rules may coexist uneasily in such a way as to produce moral conflict for officers who carefully consider them (Muir 1977:192). It is undoubtedly too much to expect that we could develop a set of criteria about the selection of disposition that is comprehensive, agreed-on and practical. Nonetheless, it may be possible for a department to focus on a particular type of problem (e.g., nonfelony domestic dispute) and articulate criteria that would allow the department to assess officer performance in one or more aspects.

Citizen Response to Police

Police in a democratic society must be concerned with how the public reacts, for they are ultimately accountable to that public and rely on it to do their work and retain institutional legitimacy. Researchers have noted how "reactive" American police are to the wishes of the citizens they encounter (Reiss 1971a; Black 1980). Police are public servants and are therefore responsible for pleasing their clientele, at least some of whom are present and directly affected by what the police do in face-to-face interactions. And community policing reformers now make it fashionable to adhere to the well-documented claim that the effective accomplishment of crime control and order maintenance tasks relies heavily on citizen compliance, cooperation and participation—whether it is providing information, testifying in court, or exercising control over oneself or others (sometimes called "coproduction" of police services). But we do not expect police to please all citizens all of the time. Justice sometimes requires that police compel people to do things they would rather not do, or that police take sides (creating losers as well as winners) (Bittner 1970). And resource limitations often mean that police must establish priorities and give some citizens less attention and effort than they feel they deserve. The art in police work under these circumstances is to minimize citizens' bad feelings and resistance to police, and if possible, secure their respect for officers doing a job that has to be done: for example, the arrest accomplished with a minimum of force, which allows the suspect to retain his or her dignity, which shows consideration for the person's feelings, which eases anxiety about what will happen next.

From the police perspective, the standard for success with citizens depends on the exigencies of the situation. It is a simple, straightforward matter to satisfy a citizen's request for traffic directions; it is seldom a simple, straightforward matter to satisfy all parties to a domestic dispute. In circumstances where the officer is responding to the requests of someone merely asking the state to help him or her—and the officer need not contend with the conflicting demands or interests of some other party present—then the criterion for success is the citizen's satisfaction with or acceptance of the police response, along with a willingness to do whatever is necessary to help. In the vast majority of such cases, the police department has bureaucratic routines (e.g., taking a report), which readily satisfy the citizen. But in some of these cases, the art of policing is in adjusting citizens' expectations, as in when they expect an intensive crime scene forensics analysis, when in fact its prospects are very poor. In other cases, it is finding a creative resolution of the problem, which may involve nonroutine police responses or even the mobilization of other agencies or community resources.

When officers confront conflicting interests in an encounter, say between a complainant and the alleged wrongdoer, then the police task is more complicated. One of the purposes of the officer's diagnosis of the situation is to determine the relative merits of the requests each party is making of police (e.g., "arrest this man" vs. "don't arrest me"). If the officer determines that there is a sufficiently large difference in the moral or legal status of such disputants, from the officer's perspective, one person becomes the client and the other the client's problem. The *client's* satisfaction becomes primary, while the *problem's* satisfaction largely disappears as the officer's concern, except insofar as the officer wishes to minimize his or her resistance and maximize cooperation and compliance. When the only citizen present is a suspected wrongdoer (e.g., in a traffic violation stop), the client becomes the state, and the only issue is whether and what sort of "problem status" the citizen will be assigned.

There are also certain circumstances in which the police officer is the supplicant, asking for assistance in a matter in which the citizen has little or no direct personal interest—other than that of a responsible community member who is entreated to act for the greater good of the neighborhood or city. When police ask citizens to watch for crime or suspicious activity and report it to them, or to provide information about their friends and acquaintances, citizens are placed in the role of informant. Police have long encouraged informants to perceive a personal stake in their cooperation (through coercive threats, promises of leniency, financial rewards, and favors), but community policing doctrine encourages officers to foster more public-spiritedness in citizens as the motivation for such cooperation (Rosenbaum 1988). Police regard such encounters as successful when they do in fact obtain the desired information or other cooperation from citizens.

What citizen participants want from police depends on the role in which they and the police cast them. Clients want results: the retrieval of property, the apprehension or punishment of a wrongdoer, the reestablishment of order, the authoritative settlement of a disagreement (in their favor), and so on. People assigned a "problem" status want a hearing of their side of the story, leniency or some other consideration.∘ Informants, at least those motivated by public-spiritedness, want appreciation from the officer—and sometimes assurances that they will be protected from retribution from citizens about whom they are informing. *All* types of citizens care about the officer's effort, concern and respect in dealing with them—the equivalent of the physician's "bedside manner" or demeanor. Perceived deficiencies in the officer's "bedside manner" are in fact the most common cause of citizens' complaints about police officers to higher or external authorities (Reiss 1968).

Police performance measurement in this dimension can be multifaceted. One might attempt to observe the extent to which police undertake actions that are routinely desired by members of the public they encounter.

Evaluators most often resort to surveying the citizen to determine his or her level of satisfaction with the police response. Usually, however, such surveys fail to determine what in particular pleased or displeased the citizen. Did the officer fulfill the citizen's expressed requests? Did the officer display a civil, caring demeanor? Was the officer thorough? To what extent was the problem *solved*—from the *citizen's* perspective? In fact, it is conceivable that officers might in some circumstances undertake all of the above behaviors and still fail to produce a positive citizen assessment. Recent research shows that citizens' assessments of police performance in particular situations are far more heavily influenced by their general attitudinal predispositions about police than are subsequent general attitudes influenced by police performance in particular situations (Brandl et al. 1994). Until we learn more about the links between police actions and citizens' assessments of those actions, evaluators would be well-advised to consider *both* objective and subjective indicators of police responsiveness. From the officer's perspective, however, the immediate impact of his or her dealings with citizens is readily observed in the extent to which citizens are deferent, compliant and cooperative, matters that the officer or an objective third-party observer might note.

People's Safety

Police and public both place a high priority on the protection of people, which is quite often the underlying concern in police involvement in a situation. However, even when the manifest problem in the situation is not a threat to life, such protection is of paramount importance. Much police training concentrates on using equipment and tactics to minimize the threats to officers' personal safety while they are engaged in traffic stops, resolving disputes, transporting suspects, handling accidents, and dealing with other potentially life-threatening situations (Bayley and Bittner 1984). Professional and craft standards, as well as the law, stress minimizing the threats to personal safety that come from police actions toward the public (Bittner 1970; Muir 1977). Economy in the use of lethal and less-than-lethal force is highly prized—using only that force that is reasonably necessary and proportional to the accomplishment of worthy ends (Klockars 1980). However, police determinations of what is reasonable and necessary force may differ from the general public's. Common examples are the tendency of police to gather in large numbers when there is a *possibility* of violence and the tendency to "gang up" on the violent citizen, something that seems like "overkill" for officers who outnumber, outweigh and outweapon the object of their physical attentions. Yet such shows of force are intended to deter the potentially rebellious, and failing that, to control them with the least physical risk to both officers and citizens. The highly skilled officer learns how to avoid "jacking up" a situation unnecessarily but sees the merit in *initiating* force in a preventive fashion, one that sufficiently exceeds the degree of force that threatening citizens are willing to use against them or others. Such officers may appear to be using unnecessary force when they are, in fact, attempting to avoid even higher levels of violence (Bayley and Bittner 1984).

The bottom line in this dimension of police performance is to minimize physical injury to self and others. It is relatively easy to measure the extent of injury police and citizens experience during encounters. What is difficult is judging whether, under those circumstances, the level of injury sustained was reasonable. From a craft perspective, the absence of injury to police and public is not an entirely useful measure of good performance, since the absence of such injury may be pure dumb luck if an officer failed to take proper precautions. Ironically, police departments require extensive documentation of incidents where someone was significantly injured, but they virtually ignore those situations where there was potential for violence that was never realized. By looking only for trouble, the departments fail to acknowledge and learn from the many instances when officers perform well, and they also fail to learn about those situations where, by failing to act with sufficient force, the officer increased the risks to him- or herself and others. There is undoubtedly some degree of risk of violence and injury in *any* police-citizen encounter, but it would be impractical to require a detailed accounting of all such occasions. A feasible alternative, however, is to obtain sufficient information to judge safety matters in those types of situations that have a heightened likelihood of violence erupting: when suspects are searched or arrested, when citizens are in a highly agitated emotional state, and when officers are dealing with people known to be violent.[7]

Lawfulness of Police Response

An important source of the legitimacy of police actions in America is the perception that they conform to the requirements of law. Most officers accept this as desirable, or at least necessary to the accomplishment of other objectives, such as securing convictions and avoiding disciplinary action and civil suits. They have also learned that, despite the profusion of substantive and procedural criminal law in the last 30 years, the law leaves officers tremendous leeway in most circumstances (Walker 1993). For the majority of police-public encounters (those dealing with noncrime matters), the law is virtually silent on what the officer should or must do. Even in crime incidents (usually those involving suspects), the law admits a diversity of interpretations about its general meaning or how it applies to the case at hand.

Nonetheless, a significant, if relatively small, portion of the police workload is routinely reviewed for the lawfulness of police practice. This may be done to some extent within the police department by supervisors who review their subordinates' reports, but the ultimate arbiter of lawfulness is the court system: judges, defense attorneys and (especially) prosecutors. Of course, many police actions targeted by the law (stops, interrogations, arrests, searches, seizures) are never reviewed in court because they are not officially reported (either because the officer had no intention of seeking prosecution in the first place or because the officer anticipated that the case would not survive legal scrutiny). Of those that are reported, only a small proportion receive anything more than a cursory legal review, due to the predominance of both formal and informal court procedures of a summary nature (e.g., plea bargaining). Of those cases that receive some legal review, at least by a prosecutor, neither police nor courts maintain tallies that would provide insight into the legal adequacy of police work. Despite the highly selective nature of this sample, this represents an unfortunate missed opportunity, since those competent to make legal judgments about such cases have indeed made those judgments and have, in many instances, recorded them.

Economy in Police Response

In addition to legal constraints, patrol officers operate under resource constraints as well. The demands for police service often outstrip the availability of officers to respond, and even when they do not, the police feel compelled to maintain a certain degree of "slack" to be prepared to respond rapidly to serious emergencies (Reiss 1971a). Police managers are under pressure of budgetary limitations and daily deal with demands for efficient service delivery (minimizing the resources used to achieve acceptable levels of service). They may attempt to deal with the demand for efficiency by various load-shedding and workload-smoothing devices, called differential police responses (Worden and Mastrofski 1992; also see chapter 8). Patrol officers experience this at the tactical level as pressure for economy or thrift in using their time—to handle incidents quickly and return to "in-service" status, available to take the next call. Management also exerts pressure to avoid unnecessary police "swarming" at certain calls (those that are exciting, interesting or may require additional presence to handle or prevent violence and disorder). At the informal level, there is also considerable workgroup pressure for officers to efficiently handle the public (Muir 1977:95; Rubinstein 1973; Van Maanen 1974). Officers are expected to handle the "load" on their assigned beat, or at least not to slack off so that others must handle their work. That means not taking too much "personal" time, handling routine calls within acceptable time periods, and calling for assistance only when situations warrant.

Other things being equal, which they rarely are, tactical economy is fairly easy to measure: it is the amount of police time devoted to a given encounter.[8] Thus, an officer who satisfactorily completes a traffic stop in five minutes is twice as thrifty as one who completes the stop in 10. An officer who handles a neighbor dispute by him- or herself is about twice as efficient as one who summons a backup officer. As with the other elements of performance, the devil is in the details. The resource commitment necessary for a good, or at least satisfactory, job relies heavily on many considerations. Does the traffic offender have outstanding warrants? Is he or she argumentative? Does he or she appear to be intoxicated? Does he or she require some special assistance? Is the location of the stop in a "dangerous" part of town?

The challenges of creating a sound basis for the comparison of police time expenditures during encounters are considerable, since the comparison factors are many, and compelling differences on any distinguishing characteristic may be subtle. The creation of hard-and-fast "standards" for handling a given type of situation will most certainly make officers chafe, and this will probably do as much to engender "creative" report writing (to justify time spent) as to provide a reliable standard for comparison. Nonetheless, officers *are* evaluated by their supervisors and peers on their tactical efficiency; introducing more systematic measurement should contribute to more reliable information about officer performance and generate new knowledge about the resource requirements for different types of situations.

The Complexity of Performance Priorities

Although not exhaustive, the above list of performance dimensions illustrates the difficulty of relying upon a single, summative measure of police performance in encounters. Police not only must be technically proficient, but they must also set priorities among the many and often conflicting standards that are applied to their work (Bayley and Bittner 1984; Muir 1977:192). Officers must maintain order, but they must be lawful. Thus, running a suspected drug dealer off a street corner may be the most effective and efficient way to protect that corner on a busy workshift, but it may also violate the suspect's right to be there—absent sufficient evidence to make an arrest. Or a police response may satisfy the requirements of law and yet be judged an unsatisfactory resolution of the problem. The correct diagnosis of a problem and an appropriate resolution may take time, yet the demands of economy call for expediency. Those actions that would most please a complainant are not necessarily legal, economical or effective.

Ethnographers have noted that street-level officers resent and invalidate any attempt to assess their performance, unless the evaluator is a skilled police officer also present. But that is probably not their strongest objection. It is, rather, that authorities (both inside and outside the department) are unable to provide workable performance priorities *a priori* (Brown 1981). Instead, managers review police performance only when things go awry and establish priorities *ex post facto*. To the officer, management seems to emphasize as the highest priority whatever aspect the officer gave the lowest. Thus, the officer who spends a great deal of time quelling a domestic dispute is chastised for being inefficient. The officer who clears the street corner of loitering juveniles is called on the carpet because the parents complain of illegal harassment. And the officer who is lenient with noisy partyers is the object of a neighbor's complaint that the police are not taking seriously the neighborhood's need for peace and quiet. Although it sometimes produces unjust or ineffective results, officers generally welcome a serious effort by department leadership to make priorities explicit—largely because it reduces their vulnerability to arbitrary performance evaluations after the fact. Developing systematic performance measures at the encounter level *without* strong leadership that establishes priorities through policy mandates, guidelines and training will doom the endeavor to tremendous rank-and-file resistance. Without such leadership, performance measurement will be viewed as another way to increase officer vulnerability without any appreciable benefit to those whose work is being assessed.

Data Collection on Encounter-Level Performance

Data on police officers' encounters with the public may be obtained in a variety of ways. The choice of method depends on the performance aspects of interest, the degree of detail required and the resources available. I will briefly discuss five different data collection approaches: officers' self-reports, reports of citizen participants, evaluations by other human service professionals who have occasion for routine review of police work, third-party indirect (video) observation, and third-party direct observation.

Officers' Self-Reports

Police departments require officers to report the features of many types of encounters and to indicate how they handled them. These include calls-for-service records; incident, citation and arrest reports; and detailed reports of special actions and situations (use of force, evidence obtained, referrals, domestic disputes). The principal benefits of data taken from these reports are that they cover a wide variety of situations and are part of the existing police routine, thus being relatively inexpensive for performance measurement purposes. Their principal drawbacks are that there are still a large number of encounters that are not covered by these reports, and their content relies on the very people who are being evaluated, calling into question the comprehensiveness and accuracy of data. The natural bias will be to exclude unfavorable information.

Departments can do a number of things to improve the quality and quantity of data available from these records. They can require documentation of all or most contacts with the public (Reiss 1971a:205). Records can be modified to require officers to provide information needed to assess performance. This means obtaining information on the officer's actions, the observable consequences of those actions, and the aspects of the situation that justify the response chosen. In some cases, this will mean providing more meaningful characterizations of what the officer did than the vague, uninformative options that are typically available. Because the possibilities of deceptive and inaccurate reports are not insignificant, departments can randomly audit a small sample of these reports via follow-up interviews with those citizens who were present. Finally, the department can ensure that performance-relevant data are routinely entered in a computer-readable format to facilitate subsequent analysis.

Reports of Citizen Participants

Follow-up customer surveys are a routine practice in many private businesses. Despite recommendations that this become a routine *police* practice (Mastrofski 1981; Parks 1982), it does not seem to have become widely practiced in the United States. There are a number of good reasons: cost, reluctance of citizens, and reliability of their responses.

Surveying citizens can be costly. The cost may be reduced by requiring the officer to provide each citizen with a brief questionnaire and postage-paid envelope at the conclusion of the encounter. Of course, officers may intentionally or unintentionally fail to offer the questionnaire; some citizens may be reluctant to complete it (with candor) for fear of officer retaliation; and if the department attempts to be comprehensive, surveying all or most citizens involved in calls-for-service incidents, then the printing, mailing and data entry costs will be substantial indeed. Resorting to follow-up telephone or in-person surveys by someone other than the police may help allay the respondent's concerns about confidentiality, but these methods are even more expensive. And finally, some citizens (e.g., the victims of violent crime) may find participation in such a survey to be traumatic.

The best resolution to the cost problem is to focus the survey on a particular type of problem or respondent and then draw a representative sample, rather than attempt to capture responses from all possible cases of interest. Resources are better spent on obtaining a representative sample than a comprehensive one. The field of survey research has well-established techniques to accomplish this (Dillman 1978). Focusing on a narrow range of respondents will also allow the surveyor to gear the method of respondent contact and survey questions to the likely concerns of the respondents and the performance issues of concern to the department. Thus, it is not inconceivable that a carefully planned survey could be conducted on even so sensitive a matter as how police respond to reports of rape.

The accuracy of citizen accounts of their contacts with police is a major consideration, since the citizens, like the police, are interested parties. In general, the higher the stakes (e.g., seriousness of the incident) and the higher the citizen's emotional state during the encounter, the greater the likelihood of a biased account of what happened. Nonetheless, there is evidence to suggest that follow-up telephone surveys of citizens can render citizen-reported accounts that closely match those of disinterested researchers who were also present at the scene (Parks 1982).

Evaluations by Other Professionals

There are occasions when the work that police do in encounters is reviewed as a matter of routine by other professionals to whom police refer cases and clients. I have already mentioned the role that prosecutors play in reviewing the legal aspects of police work. Others include professionals in health, mental health, social welfare, and insurance companies. The concerns of these people tend to be quite focused, but they offer an opportunity to learn something useful about police performance relevant to their narrow ranges of interest. For example, paramedics and hospital emergency room personnel might be able to tell us something about police performance in the medical emergencies referred to them. The coroner and crime laboratory technicians might be able to tell us something about the handling of evidence at the crime scene.

There are at least three drawbacks to using other, related professionals to gather performance data on police. First, these professionals are highly specialized, having a range of interests and competencies much narrower than that of the police. A prosecutor neither cares nor knows much about the economy of a police response or whether citizens' needs were met. The prosecutor's concern is the extent to which the police actions are supported by law. Second, the standards that the professionals apply in the narrow range of cases that interest them may not be the most appropriate for police. For example, some have measured police performance by computing the percentage of arrests that result in convictions (Petersilia, Abrahamse and Wilson 1990), but even from a purely legal perspective, probable cause—not reasonable doubt—is the appropriate standard for the police officer at the scene. Third, since the police themselves decide which of their encounters will be referred to other professionals, any sample so drawn will have biases that are hard to determine.

Video Recording

Despite the proliferation of television programs that use videotaped encounters, and despite the highly publicized use of third-party citizen videotaped material, systematic video recording of encounters is done mostly by the police. Some departments routinely videotape certain police-public encounters, such as traffic stops, drunk-driving sobriety tests at the station, and in-custody interrogation at the station. Videotaping is done to establish both evidence and that the police followed proper legal procedures. These tapes can also be used to assess a wide range of other performance considerations. They provide a tremendous amount of detail largely unfiltered by the intermediary observer's interpretation. Subtleties such as tone of voice and body position are captured, and the tapes can be replayed, slowed and thus carefully examined. They would seem to be especially valuable for recording many features of the situation that would or would not justify actions taken by the officer at the scene.

Videotaping encounters has several drawbacks, too. It is costly, requiring special equipment and, sometimes, an operator. Although it is a rich source of information, the camera nonetheless is selective about the focus of its attention. Officers may react to its presence and thus adjust their behavior to present or appear to present the desired performance. Citizens, too, may react to the camera's presence, and in some cases it could hinder police work. And if the person who is being evaluated also controls the camera's operation and the custody of the film, then the comprehensiveness and integrity of the material are an issue. The film provides no indication of what transpired before or after the period recorded and, at best, constitutes an incomplete record of events.

More experimentation with video recording of police-citizen encounters would seem warranted, especially with third-party camera operators. It may be that officers become acclimated to the camera's presence after a while, and the control of the filming by a disinterested third party reduces the threats to the integrity of the material. Videotaping may be most cost-effective when the activity of interest occurs with some degree of predictability in time or location, thus permitting the strategic location of the camera. If, for example, a department wished to assess the policing of a street corner drug-retail hot spot, it could film for extended periods the activities occurring at that corner, concentrating on what happens when the police are present. Or, if the department were interested in assessing the impact of its domestic violence training, it could send out a camera operator with a sample of officers working at locations and times of frequent domestic disputes.

Third-Party Direct Observation

Since the 1960s, social scientists have used ride-along researchers to make systematic observations of police-citizen encounters. Researchers take brief notes in the field and then later write detailed reports and code them for statistical analysis. These data have been used mostly for basic research about the nature of police work and what influences police behavior. But the data could also be used to assess performance. Trained observers can obtain much information about the circumstances of the encounter, the characteristics of participants, and the course of events. Although their presence may cause officers and citizens to alter their behavior, it is less intrusive than a video camera and less influential than many assume, once officers have become acclimated to the ride-along (Mastrofski and Parks 1990; Reiss 1971b). Further, if the researchers offer the observed officers confidentiality, such assurances will further reduce officer reactivity to the observation. This requires a large enough sample of officers to make such a guarantee meaningful, however. Finally, the researchers can make some assessment as to the extent to which officers and citizens were affected by their presence—and in what way.

Using trained third-party observers undoubtedly provides the richest, most comprehensive data on police performance of any of the methods discussed. Its major drawback is its cost. Conducting the observations and recording them are labor-intensive, requiring considerable skill from the researcher.[9] Quality control, to ensure the accuracy of data, requires considerable effort for this technique. University students are often used because their skill level is high and because they sometimes collect the data as part of their course requirements, thus greatly diminishing the cost. For the types of police-public encounters that are relatively rare and highly unpredictable as to time and location (e.g., police use of force), this method is not very cost-effective, since a great deal of observation time must be expended to capture a sufficient number of such incidents. The more frequent and predictable the type of encounter of interest, the more cost-effective this method.

Given the cost and complexity of conducting this kind of research, police departments would be well-advised to work with universities or other research organizations if they wish to use this data collection method. There is a small literature describing this method, its limitations and its potentialities, which may be drawn upon to design instruments, draw samples, train researchers, and plan logistics (Bayley 1986; Mastrofski and Parks 1990; McCall 1975; Reiss 1971b; Sykes and Brent 1983).

Developing Criteria, Designing Instruments and Interpreting Data

Performance measurement is usually considered the responsibility of police management, and many texts suggest that defining performance criteria is the job of top administrators, leaving the creation of measures and the collection of data to technical experts—social scientists who worry about validity and reliability (Mastrofski and Wadman 1991). Despite the desirability of having management-generated policies to structure police discretion (Walker 1993), the limitations of administrative rule-making are apparent (Mastrofski 1994). Not the least of these is the absence of knowledge about what actually works in the field, for whom and under what conditions. Such knowledge is essential for meaningful performance measurement. Bayley and Bittner (1984) argue that the best opportunity for obtaining this knowledge rests in developing a close working relationship between those who are the best at exercising the craft of police work and social scientists, who have the skill to submit the craftsmen's claims to systematic empirical tests. Theirs is the premise on which the following suggestions are made.

There is no aspect of the police craft richer in experiential learning and lore than how to deal with the public in encounters. However, police administrators ignore this important knowledge base when designing performance measures—whether for individual officers or for department units or programs. Social scientists, too, tend to ignore the craft knowledge of police work as framework for their studies. The spouse abuse experimental studies of the 1980s compared the impact of several possible responses to misdemeanor domestic violence incidents without drawing upon experienced officers highly regarded for their ability to deal with these situations effectively. Had they done so, they might have been able to test arrest and nonarrest strategies that had a much greater probability of success than those social scientists designed (Sherman 1992c:263; Mastrofski and Uchida 1993).

How might police craft expertise be put to better use in the development of performance measures? First, one must be able to identify who the highly skilled officers are—the master craftsmen. Bayley and Garofalo (1989) found by surveying officers that a high degree of consensus exists among them about who those people are in their department. This may vary with the type of situation, since officers often develop special interest and expertise in certain types of encounters: domestic disputes, traffic stops, traffic accidents, drunk driving, juveniles, derelicts, medical emergencies, traumatized crime victims, and so on. Even if there is consensus about who is good at these things, it remains to be demonstrated whether there is consensus among the craft experts about what constitutes good performance (Bayley and Bittner 1984). Indeed, in a pilot test I conducted with my colleagues on officer performance in domestic disputes, we found variance in the criteria experts used and in the weighting of those criteria.[10] Of course, one reason for disagreement among experts may well be based on the need for officers with different characteristics to draw on different techniques to be most effective. Physically imposing officers have one set of opportunities and constraints in handling disorders; diminutive officers have others. Thus, the selection of master craftsmen to develop performance measures should be as diverse as possible, or at least include people who have had ample opportunity to observe a wide variety of officers handle encounters.

Second, the temptation to generate all-purpose performance criteria for every type of encounter should be avoided. In line with Goldstein's "problem-oriented" approach to police work, it will be more meaningful to focus on incidents that share common features. Consequently, it may make sense to begin with the types of encounters that are the most frequent (perhaps traffic stops) or the most problematic (perhaps nonstranger disputes). It may even make sense to subdivide these kinds of problems (e.g., parent-child disputes, spouse disputes, disputes with no indication of prior violence, etc.).

Third, the format for deliberation among police experts should be one that encourages articulation of views, exploration of differences, debate on the merits, building of consensus, and—failing that—clarification of differences that might be subjected to empirical test. The scholarly format of the small seminar seems ideally suited to meet these needs (Bayley and Bittner 1984). Such a seminar might be facilitated by a person experienced in leading such groups (not a police master craftsman). The emphasis would be on the exchange of ideas among equals. It is also conceivable that nonpolice experts on the problem could participate as well (e.g., spouse-abuse shelter staff, psychologists, mediators, attorneys). Social scientists would also attend (as observers and resource people) and subsequently provide technical assistance on instrument design, data collection and analysis.

A fourth concern is how to structure deliberations. In developing performance appraisal instruments for individual officers, groups of police officers are asked to identify general traits or behaviors that represent good and bad performance—drawing on the past experiences of the master craftsmen (Mastrofski and Wadman 1991:367). Because of the way that police officers perceive encounters, it makes more sense to begin by being particular and specific and then seeing whether it is possible to move to greater levels of generality regarding performance criteria. Thus, the seminar participants might be presented with descriptions of specific encounters and asked to react to them, looking for strengths and weaknesses in the officers' performance, and ways to improve it. From these reactions, measures and standards of performance might be derived.

Although hypothetical situations might be developed, I favor using descriptions of situations that actually occurred. These could be obtained by any of the methods earlier described, although I believe that a combination of videotapes and third-party observation would work best because of the detail they offer. Where such material is unavailable, it might be possible to get police officers (even seminar participants) to volunteer to serve as observation subjects before the seminar convenes. The number and nature of such encounters used in the seminar would depend upon the features of the type of encounter that seem most relevant to performance. It is not possible, nor is it necessary, to have all variations of a particular type of encounter represented, since variations can be readily generated by participants from those selected.

Developing performance criteria that could be operationalized feasibly would undoubtedly take many seminar sessions. Once the seminar participants had articulated a set of performance criteria, the social scientists would devise data collection instruments appropriate for the department. Once a data collection instrument was developed, a pilot test would be conducted and seminar participants would evaluate the results, modifying the criteria and instruments as necessary. In some instances, one or more empirical studies might be needed to resolve issues. Such an evaluation might include obtaining reactions of officers whose work was assessed using these instruments.[11]   After review by the appropriate departmental hierarchy, these criteria might be presented to nonpolice professionals and public groups with a particular interest in the problem. After taking their reactions into consideration, the department could conduct more extensive field tests of the criteria, if thought necessary, and also obtain the reactions of patrol officers departmentwide. When managers were satisfied, these criteria could be used for issuing policy guidelines about handling the problem, training and appraising officer performance. They could also be used in evaluating programs and policies.

Conclusion

I have argued that significant advances in police performance measurement can be achieved by paying attention to what police officers do and accomplish within the time span of their encounters with the public. Having reviewed the limitations of the kinds of performance measures that have been and are in fashion, I have suggested that focusing only on crime and disorder rates, citizen perceptions and other indicators of quality of life ignores some of the aspects of policing that have long been of central concern to American society. These concerns relate to how the police treat the public in their daily encounters, and that public's immediate response. I discussed a number of dimensions of performance in encounters and described ways to collect data. I also discussed ways to involve police master craftsmen, social scientists and others in this process. As Bayley and Bittner (1984) contend, such an approach is designed to advance policing professionally by identifying the best that the police craft has to offer and making it possible to test it empirically according to standards of social science.

Because they are grounded in street-level experience, performance measures thus designed seem to have good prospects of being useful to a broad range of constituents in and outside of police organizations. Administrators have a number of needs that such a system could meet. First, they currently have little or no balanced information on how well their patrol force is performing in what Bayley calls "doing right by citizens" (1994). To the extent that organizations routinely assess how police exercise their authority, the available measures tap only the bad news: complaints filed against officers, internal affairs reviews, weapons discharged, and people shot, injured and killed. The method proposed would provide administrators with detailed information on the complete range of performance. Second, administrators could more readily identify those programs, policies and procedures that would reinforce good performance, as well as illuminate those things that detract from performance. For example, the department might use an encounter-based performance measurement system to assess whether its "verbal judo" training had a significant impact on getting citizens to comply with officers' requests and commands. Or a department might assess some aspect of its patrol resource allocation procedures, such as when backup officers are dispatched. By carefully monitoring what happens with regard to the occurrence of violence and disorder in encounters, and by documenting the presence or absence of backup units (and their degree of intervention at the scene), the department might learn the extent to which backups contribute to order and safety at these incidents.[12] With this information, administrators might determine the best level of backup to be assigned given the resources available. Third, administrators may find some encounter-based performance measures useful for personnel decisions, such as job assignment, promotion, training, and discipline. Although there are many legal and organizational difficulties in developing objective performance measures (Mastrofski and Wadman 1991), the kinds of measures proposed here are far superior to the much-disparaged "bean-counting" associated with the uninformative activity statistics (arrests, citations, field interrogations, calls answered, meetings attended). They are also potentially less vulnerable to a variety of biases that are associated with "subjective" performance appraisal methods that rely upon the impressions of supervisors who are rarely present at these events.

Patrol officers should be attracted to encounter-level performance measurement for a number of reasons. First, their own master craftsmen play the pivotal role in developing the performance criteria. This is entirely consistent with the currently fashionable "total quality management" sentiment of having those closest to the work heavily involved in finding ways to define and improve performance. It also means that the performance measurement system should have much greater face validity for the rank-and-file than do current measures for both individual and agency performance, since it would focus on aspects of the work that matter a great deal to those who do it. Second, it would be a major step forward in the development of police work as a true profession (Bayley and Bittner 1984). It would help make explicit the values and assumptions of police craftsmen. Where there are substantial differences in values about police performance, the system would facilitate debate, and it would facilitate scientific testing of craft assumptions about what works and what does not in the application of police authority.

The public—construed generally as well as by subgroups who have a special interest in police performance—should find this approach appealing. It highlights those aspects of police work that they experience most tangibly and directly, and about which they are quick to form opinions: how the police treat them. Although police would play the central role in devising performance criteria, informed and active community groups who wished to contribute would also have a role either directly in the seminars or in reviewing the performance measurement package.

Potential benefits aside, it is a fair question to ask whether this approach is feasible. Can police departments develop criteria to assess how their officers use their authority, and can reliable indicators be obtained? One of the major challenges to developing such a system is achieving a reasonable degree of consensus about the criteria for evaluation and how to measure them. Although there may be fairly high agreement among police as to who is most skilled with public encounters (Bayley and Garofalo 1989), it is not yet clear that there is agreement, even among those "elite," as to the means and ends of skilled police work. Based on impressions taken from preliminary surveys and focus group discussions on handling domestic disputes, I would speculate that there may be considerable diversity in the views of master craftsmen. I suspect, however, that through discussion it is possible to achieve greater agreement about what constitutes good and bad performance than about how either occurs. Police craftsmen may agree that avoiding injury to officers and citizens is a worthy performance objective, but they may disagree on how best to achieve it. As Bayley and Bittner (1984) argue, such differences in view present opportunities for empirical testing, which is made possible by instituting data collection for performance measurement.[13] Thus, it seems likely that much time will be spent in simply seeking consensus among the master craftsmen, and that additional time will be needed to submit their assumptions and expectations to empirical testing.

The process will be laborious, making it unlikely that a "comprehensive" system covering all types of encounters will be possible in the short run.

Perhaps the most problematic consensus problem from a management perspective is that master craftsmen may generate performance criteria and measures distasteful to the top leadership or important department constituents. Although management may reject such measures or demand alterations, it can hardly be regarded as a major advance in employee-manager relations to engage in this endeavor only to stoke controversy and combativeness. Inasmuch as there are fundamental differences in the two perspectives, as some researchers claim (Reuss-Ianni 1983), an encounter-based performance measurement system will only illuminate and clarify these differences. However, the development and validation of measures can be used as an opportunity to submit the assumptions of different viewpoints to empirical test and, possibly, to provide a starting point for negotiating an agreement over at least some differences.

Another obstacle is technical. Can objective methods be developed for making determinations about performance? The performance criteria discussed earlier may strike the reader as subjective, projective and judgmental. How can one measure objectively the level of violence or disorder in an encounter, much less determine the potential for these things? Is it possible to produce reliable indicators of citizen compliance and cooperation with police? Despite the growing use of systematic observation of patrol officers over the last 30 years to obtain such measures, there has been relatively little effort to submit the data to rigorous, intensive reliability tests (Mastrofski and Parks 1990; Reiss 1971b). More attention to this matter will be needed if the data are to be useful. It will require a particularly close working relationship between the officers asked to make these judgments at work and the researchers who will attempt to devise a data collection method. This collaboration will require a commitment of time and energy, as well as a willingness to seek common ground in the differing perspectives of the practitioner and researcher.

All of these feasibility problems raise another, the cost of the enterprise. Many departments will find it difficult to take officers off patrol, especially their most skilled, to work on such a project. Given the experimental nature of this approach, it certainly seems an enterprise appropriate for support from state and federal funding sources whose function is to support innovative efforts to improve policing. It may also be possible to secure the services of social scientists at little or no direct expense, in exchange for access to data.

Finally, even if all of the above problems are overcome, there are certain risks inherent in generating encounter-based performance measures. The principal advantage of the currently used measures is that they do not have much relevance for decisions made at both the policy and the tactical level. That allows police departments to *appear* to be accountable, when in fact, these measures tell us relatively little about what matters when the police and public face each other. Implementing a system that is designed to look at what matters will undoubtedly provide new information, much of which may trouble people within and outside of the agency. It is likely that some dearly held claims about good policy and practice will be discredited, and it may increase pressures to change ingrained organizational structures and even make consequential decisions about individual employees. Although the calls for more and better performance information are common, many concerned parties will balk at the prospect of actually getting it, because of the uncertainty of the outcome. There is no easy palliative to this concern, because high-quality evaluation research often does illuminate the inability of organizations and people to perform to expectations (Petersilia 1987). Although much can be done to create a positive environment for such a system, it ultimately rests on police leaders' willingness to accept the risks of learning that performance is not as good as we would like.

If there are many obstacles to overcome and risks to handle in implementing an encounter-based performance measurement system, there are also incentives to try it. Encounter-based performance measures speak to matters about which police officers and the public care a great deal. They focus on results that are tangible and readily observed. And they concentrate on things that police have a substantial capacity to influence. For these reasons, the prospects are good that encounter-based measures can go beyond existing measures to help improve the quality of policing experienced by the American public.

Notes

The author thanks David H. Bayley, Roger B. Parks and R. Richard Ritti for their comments and suggestions and absolves them of responsibility for any of the chapter's weaknesses.

[1] Sherman offers the most coherent and consistent line of argument on behalf of a police crime control capacity in a series of essays in which he reviews the evidence from research on police (1986, 1990, 1992a, 1992b). He finds evidence in some areas that rather consistently suggests that the police can do things to reduce crime (e.g., drunk driving), that in some cases they cannot (e.g., burglary stings), and that in some cases certain police practices are criminogenic (e.g., arresting some types of spouse abusers). Even Sherman acknowledges that the evidence is neither sufficiently extensive nor sufficiently rigorous to offer definitive judgments about most of the strategies that have been tested.

[2] See, for example, Currie (1985) and Walker (1994).

[3] I use "problem diagnosis" in a different sense than that used by Goldstein (1990) and those who advocate problem-oriented policing. The problem diagnosed in the encounter is akin to that which a physician might use in a clinical setting to deal with a patient's symptoms. The problem diagnosed in Goldstein's problem-oriented framework is akin to how someone in public health might interpret epidemiological data on a large number of patients showing similar symptoms.

[4] Of course, sometimes officers—as do decision makers generally—first decide on what they want to do and then look for evidence that supports that decision. In this case, good performance would be defined as being able to produce evidence in support of one's conclusion and being able to avoid or exclude evidence that supported some other one. Although understandable, such an approach represents a perversion of the police role of accurate and unbiased evidence gatherer.

[5] Exceptions are those encounters that are purely social or "public relations" in nature, where, in fact, the purpose is for police to step—to some extent—outside their official role and just be friendly, without responsibility for *doing* anything.

[6] A recent analysis of police officers' disposition of encounters with suspects observed during ride-alongs showed that in 28 percent of the cases, the officer dismissed the suspect without taking any action beyond investigation (Mastrofski, Worden and Snipes 1994).

[7] The National Institute of Justice is sponsoring a project to develop and validate a measurement system for monitoring police use of force during arrests.

[8] Under the doctrine of community policing, a broader conceptualization of economy may be warranted, since patrol officers are seen as the mobilizers not only of *police* resources, but also of other agencies of government. Thus, an officer who chooses to summon a social worker or mental health professional also incurs certain resource costs to the community, even if they are not within the domain of the police department.

[9]Computer software for entering coded patrol observation data and analyzing uncoded narrative descriptions has been created and will soon be in the public domain (Ritti 1993; Snipes and Ritti 1993).

[10]Thirty-three officers from several different departments in a field training officer class evaluated officer performance in five different domestic disputes. Their evaluations were based on detailed descriptions of situations observed by ride-along researchers. Although the officers varied considerably in their assessments of performance, there was little variation in the confidence with which each offered an assessment, suggesting that different styles of policing really are evident among those whom departments entrust with the training of rookies.

[11]Officers will be interested not only in how performance is defined and measured, but also in how the data will be used. This should be explained and, if possible, samples of how data will be routinely reported should be provided.

[12]If sufficient variation did not occur naturally across such incidents, the department might consider conducting a carefully controlled experiment, during which the degree of backup intervention is randomly assigned (with appropriate safeguards if things get out of hand).

[13]Differences of opinion about the relative weight given to different performance criteria seem likely to be great: for example, how to balance the need to minimize violence or disorder with the need to be economical with police time. These are issues of value, not fact, however, and are appropriately administrators' policy choices. A performance measurement system that provides information on the tradeoffs of different strategies would enable administrators to shape agency performance according to their values.

References

Bayley, D.H. 1986. "The Tactical Choices of Police Patrol Officers." *Journal of Criminal Justice* 14:329-48.

_____. 1993. "Back from Wonderland, or Toward the Rational Use of Police Resources." *Thinking About Police Resources.* Edited by A.N. Doob. Toronto: Centre of Criminology, University of Toronto.

_____. 1994. *Police for the Future*. New York: Oxford University Press.

Bayley, D.H., and E. Bittner. 1984. "Learning the Skills of Policing." *Law and Contemporary Problems* 47:35-59.

Bayley, D.H., and J. Garofalo. 1989. "The Management of Violence by Police Patrol Officers." *Criminology* 27:1-26.

Bittner, E. 1970. *The Functions of Police in Modern Society*. Washington, D.C.: U.S. Government Printing Office.

_____. 1974. "Florence Nightingale in Pursuit of Willie Sutton: A Theory of Police." *The Potential for Reform of Criminal Justice*. Edited by H. Jacob. Beverly Hills: Sage.

_____. 1983. "Legality and Workmanship: Introduction to Control in the Police Organization." *Control in the Police Organization*. Edited by M. Punch. Cambridge, Mass.: MIT Press.

Black, D. 1980. *The Manners and Customs of the Police*. New York: Academic Press.

Brandl, S.G., J. Frank, R.E. Worden, and T.S. Bynum. 1994. "Global and Incident-Specific Attitudes Toward the Police: Disentangling the Relationship." *Justice Quarterly* 11:119-34.

Brown, M.K. 1981. *Working the Street: Police Discretion and the Dilemmas of Reform*. New York: Russell Sage Foundation.

Currie, E. 1985. *Confronting Crime: An American Challenge*. New York: Pantheon Books.

Dillman, D.A. 1978. *Mail and Telephone Surveys: The Total Design Method*. New York: John Wiley and Sons.

Gilsinan, J.F. 1989. "They Is Clowning Tough: 911 and the Social Construction of Reality." *Criminology* 27:329-44.

Goldstein, H. 1990. *Problem-Oriented Policing*. New York: McGraw-Hill.

Klockars, C.B. 1980. "The Dirty Harry Problem." *The Annals* 452:33-47.

_____. 1985. *The Idea of Police*. Newbury Park, Calif.: Sage.

Manning, P.K. 1988. *Symbolic Communication: Signifying Calls and the Police Response.* Cambridge, Mass.: MIT Press.

Mastrofski, S.D. 1981. "Surveying Clients to Assess Police Performance." *Evaluation Review* 5:397-408.

_____. 1988. "Community Policing as Reform: A Cautionary Tale." *Community Policing: Rhetoric or Reality.* Edited by J.R. Greene and S.D. Mastrofski. New York: Praeger.

_____. 1994. "The Police." *Criminology: A Contemporary Handbook.* Edited by J.F. Sheley. 2nd ed. Belmont, Calif.: Wadsworth.

Mastrofski, S.D., and R.B. Parks. 1990. "Improving Observational Studies of Police. *Criminology* 23:475-96.

Mastrofski, S.D., and C. Uchida. 1993. "Transforming the Police." *Journal of Research in Crime and Delinquency* 30:330-58.

Mastrofski, S.D., and R. Wadman. 1991. "Personnel and Agency Performance Appraisal." *Local Government Police Management.* Edited by W.A. Geller. Washington, D.C.: International City Management Association.

Mastrofski, S.D., R.E. Worden, and J.B. Snipes. 1994. "Law Enforcement in a Time of Community Policing." University Park, Pa.: Pennsylvania State University.

McCall, G.J. 1975. *Observing the Law: Applications of Field Methods to the Study of the Criminal Justice System.* Washington, D.C.: U.S. Government Printing Office.

Miller, W.B. 1977. *Cops and Bobbies: Police Authority in New York and London, 1830-1870.* Chicago: University of Chicago Press.

Muir, W.K., Jr. 1977. *Police: Streetcorner Politicians.* Chicago: University of Chicago Press.

Pate, A.M., and L.A. Fridell. 1993. *Police Use of Force: Official Reports, Citizen Complaints and Legal Consequences.* Washington, D.C.: Police Foundation.

Pate, A.M., and W.G. Skogan. 1985. "Reducing the Signs of Crime: The Newark Experience." Technical report. Washington, D.C.: Police Foundation.

Parks, R.B. 1982. "Citizen Surveys for Police Performance Assessments: Some Issues in Their Use." *The Urban Interest* (Spring):17-26.

Petersilia, J. 1987. *The Influence of Criminal Justice Research.* Santa Monica, Calif.: RAND.

Petersilia, J., A. Abrahamse, and J.Q. Wilson. 1990. "The Relationship Between Police Practice, Community Characteristics and Case Attrition." *Policing and Society* 1:23-38.

Prottas, J.M. 1978. "The Power of the Street-Level Bureaucrat in Public Service Bureaucracies." *Urban Affairs Quarterly* 13:285-312.

Reiss, A.J., Jr. 1968. "Police Brutality—Answers to Key Questions." *Transaction* (July/August):10-19.

_____. 1971a. *The Police and the Public.* New Haven, Conn.: Yale University Press.

_____. 1971b. "Systematic Observation of Natural Social Phenomena." *Sociological Methodology, 1971.* Edited by H.L. Costner. San Francisco: Jossey-Bass.

Reuss-Ianni, E. 1983. *The Two Cultures of Policing.* New Brunswick, N.J.: Transaction Books.

Ritti, R.R. 1993. *Qualitat User's Manual.* University Park, Pa.: Pennsylvania State University.

Rosenbaum, D.P. 1988. "Community Crime Prevention: A Review and Synthesis of the Literature." *Justice Quarterly* 5:323-95.

Rubinstein, J. 1973. *City Police.* New York: Garrar, Straus and Giroux.

Sherman, L.W. 1986. "Policing Communities: What Works?" *Communities and Crime.* Edited by A.J. Reiss Jr. and M. Tonry. Chicago: University of Chicago Press.

_____. 1990. "Police Crackdowns: Initial and Residual Deterrence." *Crime and Justice.*   Edited by M. Tonry and N. Morris.   Chicago: University of Chicago Press.

_____. 1992a. "Attacking Crime: Policing and Crime Control." *Crime and Justice.*   Edited by M. Tonry and N. Morris.   Chicago: University of Chicago Press.

_____. 1992b. "Book Review: Problem-Oriented Policing." *Journal of Criminal Law and Criminology* 82:690-707.

_____. 1992c. *Policing Domestic Violence: Experiments and Dilemmas.* New York: Free Press.

Sherman, L.W., P.R. Gartin, and M.E. Buerger. 1989. "Hot Spots of Predatory Crime: Routine Activities and the Criminology of Place." *Criminology* 27:27-55.

Skogan, W.G. 1990. *Disorder and Decline: Crime and the Spiral of Decay in American Neighborhoods.* New York: Free Press.

Skolnick, J.H. 1966. *Justice Without Trial: Law Enforcement in a Democratic Society.* New York: John Wiley.

Snipes, J.B., and R.R. Ritti. 1993. *Codit User's Manual: A Guide for Qualitative Data Entry.* University Park, Pa.: Pennsylvania State University.

Sykes, R.E., and E.E. Brent. 1980. "The Regulation of Interaction by Police: A Systems View of Taking Charge." *Criminology* 18:182-97.

_____. 1983. *Policing: A Social Behaviorist Perspective.* New Brunswick, N.J.: Rutgers University Press.

U.S. Department of Justice.   1992.   "Operation 'Weed and Seed.'" Washington, D.C.: U.S. Department of Justice.

Van Maanen, J. 1974. "Working the Street: A Developmental View of Police Behavior." *The Potential for Reform of Criminal Justice.* Edited by H. Jacob. Beverly Hills: Sage.

Walker, S. 1985. "Setting the Standards: The Effort and Impact of Blue-Ribbon Commissions on the Police." *Police Leadership in America: Crisis and Opportunity.* Edited by W.A. Geller.   New York: Praeger.

_____. 1993. *Taming the System: The Control of Discretion in Criminal Justice, 1950-1990.* New York: Oxford University Press.

_____. 1994. *Sense and Nonsense About Crime and Drugs: A Policy Guide.* 3rd ed. Belmont, Calif.: Wadsworth.

Westley, W.A. 1970. *Violence and the Police.* 2nd ed. Cambridge, Mass.: MIT Press.

Whitaker, G.P., S.D. Mastrofski, E. Ostrom, R.B. Parks, and S.L. Percy. 1982. *Basic Issues in Police Performance.* Washington, D.C.: National Institute of Justice.

Worden, R.E., and S.D. Mastrofski. N.d. *Differential Police Response: A Program Evaluation Package.* Huntsville, Texas: Bill Blackwood Law Enforcement Management Institute of Texas (unpublished).

Chapter 12

Community Policing and Accreditation: A Content Analysis of CALEA Standards

Gary W. Cordner
Gerald L. Williams

Introduction

This content analysis of the standards used by the Commission on Accreditation for Law Enforcement Agencies (CALEA) is part of a larger study of the compatibility of community policing and police agency accreditation, two of the most significant programmatic developments now under way in American policing,[1] both linked to quantifying quality. The research project, funded by the National Institute of Justice, also involves case studies of 12 accredited law enforcement agencies currently implementing community policing.[2]

The 897 standards in effect as of February 1993, following issuance of Change Notice No. 8 to *The Standards Manual of the Law Enforcement Agency Accreditation Program*,[3] were subjected to analysis. This analysis included both the standards and their commentaries; although the commentaries are not officially binding, they were included in the analysis because it has been the experience of some departments that assessors require compliance to commentaries as well as to standards.

It should be noted that a major revision of the CALEA standards was completed in 1994. This revision reduced the number of standards from 897 to

436.   Whether the revision substantially altered the substance of the standards or merely altered their style and organization is the subject of a second content analysis now under way.

Method

Each standard was coded on 27 variables reflecting four major dimensions: community policing, problem solving, organization/management, and overall assessment.   The community policing and problem-solving variables represented major elements of these strategies as identified in the literature.[4]   The organization/management variables represented key aspects of structure and process thought to be affected by accreditation or to affect the implementation of community policing.[5]   The overall assessments represented subjective judgments about the focus and impact of the standards.

Pretesting of the original coding instrument in the spring of 1993 led to revision of several items and extensive discussion of the meaning of variables and coding values.   Following this pretest, a final data collection form was prepared, as well as a codebook that described each variable and its values.

The content analysis was conducted as follows:

1.   Each of three researchers[6] independently coded the same subset of the standards (usually several chapters' worth).
2.   The three researchers compared and discussed their coding of the assigned subset of the standards.
3.   They reached a consensus on the coding of each of the assigned standards.
4.   They then repeated the process for the next subset of the standards.
5.   When they completed all the coding, they were each assigned a subset of the variables.   They rechecked the standards coded with each value to ensure that coding had been internally consistent throughout the entire 897-standard content analysis process.

Community Policing

The direct impact of accreditation on community policing (COP) was measured by seven variables.   For the most part, the standards were found to be silent or neutral about COP.   The few standards that pertained directly to COP were more often supportive than contradictory of COP principles.

Source of Legitimacy

Twenty-six standards (3% of the total) cited the law or legal institutions as their basis. Typical examples were 1.3.1, "A written directive states personnel will use only the force necessary to effect lawful objectives," and 42.2.12, "A written directive governs procedures assuring compliance with constitutional requirements during criminal investigations."

The profession and the community were each cited by less than 1 percent of the standards, while no standards cited politics or political institutions. Examples of standards citing the profession as a basis for legitimacy were 11.1.2, which recommended "grouping by function" those units reporting directly to the chief as "the most accepted basis"; two standards pertaining to radio communications that cited technical procedures and criteria; and three standards related to evidence processing that were clearly derived from principles of scientific criminal investigation.

The three standards based on community norms were 43.1.3, which suggested targeting those vice-related activities of concern to the community; 45.2.4, which encouraged incorporating community interests in crime prevention plans and programs; and 54.2.1, which committed the agency to responding to the community's needs. Over 95 percent of the standards cited no clear or explicit source of legitimacy.

Community Input

Eight standards (1% of the total) encouraged or required community input in police policy making or decision making: two in the area of recruitment, two in crime prevention, and four in community relations. No standards prohibited or clearly discouraged community input; 99 percent of the standards were silent on this issue.

Community Reciprocity

Only one standard clearly encouraged a greater community role in the production of public safety; all the rest were silent or neutral. This one standard, 45.2.2, required agencies to assist in organizing residential crime prevention groups and referred to "10 to 15 neighbors working together and with the law enforcement agency."

Geographic Responsibility

Only three standards directly pertained to geographic responsibility as a basis for police operations or organization. Two standards favored geography as a criterion: 41.1.8, which encouraged agencies "to specify the period of time that an officer is assigned to a particular beat" (but did not recommend any length of assignment); and 44.2.10, which recommended having school liaison officers serve the same schools on an ongoing basis. The standard that opposed geography as the basis for responsibility was 11.1.2, noted above, which suggested grouping the chief's staff by function rather than by geographical assignment.

Reoriented Operations

The reoriented operations variable focused on alternatives to traditional patrol, call handling and investigative operations. Five standards encouraged such reoriented operations, while one standard opposed them. The standards coded as encouraging reoriented operations gave generally lukewarm support for alternative patrol conveyances (bicycles, horses, etc.) and for differential responses to some types of calls. The oppositional standard specified traditional criteria (inspections and calls) for determining whether foot patrol was needed in an area.

Civilianization

Fifteen standards favored civilianization of some police functions, while five standards discouraged some aspect of civilianization. Specific support for civilianization in crime analysis, reserves, victim-witness assistance, and traffic direction and control was evident. Two additional standards (16.6.1 and 16.6.2), though not mandatory for any agencies, backed the general principle that positions not requiring sworn authority should be filled by civilians. Four of the five standards opposing civilianization simply prohibited civilians from performing duties that require sworn status, such as serving arrest warrants. Surprisingly, the fifth discouraged using civilians to conduct background investigations.

Broadening of Functions

The broadening-of-functions variable was used whenever a standard or commentary encouraged or discouraged broadening the police function beyond the traditional roles of crime fighting and law enforcement. About 4 percent (37) of the standards favored broadening the police function, while only one opposed it. Examples of standards supporting the broadening of police function included 44.2.10, which encouraged school liaison programs; 45.2.5, which recommended crime prevention input to zoning policies; and 54.2.9, which backed annual surveys of citizens. The standard that opposed broadening the police function was the one mentioned above that based the deployment of foot patrol on calls and building inspections, without mentioning disorder, fear, community relations, or other alternative criteria.

The community policing approach that received some support from the accreditation standards was a relatively limited and conservative brand of COP. Departments were encouraged to broaden the police function and to civilianize nonoperational positions. Community input, community reciprocity, geographic responsibility, and reorientation of police operations received less support, however. On the other hand, very few of the standards seemed to seriously interfere with the implementation of more far-reaching forms of COP.

Problem Solving

The compatibility of the accreditation standards with the problem-solving or problem-oriented approach to policing (POP) was measured with five variables. The standards were found to be generally supportive of analysis and collaboration, but they tended to reflect an incident-level view of policing and to focus on traditional types of police problems.

Level of Analysis

Thirteen percent (113) of the standards described the focus of police work, or the level of police analysis, in terms of individual events (cases, calls for service, incidents). For example, analysis of *incidents* was specified as the basis for allocating and distributing personnel, and 25 of the 26 standards in the patrol and criminal investigation chapters coded on this variable referred to the incident level of policing.

Only 23 standards reflected a problem-oriented perspective. Of these, 17 were found in the chapters on the traffic function. Examples of nontraffic POP standards were 43.2.2, which recommended analyzing vice and organized crime complaints to "evaluate both the community problem and public attitudes toward the problem"; and 45.2.1, which encouraged targeting crime prevention programs based on analysis of data on crime and public perceptions of crime.

Empirical Analysis

About 9 percent (77) of the standards encouraged or required empirical analysis, while none seemed to discourage it. These standards supported data collection and analysis in such areas as planning and research, crime analysis, allocation and deployment, budgeting, grievances, recruitment, selection, training, investigative management, intelligence, internal affairs, victim-witness assistance, and traffic safety.

Collaboration

Similarly, 76 of the standards encouraged or required collaboration with outside agencies or officials (collaboration with other law enforcement agencies was not counted toward this variable). Over 30 different entities were identified at least once in the standards; those receiving five or more mentions were courts, prosecutors, fire departments, emergency medical services, social services (including victim-witness assistance), traffic safety and engineering groups, juvenile authorities, and the media. None of the standards discouraged collaboration.

Evaluation/Assessment

Somewhat fewer of the standards (34, 4% of the total) encouraged or required evaluation and/or assessment of tactics, strategies or programs (routine internal inspections and individual performance appraisals were not counted toward this variable). Among the topics covered were an annual written evaluation of each organizational component, an annual assessment of the utilization of crime analysis information, an annual recruitment evaluation report, and an evaluation of investigative task force results. No standards opposed evaluation/assessment.

Nature of Problems

Crime, traffic and emergencies were the substantive community problems (as opposed to within-organization problems) most often mentioned in the standards. Rarely mentioned were such problems as drugs (once), fear (twice), disorder (three times), and community relations (seven times).

None of the standards specifically referred to POP, nor did any require use of the full-fledged problem-solving process. Rather, the standards tended to encourage using analysis and collaboration within a largely traditional and incident-oriented framework. And although the standards did not prohibit giving attention to fear of crime, disorder and similar conditions, they tended to focus police attention on the more traditional issues of crime and traffic.

Organization/Management

Eleven variables measured the effects of the CALEA standards on organizational structure and management process within police departments. Overwhelmingly, the standards required formalizing organizational practices. To a lesser extent, the standards tended to narrow police discretion and to encourage specialization, specific accountability, employee notification, and a customer orientation toward the police business.

Formalization

Most of the standards (755, 84% of the total) encouraged or required formalizing police organizational practices. This was usually accomplished with written directives, but it was also accomplished with files, forms, systems, contracts, periodic reporting, and other devices. Typical standards began with "A written directive ...," followed by "requires," "establishes," "specifies," "identifies," "governs," "authorizes," "describes," or "states." No standards discouraged formalization.

Specialization by Task

Forty-seven standards (5% of the total) encouraged specialization by task or function, while eight standards opposed such specialization. Many of the pro-task specialization standards simply required that responsibility for some organizational function be vested in an identifiable person or position or that specialized training be provided. Others encouraged specialization in such tasks as background investigation, court liaison, criminal investigation, crime analysis, juvenile operations, school liaison, crime prevention, victim-witness assistance, traffic analysis, photography, and crime-scene processing.

Standards opposed to task specialization or more in favor of a generalist approach included 16.3.1, which cautioned against overspecialization; 31.1.5, which recommended involving all personnel in recruitment; 42.1.17, which encouraged temporary assignment of patrol officers to the criminal investigation function; 44.1.6, which required all personnel to participate in or support the juvenile operations function; 53.1.1, which required ongoing line inspections by all supervisors and managers; 54.2.4 and 54.2.5, which mentioned that "each officer is responsible for promoting community relations"; and 61.1.4, which called for all uniformed personnel to share the responsibility for traffic enforcement.

Specialization by Unit

Thirteen standards encouraged or required specialization by unit or component, while only one standard discouraged it. Reducing the extent to which specialization by unit was required to achieve accreditation had been an objective of earlier revisions of the CALEA standards; the term *organizational component* had been replaced in several standards by the term *organizational function*. Unit specialization was still encouraged, though, at least for larger agencies, in such areas as planning and research, crime analysis, employee services, background investigation, criminal investigation, vice control, intelligence, staff inspections, public information, victim-witness assistance, and communications. The one standard opposing specialization by unit was 16.3.1, mentioned above, which cautioned against overspecialization and required annual review of any specialized assignments.

Centralization

The centralization variable was used whenever a standard or commentary had clear implications for either the centralization or the decentralization of authority, control or decision making. Few standards had such implications—six were pro-centralization, and seven were pro-*de*centralization. Pro-centralization standards included 42.1.16, which required management to decide how much follow-up investigation a case should receive; 52.1.5, which specified that the internal affairs function should report directly to the chief; and several standards that pertained to records, property and forms control. Anti-centralization standards included 26.1.5 and 52.3.3, which gave each supervisor the authority to dispense discipline under certain conditions; 31.7.3, which encouraged "application and testing processes at decentralized locations"; 52.3.2, which allowed line supervisors to investigate some citizen complaints; and three standards that permitted some records to be maintained apart from the central records function.

Levels/Hierarchy

Even fewer of the standards had clear implications for the degree of hierarchy in police organizations. Only two standards had the effect of encouraging a taller hierarchy, while none encouraged a flatter organizational structure. These two standards suggested limits on supervisors' span of control, the effect of which could have been to require additional levels of management.

Specific Accountability

Quite a few standards (82, 9% of the total) established some form of specific accountability, while no standards opposed accountability. Most of this accountability (72% of these standards) pertained to general management, supervisors or special functions, however, rather than to employees directly providing police service. The 23 standards that did establish specific accountability for patrol officers and detectives covered such topics as use of force, crime-scene processing, accident-scene responsibilities, transporting prisoners, and traffic-citation accountability. Even these 23 standards leaned more toward administration than operations, however; they tended to emphasize formal systems, reports and record keeping more than actual performance standards or standards of service to the public.

Officer Discretion

Twenty-one standards supported narrowing police officer discretion in decision making, while only one standard encouraged broadening discretion. Limiting officer discretion was recommended in such areas as alternatives to arrest, use of force, field interviews, emergency driving, follow-up investigations, juvenile processing, and traffic enforcement. The one standard that leaned more toward broadening discretion, 44.2.3, emphasized the range of alternatives available for handling juvenile offenders. The bulk of the standards did not seem to directly affect police officer discretion (standards that pertained strictly to management or administrative discretion were not counted).

Employee Notification

Quite a few of the standards (44) encouraged or required that employees be notified of decisions, personnel-related opportunities (promotion, assignment, etc.) or benefits available to them. No standards were anti-employee notification.

Employee Involvement

Only one-quarter as many standards encouraged employee involvement in decision making and policy making (11) as supported employee notification (44). The areas in which employee involvement (sometimes limited to managerial involvement) was suggested included establishment of agency and unit goals and objectives, development of policy, preparation of budgets, development of individual careers, recruitment of new employees, evaluation of training needs, evaluation of individual employees, and development of new forms. No standards prohibited or discouraged employee involvement.

Employee Rights

Twenty-one standards specified employee rights that should be protected (contractual employment rights, insurance for reserve officers, career development, due process, appeals, adequate notice, etc.), while only two standards restricted or opposed employee rights. The two standards coded anti-employee rights recommended restrictions on off-duty and extra-duty secondary employment.

Customer Orientation

The customer orientation variable was used whenever a standard or commentary clearly focused attention on serving customers, clients or citizens. About 3 percent of the standards (23) encouraged departments to adopt a customer-oriented approach, while no standards opposed such an approach. These included 15.1.8, which supported disseminating crime analysis information "to enhance public information"; 42.2.5, which suggested "second contacts" of victims and witnesses to express genuine concern about their welfare; 45.1.4, which required access to foreign language specialists; and 84.1.14, which encouraged prompt return of evidence and property to rightful owners.

The viewpoint that holds that accreditation promotes formalization received strong support, but the standards did not seem to encourage either centralization or increased levels of hierarchy, two other characteristics of traditional organizational structure. The standards tended to require specialization by task much more than creation of special units. Managerial accountability was stressed more than operational accountability. A number of the standards encouraged police departments to be more concerned about employees and customers. Perhaps surprisingly, given the accreditation program's emphasis on promulgating written directives, relatively few standards directly impinged on police officer discretion.

Overall Assessments

Four variables reflected overall assessments of the accreditation standards. The vast majority of the standards were judged to be closely affiliated with neither the community nor the professional strategy of policing, but a number of the standards did seem to support COP. The standards were found to focus much more on administrative matters than on police operations. Finally, the standards were deemed much more process-oriented than outcome-oriented.

Strategic Affiliation

Fewer than 1 percent of the standards were primarily affiliated with the COP strategy of policing; similarly, fewer than 1 percent were clearly affiliated with the professional model. Standards affiliated with COP included 31.3.1, which stated that "[t]he agency seeks recruitment assistance, referrals and advice from community organizations and key leaders"; and several standards in the community relations section. Those affiliated with the professional model included several already mentioned pertaining to grouping by function, allocating on the basis of incidents, and maintaining strict criteria for foot patrol, as well as very traditional standards focused on the oath of office, ethics and proper traffic enforcement demeanor. The rest of the standards (885) were neutral or associated equally with both strategies.

Overall Compatibility

Several of the standards (43, 5% of the total) were judged to be supportive of COP, while only one standard directly conflicted with COP. Supportive standards included ones requiring or encouraging social service referrals, consistent beat assignment, school liaison, crime prevention programs, feedback on citizen complaints, citizen surveys, victim-witness assistance, and similar activities. The one conflicting standard specified restrictive and traditional criteria for deploying foot patrols. The rest of the standards were essentially neutral.

Operations/Administration

Standards were coded as operations-oriented when they pertained primarily to the work of police officers in the field, to issues and problems in the community, or to direct service to the public. Standards that focused primarily on internal organizational matters were coded administration. A total of 140 standards (almost 16%) were found to focus on operations; the rest (84%) were primarily administrative in nature.

Even standards located in chapter subsections titled "Operations" were often found to pertain more to administration. For example, only one of the 18 standards in the "Operations" section of the "Organized Crime and Vice Control" chapter was coded operations. The remainder dealt with complaint processing, records, files, funds, equipment, intra- and interagency coordination, resources, and plans, all of which were deemed more administration than operations.

Process/Outcome

Standards and their commentaries were deemed to be process-oriented when they primarily focused on methods, procedures and how to perform a function; they were deemed outcome-oriented when they primarily specified a goal, objective, product, effect, or other outcome to be accomplished. Only 23 of the standards (less than 3% of the total) were judged to be outcome-oriented; the rest were primarily process-oriented.

A good example of an outcome-oriented standard was 84.1.14, which stated, "Final disposition of found, recovered and evidentiary property is accomplished within six months after legal requirements have been satisfied." The commentary accompanying this standard reinforced its importance, without telling the agency how to accomplish it. Another example was 41.1.4, which stated, "Law enforcement response to emergencies is available 24 hours a day, every day of the week, within the agency's service area." This standard's commentary did make suggestions for meeting the standard, but the overall effect was to emphasize the objective of 24-hour emergency availability.

The overwhelming majority of the standards were more process- than outcome-oriented. Many suggested some kind of an outcome in the standard itself, but then, in the commentary, specified precise methods and procedures that had to be used. Many others simply identified an administrative process that had to be adopted, without clearly or strongly emphasizing the outcome that should or must result.

Other standards were written in a particular style that stopped just short of being outcome-oriented. For example, 83.4.4 stated, "A written directive requires that the commanding officer of investigations and the director of the agency laboratory, or their designees, take the initiative and attempt to meet at least annually with the prosecutor and judges of the courts for coordination purposes." This standard, and dozens like it, did not require that coordination be accomplished, or even that the suggested meetings take place, but only that a written directive require that such meetings be attempted. Similarly, 25.1.8 read, "A written directive requires an annual analysis of grievances," rather than "An annual analysis of grievances is conducted," or better yet, "The agency conducts an annual analysis of grievances to identify and correct internal organizational problems."

It should be emphasized that coding these overall assessment variables was more subjective and generally more difficult than coding the variables previously discussed. This was particularly true of the process/outcome variable. First, many standards mentioned both an outcome and methods for achieving it, making the coding task one of judging degree and emphasis. Second, some standards specified immediate-level outcomes that were also means to higher-level outcomes. Again, the coding task was then one of judging whether the standard and its commentary were *primarily* focused on what to accomplish (an outcome) or on how to accomplish it (a process).

Discussion

The hypothesis that the police agency accreditation standards were directly contradictory to community policing principles received very little support. Only one standard out of 897 was judged to be in overall conflict with COP, and only a few clashed with specific elements of COP. No standards were found that opposed community input or community reciprocity.

The opposite hypothesis that the standards supported, or at least complemented, community policing, received somewhat more support. More standards favored community input, community reciprocity, geographic responsibility, reoriented operations, civilianization, and broadening of functions than opposed these characteristics of COP. Overall, 5 percent of the standards were judged to support COP. The degree of support for COP was modest, however, and it was a relatively conservative or limited variety of community policing that was encouraged.

The standards encouraged police departments to gather and analyze data and to collaborate with other public and private agencies, but they did not require any systematic adoption of problem-oriented policing. The standards cast police work and police administration more in terms of incidents than problems, and they tended to emphasize the traditional police concerns with crime and traffic. Such problems as drugs, fear, disorder, and community relations were mentioned in fewer than 2 percent of the standards, while crime, traffic or emergencies were cited in about 30 percent of the standards. In general, the standards did seem to encourage police agencies to "work smarter, not harder,"[7] but not necessarily to reconsider their basic assumptions about police work and their basic methods of providing police service.[8]

Taken as a whole, the standards reflected greater concern with internal organizational issues than with substantive community problems. In this sense, they may have reinforced the efficiency orientation of the professional model rather than the effectiveness orientation of community and problem-oriented policing. In Goldstein's view, greater attention to substantive problems rather than administrative processes is a key ingredient of COP and POP.[9]

From the standpoint of organization and management, the standards reflected a plurality of interests and viewpoints. From the classical school came a strong emphasis on formalization and some emphasis on specialization, accountability and control of discretion. From the human relations approach came the concern for employee notification, involvement and rights. The customer orientation found in a number of the standards probably derived from, or was at least consistent with, the managing-for-excellence and quality-management perspectives.

The impact of these administratively-oriented standards for community policing is not clear-cut. One can argue that heavy reliance on formalization creates organizational rigidity and discourages employee initiative and creativity.[10] Restricting police officer discretion may similarly interfere with police officer efforts at problem solving and community service. Organization theory generally holds that informal and organic structures, rather than formal and mechanistic ones, provide the best fit with work that involves problem solving and truly discretionary decision making instead of the mere application of predetermined choices.[11] However, accreditation advocates argue that the standards merely specify broad parameters within which agencies and officers retain considerable freedom and discretion.

It seems likely that police officials who envision a fairly limited version of COP found nothing in the accreditation program's administratively-oriented standards that interfered with their management of community policing. Police officials whose greatest concerns are with empowering their officers, encouraging risk-taking and removing organizational barriers to employee creativity may have found the accreditation standards more constraining to the implementation of their versions of COP, however.[12]

The overall assessment variables perhaps hold one key to the question of conflict or compatibility between community policing and police agency accreditation. The accreditation program's standards were overwhelmingly process-oriented and predominantly focused on administration. For the most part, the standards told police executives how to set up and run their organizations. They did not specify philosophy or strategy to any great extent, and they left most questions about day-to-day operations and service delivery to each agency's discretion. Thus, agencies committed to COP would not have found much in the accreditation standards that interfered with their strategic orientation. By the same token, agencies that looked to the accreditation standards for strategic guidance would not have been directed toward community policing to any great extent.

Conclusion

The results of this content analysis of CALEA standards bear on a number of hypotheses about the compatibility of community policing and police agency accreditation, as follows:

I. *Direct-Conflict   Hypotheses*

H1 *The Anti-COP Hypothesis*: Police agency accreditation directly conflicts with community policing (COP).   This hypothesis received little or no support from the content analysis.

H2 *The Anti-POP Hypothesis*: Police agency accreditation directly conflicts with problem-oriented policing (POP). This hypothesis received little or no support from the content analysis.

II. *Indirect-Conflict   Hypotheses*

H3 *The Rigid Bureaucracy Hypothesis*: Police agency accreditation (1) creates a formal administrative/management system that (2) interferes with COP/POP.   The first part of this hypothesis received some support from the content analysis. The second part remains to be explored and will be a particular focus at the case-study sites.

H4 *The Efficiency Hypothesis:*   Police agency accreditation (1) focuses administrative attention on internal organizational matters (2) to the detriment of external substantive problems in the community.   The first part of this hypothesis received strong support from the content analysis.   The second part will be explored at the case-study sites.

H5 *The Thin-Blue-Line Hypothesis*: Police agency accreditation (1) emphasizes police responsibility and accountability for policy making and operations (2) to the detriment of community input and community reciprocity.   The first part of this hypothesis received some support from the content analysis. The second part will be explored at the case-study sites.

H6 *The   Style-Over-Substance   Hypothesis:* Police agency accreditation (1) focuses attention on process (2) to the detriment of concern for outcomes. The first part of this hypothesis received strong support from the content analysis. The second part will be explored at the case-study sites.

H7 *The Incident-Driven Hypothesis*: Police agency accreditation (1) reflects an incident-oriented perspective of police work (2) to the detriment of the problem-oriented perspective. The first part of this hypothesis received substantial support from the content analysis. The second part will be explored at the case-study sites.

H8   *The Professional-Model Hypothesis*: Police agency accreditation (1) implicitly favors professional-model strategies, tactics and values (2) to the detriment of COP/POP. The first part of this hypothesis received support from the content analysis when viewed in its entirety, although the atomistic nature of the analysis found relatively few overt references to professional model characteristics.[13] The second part will be explored at the case-study sites.

H9   *The Scarce-Resources Hypothesis*: Police agency accreditation and COP/POP are competitors within police agencies for scarce resources and sustained managerial attention. The content analysis did not address this hypothesis, but it will be explored at the case-study sites.

H10   *The Police-Politics Hypothesis*: Supporters of police agency accreditation and supporters of COP/POP compete within police agencies and within the police industry for status and influence. The content analysis did not address this hypothesis, but it will be explored at the case-study sites.

III.   *No-Conflict Hypotheses*

H11   *The Support Hypothesis*: Police agency accreditation positively affects community policing because the standards directly support COP/POP. This hypothesis received limited support from the content analysis.

H12   *The Neutrality Hypothesis*: Police agency accreditation has no direct effect on community policing because the standards are neutral in regard to COP/POP. This hypothesis received substantial support from the content analysis.

H13   *The Flexibility Hypothesis*: Police agency accreditation has no direct effect on COP/POP because the standards are flexible enough to permit agencies to adopt whatever strategies and philosophies they choose. This hypothesis received substantial support from the content analysis.

H14   *The Null Hypothesis*: Police agency accreditation and/or community policing has no impact, and therefore the two do not conflict. The content analysis did not address this hypothesis, but it will be explored at the case-study sites.

This detailed content analysis provides strong evidence that the CALEA standards in effect until mid-1994 did *not* directly conflict with commonly accepted principles of community policing. Whether the standards *indirectly* or *implicitly* conflicted with community policing, and whether the recent revision of the standards has affected their interface with community policing, await further investigation.

In the meantime, it will be interesting to see whether the standards' apparent neutrality toward, or at most, weak support for, community policing enhances or endangers the accreditation program's survival and growth, given the tremendous outpouring of popular, political and professional support for community policing in the 1990s. Through the early fall of 1994, culminating in the passage of the federal crime bill, community policing appeared firmly ensconced and politically very correct. In this context, accreditation seemed in danger of becoming irrelevant and of being flattened by the community policing steamroller.

Since then, however, rumblings about community policing's being too soft, too liberal and too costly have grown louder; some believe the new Republican Congress might reduce or even eliminate the community policing features of the 1994 crime bill. If this should occur, the accreditation program's reticence about embracing community policing or any other particular philosophy or strategy of policing might prove to have been wise, at least politically.

Ideally, of course, the law enforcement agency accreditation program's standards should support and encourage "best practice"—the most effective programs and techniques known to the profession—without regard to ideology or temporary fads. At least three impediments limit the accomplishment of this ideal, however: (1) on many topics, we lack authoritative knowledge about which operational and administrative practices actually work best; (2) because of the multiple objectives of policing and the pluralistic nature of our society, it is often impossible to identify *the* best practice, even when authoritative knowledge is available; and (3) the accreditation program must inevitably balance its pursuit of ideal standards against practical, financial and political realities. Consequently, we will probably continue to see played out in the accreditation program many of the same fundamental issues and dilemmas that confront all of modern policing and police administration in a free society.

Notes

[1]Supported under award #92-IJ-CX-K038 from the National Institute of Justice, Office of Justice Programs, U.S. Department of Justice. Points of view in this document are those of the authors and do not necessarily represent the official position of the U.S. Department of Justice. This chapter is a revision of a presentation to the 1994 annual meeting of the Academy of Criminal Justice Sciences in Chicago.

[2]The case-study sites are Arlington, Texas; Baltimore County, Md.; Berkeley, Calif.; Colorado Springs, Colo.; Fort Pierce, Fla.; Fort Wayne, Ind.; Greenville County, S.C.; Kettering, Ohio; Knoxville, Tenn.; Salisbury, Md.; St. Petersburg, Fla.; and Tempe, Ariz.

[3]Commission on Accreditation of Law Enforcement Agencies, *Standards for Law Enforcement Agencies: The Standards Manual of the Law Enforcement Agency Accreditation Program* (Fairfax, Va., 1991, as updated in February 1993).

[4]Jerome H. Skolnick and David H. Bayley, *The New Blue Line: Police Innovation in Six American Cities* (New York: The Free Press, 1986); John E. Eck and William Spelman, *Problem Solving: Problem-Oriented Policing in Newport News* (Washington, D.C.: Police Executive Research Forum, 1987); George L. Kelling and Mark H. Moore, "The Evolving Strategy of Policing," *Perspectives on Policing* (Washington, D.C.: National Institute of Justice, 1988); Herman Goldstein, *Problem-Oriented Policing* (New York: McGraw-Hill, 1990); Robert Trojanowicz and Bonnie Bucqueroux, *Community Policing: A Contemporary Perspective* (Cincinnati: Anderson, 1990).

[5]Stephen Mastrofski, "Police Agency Accreditation: The Prospects of Reform," *American Journal of Police* 5, 2 (1986):45-81; Gary W. Cordner, "Written Rules and Regulations: Are They Necessary?", *FBI Law Enforcement Bulletin* 58, 7 (1989):17-21; David C. Couper and Sabine H. Lobitz, *Quality Policing: The Madison Experience* (Washington, D.C.: Police Executive Research Forum, 1991); Robert H. Langworthy, "Organizational Structure," in Gary W. Cordner and Donna C. Hale, eds., *What Works in Policing? Operations and Administration Examined* (Cincinnati: Anderson, 1992), pp. 87-105; Larry T. Hoover, ed., *Police Management: Issues and Perspectives* (Washington, D.C.: Police Executive Research Forum, 1992).

[6]The authors and Robert Hardesty of Eastern Kentucky University.

[7]James K. Stewart, "Research and the Police Administrator: Working Smarter, Not Harder," in William A. Geller, ed., *Police Leadership in America: Crisis and Opportunity* (New York: Praeger, 1985), pp. 371-382.

[8]Goldstein, *Problem-Oriented Policing.*

[9]*Ibid.*

[10]Timothy N. Oettmeier, "Matching Structure to Objectives," pp. 31-60; and Mittie D. Southerland, "Organizational Communication," pp. 281-303; both in Hoover, *Police Management.*

[11]Langworthy, "Organizational Structure."

[12]Couper and Lobitz, *Quality Policing.* Also see Mary Ann Wycoff and Wesley K. Skogan, *Community Policing in Madison: Quality From the Inside Out* (Washington, D.C.: National Institute of Justice, 1993).

[13]This observation was initially made by several participants in a roundtable discussion of the content analysis at the 1994 meeting of the Academy of Criminal Justice Sciences in Chicago, particularly Vic Strecher and Jack Greene.

Appendix

Potential Quality Measures for Law Enforcement

The issue of quality in policing was addressed in a two-year sequence of Executive Issues Seminars sponsored by the Bill Blackwood Law Enforcement Management Institute of Texas. The initial year's theme, September 1992 through August 1993, was "Applying Total Quality Management to Policing." During that year, the instructors were Professor Larry Hoover of SHSU and consultant J.W. "Bill" Streidl. Mr. Streidl is retired from Tenneco Corp., where he was director of management development. Additionally, during that year, executives from several Texas-based corporations participated as guest speakers. The second year of the two-year sequence, September 1993 through August 1994, focused on the theme of this book, "Quantifying Quality in Policing." The instructors were the chapter authors.

During the first year's seminar sessions, participants were assigned to small groups to consider the law enforcement applications of TQM principles and possible areas for measuring service quality. Discussion results were preserved on flip-chart paper. Summarized results follow.

WHAT MEASURES OF QUALITY MIGHT BE EMPLOYED FOR THE WORK OF

Complaint desk personnel?
 Accurate transfer of telephone calls
 Dress and area appearance
 Number of cases rejected/reported
 Number of reports taken—number rejected by supervisor
 Number of problems solved/resolved without further appeal
 Instant error-free transmission of information

Number of data entry errors
Continuity of assignments
Acceptance of authority and responsibility (based on written standards)
Staff review
Citizen survey—supervisory/random
Survey of telephone etiquette
Citizen complaints—citizen commendations

Dispatchers?

Supervisory review of tapes
Internal reports from officers
Citizen contacts, satisfaction
Citizen satisfaction survey
Survey of contract services
NCIC, TCIC errors
Complete dispatch information to responding officers
Timely response to incoming calls, calls in queue
Timely dispatch
Articulate, understandable speech
Geographic knowledge of area
Courtesy to complainants

Record clerks?

Demeanor—courtesy to officers and public
Internal and external user complaints
Production volume of reports, etc.
Response time for requests—same-day delivery
Speed of report preparation
Complete, accurate and reliable information
Minimum error rate
Timely response to walk-in requests
Fingerprint rejections
Lost reports

Data services?

Accuracy/integrity of data
Timeliness
Cost
Downtime

Patrol officers?

Response time consistent with area and support provided
Number of repeat calls
Communication errors—crime classification, wrong address, etc.
Citizen surveys and feedback—planned and random
IAD and other complaints
Reports rejected

Reports—complete and accurate
Cases rejected
Courtesy comments and complaints received
Officer-initiated incidents
Safety record (traffic accidents, etc.)
Internal/external coordination (dispatch, detective, etc.)
Supervisor follow-up and observation
Demonstrated initiative, judgment and reliability
Feedback from other criminal justice agencies
Comments in neighborhood meetings

Detectives?

Checklist of solvability—follow-up on cases pending
District attorney case acceptance
Patrol coordination activities
Citizen satisfaction
Peer surveys
Clearance rates
Quality of clearances
  Initiative
  Follow-up through notes
Case preparation for court

Crime prevention/community relations specialists?

Customer survey
Professional development of officer
Supervisory monitoring of meetings
Coordination with crime analysis
Appearance/acceptance of officer in role
Active coordination with other units
Personal and service complaints received
Successful follow-up actions
District attorney follow-up
Number of public contacts
  Neighborhood watch programs
  Number of crime surveys
  Number, quality, effectiveness of programs presented
    (citizen feedback)

WHAT METHODS MIGHT BE EMPLOYED TO INCREASE A SENSE OF
OWNERSHIP OVER ROLES/WORK PRODUCTS?   ILLUSTRATE IN
TERMS OF THE ROLES OF

- Complaint desk personnel

- Dispatchers

- Record clerks

- Patrol officers

- Detectives

- Crime prevention/community relations specialists

EDITOR'S NOTE: Most seminar participants felt that "ownership ideas"
were useful for all positions noted above. Their generic responses follow.
Position-specific responses follow generic responses.

Generic Responses

Provide extended assignment opportunities and work on feeling of
"belonging"

Involve concerned personnel in decision making at lowest possible level

Assign specific accountability

Delegate real authority

Solicit recommendations and complaints through quality circles/group
meetings

Provide management training

Implement reward systems for good job performance

Facilitate mutual/shared understanding of organization role (e.g., through
a complaint desk)

Participate in management of change

Stress importance of team building (e.g., have records clerk design work
schedule)

Develop feedback system (e.g., let employees know the results of their
work)

Involve employees in development of police policies and procedures

Involve employees in budget preparation

Involve employees in uniform and equipment design and selection

Involve employees in area-specific tactical patrol

Recognize and reward successes

Train managers to handle communications, conflict resolution problems

Provide time and support to implement human resource strategies

Participate in problem identification and solution

Have systems support for organization goals and employee ownership

Solicit employee feedback on performance measures and evaluation

Decentralize—"small is better"

Change attitudes about the way we do business
    Get selective valuations of management from internal groups
    Make serious commitment to well-being of department personnel
    Strive to get practical, realistic input about needed changes

Work on public service statements and better media image
    Provide individual recognition in media and elsewhere
    Include several levels in staff meetings (focus on low-hanging fruit)
    Eliminate fear of retaliation when we disagree with messenger
    Quantify and statistically chart our empowerment results

Position-Specific Responses

Dispatchers
    Solicit input regarding collection/dissemination methods
    Implement peer scheduling to address peak loads
    Attend briefings/training with officers
    Trade positions—officers in dispatch, dispatchers on patrol
    Recognize excellence in dispatch delivery: clarity, composure,
        reliability

Patrol officers
    Allow latitude to develop alternative patrol strategies
    Solicit officer input to determine specific traffic enforcement areas
    Let officers develop alternative responses to problem crime areas

Crime prevention/community relations specialists
    Support innovation
    Allow latitude to specialize (DARE, Boy Scouts, adults, etc.)
    Provide support for unique in-house programs

IDENTIFY SEVERAL "IN-HOUSE" VENDORS IN POLICE AGENCIES. SUGGEST SOME QUALITY MEASURES FOR THE PRODUCTS RECEIVED FROM THE "IN-HOUSE" VENDORS.

Training
   Timely delivery of required hours
   Specialized schools
   OSHA/hazardous materials management
   Number of lawsuits related to training

Jail operations
   Speed in booking process
   Number of medical claims
   Number and intensity of jail population conflicts
   Operational costs vs. jail population

Fleet maintenance
   Operating cost per unit
   Costs of service compared with private sector
   Reoccurrence of repair problems
   Number of miles of road service vs. downtime
   Preventive maintenance—turnaround time
   Replacement frequency
   Scheduling of timely repairs
   Record-keeping capability
   Priority for emergency vehicles
   User satisfaction survey

Communications
   Call screening
   Percentage of calls diverted to direct entry
   Number of duplicate calls
   Information gathering
      Type of situation
      Safety factors
      People/weapons involved
   Systems
      Dispatch timeliness
      Number of calls sent to wrong unit
      Number of calls with wrong address
   Unit tracking
      Accuracy of information on hits
      Patrol complaints
   Direct entry—accuracy and timeliness
   Departmental evaluation of work standards

Records
    Standards for paperwork evaluation and review
    Timely data entry and retrieval
    Accuracy—minimum error rate
    Timeliness—same-day delivery
    Courtesy—minimum complaints

Patrol
    Complete offense reports
        Correct name
        Address—complete and correct
        Phone numbers—complete and correct
        Accurate property descriptions
            Brand names
            Serial numbers
            Entries all legible
    Intelligence information
        Field interrogation cards filled in
        Reports routed to correct units
        Reports routed in timely manner
    Identification
        Fingerprint rejections
        Accurate and positive suspect identification
        Systematic maintenance of filed information
        High-quality prints, photos, etc.

WHAT ARE SOME PRACTICAL METHODS TO TRACK CUSTOMER SATISFACTION?

Internal

Interoffice memos, evaluations

Staff meetings

Complaint monitoring

MBWA (management by walking around)

External

Liaison officers (e.g., DA's office)

Citizen feedback

Meet-the-chief sessions

Victim's assistance (monitor service)

Complaints and congratulations

Community surveys, both written and telephone

Participation in civic organizations

IDENTIFY SERVICE MEASURES BEST MONITORED BY A STATISTICAL CONTROL CHART. ILLUSTRATE POTENTIAL SERVICE MEASURES.

Time spent on different types of calls

Traffic enforcement—control charts show range of enforcement efforts/ results

Accident locations

Caseload and case clearances
  Number of cases presented to district attorney
  Number of cases accepted by district attorney
  Number of cases prosecuted by district attorney
  Number of arrests, etc.

Drug case assignments

Citizens on Patrol (C.O.P.) cost analysis
  Training
  Communication
  Uniforms
  Transportation
  Other expenses

Sick-leave usage—average days taken, + or - $x\%$

High usage of doctor excuses

Reports returned for correction

Surveys of internal/external customers

Allegations of misconduct

Lawsuits

Case acceptance/rejection

Voter approval of bond proposals for capital improvements

Jury verdicts

Letters to the department (good vs. bad)

IDENTIFY SERVICE MEASURES THAT WOULD LEND THEMSELVES TO QUALITY-CONTROL CHARTING (PARETO CHARTING).

Types of calls dispatched

False burglar-alarm responses
    Lack of maintenance
    Power surges
    Weather
    Installation

Property recovery rates

Municipal courts—not-guilty rates

Nonenforcement service requests

Alternative service requests (e.g., citizen requests for foot patrol)

Traffic enforcement—accident locations

Assaults on officers
    By beat
    By time of day

Recruiting efforts

Exit-interview results

Use-of-force incidence data

Quality-perception surveys
    Department personnel
    Citizens

Causes of fleet accidents
    Officer inattention
    Driving conditions
    Speed
    Backing up
    Violation by officer
    Age/experience of officer
    Training
    On service calls
    Equipment defect
    Not officer's fault

Vehicle maintenance
    Routine
    Accidents
    Times to maintain and repair

Excessive equipment downtime
    Accidents
    Inadequate maintenance
    Officer abuse
    Purchasing delays
    Equipment age

Unanticipated absences
    Sick
    Duty-related injury
    Extended court duty

Citizen complaints
    Rudeness
    Excessive force
    Harassment
    Improper conduct

About the Authors

David H. Bayley is a professor in the School of Criminal Justice, State University of New York at Albany. He earned his bachelor's degree at Denison University, his master's degree at Oxford University, and his doctorate at Princeton University. He is a specialist in international criminal justice, with particular interest in policing. He has done extensive research on the police in India, Japan, Australia, Canada, Britain, Singapore, and the United States. His work has focused on strategies of policing, evolution of police organizations, organizational reform, accountability, and tactics of patrol officers in discretionary law enforcement situations. His most recent publications include *Police for the Future* (Oxford University Press, 1994); *Forces of Order: Policing Modern Japan* (University of California Press, 1991); *Patterns of Policing: A Comparative International Analysis* (Rutgers University Press, 1985); *Community Policing: Issues and Practices Around the World* (National Institute of Justice, 1988), with Jerome H. Skolnick; *A Model of Community Policing: The Singapore Story* (National Institute of Justice, 1989); and "The Organization of the Police in English-Speaking Countries," in *Modern Policing* (University of Chicago Press, 1992).

Dorothy H. Bracey is an anthropology professor at John Jay College of Criminal Justice, The City University of New York. She received her bachelor's degree from the College of William and Mary in Virginia, her master's degree in studies in law from Yale Law School, and her doctorate from Harvard University. She has been a visiting professor at the University of Illinois at Chicago, a distinguished scholar in residence at American University, and the 1986 George J. Beto Professor of Criminal Justice at Sam Houston State University. Dr. Bracey has studied juvenile prostitution, police corruption and criminal justice education. Her main interest has been comparative studies of policing; she has studied police in China, Taiwan, England, Germany, France, Australia, and the Netherlands. She has taught at police colleges in several countries, and for 10 years she was the editor of *Police Studies: The International Journal of Police Development*. Dr. Bracey was the 1984 to 1985 president of the Academy of

Criminal Justice Sciences and was appointed by the Academy to be editor of its publication, *The Journal of Criminal Justice Education.* She has received the Academy Fellow Award and was the American Academy for Professional Law Enforcement's 1990 Person of the Year.

David L. Carter is a professor in the School of Criminal Justice and director of the National Center for Community Policing, both at Michigan State University. In addition, he is a research fellow with the Police Executive Research Forum. He received his bachelor's and master's degrees in criminal justice from Central Missouri State University, and his doctorate in criminal justice administration from Sam Houston State University in Huntsville, Texas. He has provided community policing training and technical assistance nationwide and has also conducted research on a wide range of policing issues both in the United States and in Europe. Dr. Carter's most recent book (with the late Louis Radelet) is *The Police and Community,* fifth edition, Macmillan Publishing Co.

Gary W. Cordner is a professor in the Department of Police Studies at Eastern Kentucky University and a visiting fellow at the National Institute of Justice (NIJ). Previously, he taught at Washington State University and at the University of Baltimore. He has also been a police officer and police chief in Maryland. He received his doctorate from Michigan State University. Dr. Cordner has coauthored textbooks on police administration and criminal justice planning, coedited the volume *What Works in Policing?* in the Anderson/ACJS series, edited the *American Journal of Police* from 1987 to 1992, and coedits the *Police Computer Review.* He is currently engaged in an NIJ-funded national study of the compatibility of community policing and police agency accreditation, and in an NIJ-funded study of problem-oriented policing in Lexington, Ky.

John E. Eck is the executive director of the Crime Control Institute, where he studies policing and crime patterns. Dr. Eck also directs evaluations for the Washington/Baltimore High-Intensity Drug Trafficking Area (W/B HIDTA), a regional multi-agency drug enforcement and treatment group. Before joining the Crime Control Institute and W/B HIDTA, he was the associate director for research at the Police Executive Research Forum (PERF). He has conducted studies of burglary case screening, criminal investigations management and citizen reporting of serious crimes. In 1984, he led a study team examining investigative practices and management at the London Metropolitan Police (Scotland Yard). Since 1984, he has conducted research on problem-oriented policing in police agencies throughout North America. This has included the development of problem-oriented approaches to drug and gang problems. Dr. Eck has written extensively on investigative management, police problem-solving, community policing, crime displacement, and the geography of drug markets. His articles have appeared in such publications as *Crime and Delinquency*, the *Journal of Criminal Justice*, the *American Journal of Police*, and *Criminal Justice Abstracts*, as well as in many PERF publications. He received his master's in public policy from the Institute of Public Policy Studies at the University of Michigan, and his doctorate in criminology from the University of Maryland.

Larry T. Hoover received his bachelor's, master's and doctorate degrees from Michigan State University and has been on the criminal justice faculty at Sam Houston State University since 1977. Before that, he taught at Michigan State University, served on the staff of the Michigan Law Enforcement Officers Training Council, and held assignments in the patrol, communications and personnel divisions of the Lansing, Mich., Police Department. A past president of the Academy of Criminal Justice Sciences, Dr. Hoover now directs the Police Research Center at Sam Houston State University. Since 1980, he has been coprincipal of Justex Systems, a personnel relations consulting firm that markets promotional examinations for public safety agencies and publishes the newsletters *Police Labor Monthly* and *Fire Service Labor Monthly*. His publications include articles in the *Journal of Criminal Justice, Police Science and Administration, American Journal of Police, Texas Police Journal, Public Personnel Management, Monthly Labor Review, Security Administration*, and *Liberal Education*, as well as a research monograph for NIJ. He is also coeditor of the *Encyclopedia of Police Science* and editor of *Police Management: Issues and Perspectives*.

George L. Kelling is a criminal justice professor at the College of Criminal Justice, Northeastern University, and a fellow in the Program in Criminal Justice at the Kennedy School of Government at Harvard University. He received his bachelor's degree from St. Olaf College, his master's degree from the University of Wisconsin-Milwaukee, and his doctorate from the University of Wisconsin-Madison. He has been involved in police research, consultation and teaching since the 1960s. From 1971 to 1980, Dr. Kelling was director of field research for the Police Foundation. In that capacity, he conducted the Kansas City Preventive Patrol Experiment and the Newark Foot Patrol Experiment. One of his most noteworthy publications was coauthored with James Q. Wilson in *Atlantic* and is popularly known as "Broken Windows." His book, *Fixing Broken Windows: Restoring Order in American Cities*, coauthored with Catherine M. Coles, will be published by Free Press in Spring 1996.

Dennis J. Kenney has over 21 years of experience in varied aspects of criminal justice—as a Florida police officer; as a research and planning director in Savannah, Ga.; as a project director for the Police Foundation in Washington, D.C.; and as a professor at both the Western Connecticut State University and the University of Nebraska at Omaha. Currently, he is the research director at the Police Executive Research Forum (PERF). He is the author, coauthor or editor of numerous articles, monographs and books, including *Crime, Fear and the New York City Subways* and *Police and Policing: Contemporary Issues.* Additionally, Dr. Kenney has provided consulting services to police agencies around the country, has managed federally sponsored research and technical assistance projects, and is the editor of the *American Journal of Police.* At present, he is completing funded research projects on police pursuits; methods of reducing crime, fear and disorder in urban high schools; and the application of problem-solving techniques to urban gang problems. Dr. Kenney holds a doctorate in criminal justice from Rutgers University.

Stephen D. Mastrofski is an associate professor of administration of justice at Pennsylvania State University and is currently a visiting fellow at the National Institute of Justice. Dr. Mastrofski has done research on a number of police-related topics, such as program evaluation and performance measurement, police reform, police agency consolidation, accreditation, and drunk driving enforcement. He serves on the editorial boards of the *American Journal of Police* and *Criminology.* In addition to scholarly journals, his work has appeared in police professional journals and the International City Management Association's *Local Government Police Management.* Dr. Mastrofski has written several essays and articles on community policing and coedited a volume titled *Community Policing: Rhetoric or Reality.* He has provided technical assistance on community policing to a number of departments in the United States and Canada. He is currently conducting an NIJ-sponsored observational study of patrol officers engaged in community policing.

Darrel W. Stephens is currently chief of police in St. Petersburg, Fla. He served as executive director of the Police Executive Research Forum from 1986 to 1993. Since beginning his career as a patrol officer in Kansas City, Mo., in 1968, he has served in a number of police executive positions: first as assistant chief in Lawrence, Kan., and later as chief in Largo, Fla., and Newport News, Va. While he was chief in Newport News, the police department gained national recognition for developing and implementing the problem-oriented policing concept. The department was also among the first in the United States to be accredited. Stephens, who also spent a year as an NIJ fellow, has coauthored several books, including *Beyond Command and Control: The Strategic Management of Police Departments; The State of Police Education: Policy Direction for the 21st Century;* and *Drug Abuse by*

Police Officers: An Analysis of Critical Policy Issues. He holds a bachelor's degree in administration of justice from the University of Missouri at Kansas City, and a master's degree in public services administration from Central Missouri State University.

Gerald L. Williams is the executive director of the Bill Blackwood Law Enforcement Management Institute of Texas at Sam Houston State University. Previously, he was the director of the Law Enforcement Education and Research Project at North Carolina State University. Before that, he served as police chief in Aurora and Arvada, Colo. Williams holds a bachelor's degree in sociology from Metropolitan State College, and a master's in criminal justice administration and a doctorate in public administration from the University of Colorado. He is a past president of the Police Executive Research Forum (PERF), a former chairman and commissioner of the Commission on Law Enforcement Accreditation, and a member of the executive sessions on policing at Harvard University's Kennedy School of Government. He has been an exchange representative in Israel for the Anti-Defamation League, and is a graduate of the FBI National Academy. His publications include *Making the Grade: The Benefits of Law Enforcement Accreditation* (PERF), and *Turning Concept into Practice: The Aurora, Colorado, Story* (National Center for Community Policing). He was coauthor of the chapter "Criminal Investigations" in *Local Government Police Management.*

Robert E. Worden is an assistant professor of criminal justice and of public policy at the Rockefeller College of Public Affairs and Policy, University at Albany, State University of New York. He holds a doctorate in political science, with a specialization in public administration and policy analysis, from the University of North Carolina at Chapel Hill. He previously served on the faculties of the University of Georgia and Michigan State University. Worden's studies on the police have included both basic and applied research, and his articles have appeared in a number of academic journals, including *Justice Quarterly, Law & Society Review, Law & Policy,* and the *American Journal of Police.* He first undertook research on drug enforcement in 1989, with support from NIJ, as coprincipal investigator on a process and outcome evaluation of police drug crackdowns in Detroit. He is currently coprincipal investigator on an NIJ-funded demonstration and evaluation of the New York State police's application of problem-oriented policing to local drug problems.